ETHNOGRAPHIC STUDIES IN SUBJECTIVITY

Tanya Luhrmann and Steven Parish, Editors

Under a Watchful Eye

Under a Watchful Eye

Self, Power, and Intimacy in Amazonia

HARRY WALKER

University of California Press

BERKELEY   LOS ANGELES   LONDON

University of California Press, one of the most distinguished
university presses in the United States, enriches lives around the
world by advancing scholarship in the humanities, social sciences,
and natural sciences. Its activities are supported by the UC Press
Foundation and by philanthropic contributions from individuals
and institutions. For more information, visit www.ucpress.edu.

University of California Press
Berkeley and Los Angeles, California

University of California Press, Ltd.
London, England

Library of Congress Cataloging-in-Publication Data

Walker, Harry, 1977–
    Under a watchful eye : self, power, and intimacy in Amazonia /
Harry Walker.
        p.   cm. — (Ethnographic studies in subjectivity vol.9)
    Includes bibliographical references and index.
    ISBN 978-0-520-27359-7 (cloth : alk. paper)
    ISBN 978-0-520-27360-3 (pbk. : alk. paper)
    1. Urarina Indians—Psychology. 2. Urarina Indians—Social
networks. 3. Urarina Indians—Social life and customs. I. Title.
    F3430.1.U83W35   2013
    305.898—dc23   2012025913

22   21   20   19   18   17   16   15   14   13
10   9   8   7   6   5   4   3   2   1

Contents

Illustrations

Acknowledgments

Getting started on this project was certainly a lot easier than finishing it, and it is consoling to think that an undertaking of this nature is never truly finished. There is always so much more to say; the subject matter will always resist finalization. That this book exists owes a great deal to the patience and goodwill of the inhabitants of the communities of the upper Chambira River, where I spent one of the most rewarding and challenging chapters of my life. To the many Urarina who contributed to my project, each in his or her own way, I am profoundly grateful. I wish especially to acknowledge my debt of gratitude to Luis Ojaicate Ignacio and Elias Ojaicate Ahuite, without whose innumerable reflections and articulate, intelligent insights this book would have been much impoverished. Their amicable hospitality and kindness greatly enriched my time in the field.

In Iquitos and along the Chambira and Marañon Rivers, the Tuesta brothers, Marlo, José Luis, Marco Antonio, and especially Orlando, offered me friendship and crucial logistical support and taught me much about commerce in the region. Ron and Phyllis Manus warmly extended to me their hospitality in Iquitos and generously gave me a copy of their unpublished data on the relationship terminology. I wish to thank all the doctors, nurses, and support staff of the Clinica Tucunaré, for their much-appreciated hospitality during my brief visits, especially Berbel Würth, Arjan Noot, Eva Ackermann, and Malte Bräutigam, as well as Patricio Zanabria of CEDIA for his help and friendship. Ana Monge Sandoval provided invaluable support, assistance, and companionship throughout, for which I am deeply grateful.

Conversations with Filip Rogalski helped to shape many of the key ideas in this book, and his brief visit to the Chambira opened my eyes to several important aspects of Urarina life and culture that I had hitherto neglected. He also introduced me to the work of Peter Sloterdijk, which has influenced my thinking on many of the themes treated here. I was also lucky to have Jorge Gasché and Andrea-luz Gutierrez Choquevilca as colleagues and friends during my time in Iquitos. Jorge offered me endless good advice as well as provocation, and his study/courtyard was a fertile forum for many stimulating discussions and memorable debates. Before I arrived in Peru, Knut Olawsky generously offered me a draft of his then-unpublished grammar of the Urarina language, as well as a lexicon and a set of translated texts, all of which proved indispensable tools.

A Commonwealth Scholarship supported the doctoral research on which this book is based, and St. John's College, Oxford, also provided financial support in the form of travel grants and other allowances. The Institute of Social and Cultural Anthropology provided me with a productive academic environment, and I am grateful to Robert Parkin and Elizabeth Ewart for their intellectual input and to Vicky Dean for support with endless practical matters. My doctoral supervisor, Laura Rival, proved a remarkably stimulating and astute guide through the world of Amazonian anthropology, and her support and critical engagement with my work are greatly appreciated. I would also like to thank the Graduate School of Human Sciences at Osaka University for hosting me for a year, allowing me to prepare the final manuscript. Peter Dwyer and Monica Minnegal, from the University of Melbourne, deserve special credit for inspiring me to pursue this path in the first place and for greatly enriching my conception of what anthropology might be capable of.

I am especially grateful to my parents, David and Felicity, for their love and support throughout, even across great distances for much of the time. Finally, I wish to thank Iza Kavedžija for her unflagging patience and encouragement and for making the journey so much more enjoyable.

Prologue

Learning to Stand-Leaned-Together

Upon returning from fieldwork in the Peruvian Amazon I was often asked, as many returning anthropologists must surely be, what I missed most from life in the field. After contemplating for a moment the peaceful beauty of the river just before dawn and the agreeable challenge of drinking abundant manioc beer in good company, I was often led to ponder a certain hard to define aspect of the quality of life that I suspected had something to do with the sense of freedom that comes with self-sufficiency, or more precisely mastery over the entire range of productive techniques and resources necessary for living well. I was impressed by the way my Urarina hosts were equally competent in a diverse range of activities, between which they would continually switch, more or less as they pleased, forever varying the daily round. If they felt like fishing, they went fishing; if there was manioc beer to drink, they would drink it. If they were hungry, they assured me, they need simply wander into the forest and find an animal, or go to the river and pull out some fish. Of course, matters were not always quite so simple, but as I gradually learned some of the practical skills basic to jungle life, I came to experience firsthand a new kind of competence and satisfaction that could only arise from the knowledge that virtually anything that needed doing could be achieved, with a little creative improvisation, using materials and instruments all ready to hand. I also learned that this ability to meet the full range of one's needs and desires was basic to earning the respect of others. I am sure I gained in people's esteem after learning a few basic skills, such as how to build a fire and carry plantains, but above all when I made my first garden, admittedly on the small side but of unmistakable symbolic significance. I remember well my feeling of satisfaction, which I am similarly sure was both noted and appreciated by others.

The importance placed on enskillment was but one dimension of a far-reaching prioritization of, and respect for, the autonomy of individuals. For example, I learned that invitations, greetings, and farewells must be addressed fastidiously to every person in turn and were ineffectual otherwise. In the course of fieldwork I was often frustrated by a steadfast refusal to presume to know the mind of another, and had to accept the futility of asking informants about the behavior or intentions of others. People seldom invoked collective or categorical identities, preferring instead to define persons and things through the particular relationships in which they were embedded. Much work was undertaken collectively, for example, clearing gardens and lumbering, but inevitably for the ultimate benefit of a single person, for ownership is only by individuals, not by groups. Parity was achieved by rotating beneficiaries over successive work efforts rather than distributing the proceeds among many. And, of course, people rarely told others what to do. There were some important exceptions. Men, for example, often gave the impression of commanding their wives. But it was also understood there was little a man could do should his wife choose not to obey; at worst, she could always leave him and find another husband. I noticed that many such orders, particularly the more strident ones, were quietly ignored. The contribution of this style of individualism to a pervasive sense of social equality seemed undeniably strong.

Of course, familiarity with the literature on Amazonian societies had led me to expect such an emphasis on individual autonomy. But perhaps what impressed me most about this strong sense of personal liberty, underwritten by a hard-won practical mastery, was how it combined with an equally strong sense of doing things with and for others. As much as people were adamant that they did whatever they pleased, the stated reason for doing any particular activity involved meeting the needs and desires of one's kinfolk. A man went hunting because his wife was hungry for meat; he went fishing so his newborn baby could eat some fish soup; he went to extract palm hearts because he owed his *patron*, or labor boss. These debts and obligations—even to apparently exploitative *patrones*—were not seen in a negative light; on the contrary, they seemed to index a healthy relationship. The fact that I arrived in the field single caused some consternation, and I was continually asked when I was going to "take a wife." I was clearly not a grown man without one; self-realization could only come through starting a family. Even enskillment itself depended on the involvement of others, although it was not conceived in terms of a transmission of knowledge from parent to child, whether through instruction or mimesis. Neither was it generated internally. Virtually all physical skills, from complex movements such as weaving, spear throwing, or playing the flute to something as seemingly basic as learning to walk, were the object of extensive interventions directed at the appropriation of knowledge from external sources, particularly plants, animals, and other, nonhuman beings. The conditions for individual autonomy were, in short, to be found in the literal introjection into the self of qualities and relations defining a variety of "others." The very soul itself, as one of the purest expressions of individual uniqueness and closure to others, was thought to come into existence through the intentional, caring actions of parents and others, who inevitably grew closer to each other as a result.

Paramount among all social values was the injunction against being "stingy," particularly with food. I had to learn to share what I had widely if I wanted to participate in the life of the community. The way old Manuel educated me in this foundation stone of morality was itself illuminating. "Whenever I have some food, I always share it with everyone so we can eat together," he would tell me solemnly, making his point carefully without scolding or recrimination. I expect that the challenges and tribulations of successfully negotiating one's incorporation into the demand-sharing economy will be a familiar experience for many researchers who have lived and worked in an Amazonian society. I realized I was trying to adapt to a society that was somehow both more individualistic and more communal than the one I had grown up in. If there was any kind of paradox or contradiction here, my hosts didn't seem particularly troubled by it; on the contrary, they seemed to revel in finding ways to articulate the idea of autonomy within dependency. A pleasingly concise expression emerged from the dense symbolism of the improvised shamanic chanting of hallucinogenic trance. Though voiced from the perspective of the spirit "mother" of the ayahuasca and brugmansia plants, these often served as a platform for the expression, by senior men, of the moral values associated with correct and harmonious living. One of the formulaic expressions I heard again and again was *temerequiin*, or its several variants, which can be translated as "standing-leaned-together." People willingly demonstrated the meaning with whatever two long, flat objects were lying at hand, standing each on its end and leaning the other ends together to balance them, each supported by the other. The expression was used, in the context of the songs, both as a description of how real people do live and as a moral injunction concerning how they *should* live. The image seemed to capture perfectly how autonomy and mutual support are to be brought into conjunction in order to live well.

The relationships with those for or with whom one acts were very often articulated through idioms other than those of consanguinity or shared substance, highlighting for me their voluntary nature. A far-reaching notion of fellowship or companionship, typically conceived as dyadic in form, irreducible to kinship but more formal than friendship, seemed particularly salient for many. "Everyone has a companion," I was informed, "otherwise they could not live in peace. No one can live alone." A spouse is literally one's "sleeping companion" (sinijera), while a lover is one's "walking companion" (amujera). Men who work or undertake journeys together are prototypical companions (coriara or corijera, lit., "shadow-soul-fellow"), even more so if they are also ritual co-fathers. Many myths and oral histories document the exploits of individuals acting not alone but in pairs, though the emotional tenor of the relationship was variable, and not always amicable, particularly where they concerned male affines. In some stories the relation between the men was not specified. In response to my questions, I was simply told that "the ancients always went around together in twos."

The possibilities of companionship extend beyond human society to embrace manifold nonhumans. All newborn babies have their companions, in the form of lovingly prepared string hammocks, to which they are said to form strong emotional and physical bonds, and which blur the boundaries between persons and artifacts. I was told that a companion may be "of the same race or group" or "of the same activity." Birds accompany those who walk in the forest, advising through song on a range of topics, from rising water levels to the imminent death of a loved one. Trees were often classified into sets of companions reflecting species found together or held in similar esteem. Cultigens have companions "in order to produce." Thus sweet potato, the companion of manioc, is the latter's "support" and "resistance," and each helps the other to grow. "Without help, one cannot work." A thing, too, can be a companion of another thing, or even of a human, though the relation must be established through continual use and ever-increasing familiarity, until the identity of each entwines with the other.

Most of these relationships, I realized, were inherently asymmetrical. This was true even when those so related were typically social equals, as in ritual co-parenthood. In some cases, there was a more or less explicit power differential. Experienced shamans, for example, initiate intimate companionships with small stone bowls, considered both powerful and dangerous, in order to learn the arts of mystical attack. The man must "tame" the bowl by subduing it and establishing his complete authority over it, becoming its trusted friend as well as its "owner" and "master." Most animals and plants are similarly said to each have their owner or mother, who controls their distribution in the forest and is responsible for their "protection" or "defense," always "watching over" them attentively. Large game animals have a special type of companion, known as *cojoaaorain*, who takes the form of a small bird and advises the animal on a daily basis, warning of approaching predators and other dangers. If the animal is slain by a hunter, it is because this bird had earlier ceased this communication, terminating the relationship. The inherent asymmetry of a relationship was often advantageous, not least insofar as people not only strived to be in the more powerful position of a master or controller; on the contrary, they would often appear to subordinate themselves voluntarily to others, emphasizing their helplessless and vulnerability as a way of eliciting love and pity along with benevolent acts of caring and giving that, in the end, served to further their own interests anyway.

In sum, the striking importance accorded to individual autonomy, enskillment, and personal liberty turned out to be closely and somewhat paradoxically wedded to equally salient notions of mutuality, dependency, and responsibility. Central to being an individual were the practices of living together with others; each was possible only with and through the other. The particular relationships that seemed most directly constitutive of personal autonomy were articulated in ways that often overflowed the language of kinship and commensality. Though basically or ideally dyadic in form, they varied in degree of asymmetry. Some seemed expressive of solidarity between social equals; others were more explicitly structured around notions of authority, ownership, or even filiation. How were these to be reconciled with the purportedly egalitarian character of Amazonian societies? How can autonomy and dependency coexist, and do even the most hierarchical relationships still somehow condition or even enhance the agency of the "owned" or subjugated? It was apparent that individualism and equality, power and dependency could be read in a variety of ways. Yet it was their expression, in discourse and practice, that seemed to lie at the heart of Urarina social life, both as salient values and as organizational principles. This book represents an attempt to trace these values and principles across some of the many overlapping practices and discourses through which personal identity unfolds alongside the fragile re-creation of society itself.

1. Spaces of Refuge

This book is about the shared nature of human existence: how we live our lives in the close company of others, in whose very being we come to participate. We come into the world accompanied, and this remains our defining condition: who we are, how we come to experience ourselves as conscious subjects, with the capacity to act on the world, are fundamentally conditioned by our constitutively accompanied nature. This mutuality does not undermine individuality but precedes it and is its condition of existence. Typically grounded in intimate but often asymmetrical relations of care and protection, mutuality nevertheless also establishes a certain vulnerability. This can manifest as a willingness to be dominated, if our continued sense of identity, our sense of self, can thereby be assured.

The Urarina, a hunting and horticultural people of the Peruvian Amazon with reference to whom these arguments are developed, recognize and elaborate these relational qualities of human experience to a high degree. Yet they never lose sight of the importance of individuality and uniqueness. A range of factors have shaped this dual emphasis on mutuality and autonomy, from low population density and the immediate, largely face-to-face nature of the social environment to limited access to modern technologies and manufactured goods to the exuberant, formidable expanse of the seemingly endless jungle, teeming with diverse forms of life. Then there is the extraordinary, turbulent history of the Amazon basin itself, marked by complex networks of trade and warfare, demographic expansion and contraction, high mobility, and brutal clashes between radically different civilizations. The struggle for survival of the

7

indigenous inhabitants of the region has not diminished over the centuries, and their enemies today remain as powerful as ever. Despite historical trajectories and environmental conditions that are in many ways unique, peoples such as the Urarina also grapple with answers to fundamental existential conundrums that apply equally to us all, concerning what it means to be alive, to be human, and to live with others.

Despite the commonality of our human predicament, the responses that Urarina have developed—not to mention the distinctive cultural forms through which these are expressed—are their own, and must be understood with reference to the social and cultural milieu in which they are embedded. Careful analysis of a diverse range of practices and events together with commentaries and explanations offered by my hosts and interlocutors over the course of fieldwork reveal a set of basic assumptions and presuppositions, often more or less taken for granted, about the nature of the self and its coming into being through relations with others. How well these square with our own theories or intuitions may vary considerably. Some of the most important rites and practices of child care from an Urarina perspective—ceremoniously cutting the umbilical cord and burying the placenta, or going out of one's way to keep a newborn baby feeling warm and safe—differ only slightly from our own experiences, while others—the performance of esoteric chants that can last for hours, or the receipt and bestowal of personal names by shamans in the throes of powerful visionary experiences—offer a striking contrast. The common Amazonian wisdom that certain animals, plants, or material objects are themselves essentially persons who share many basic qualities of humanity, including a mind or soul, intentionality, and even human culture, are still more difficult to reconcile with our scientifically informed understandings. Reflecting on these ideas and practices may not only help to draw our attention to implicit assumptions and prejudices in our own worldview; they may be seen to offer insights into the nature of human experience that we can recognize as valid in some important sense despite being largely overlooked or even suppressed by dominant Western discourses.

In everyday language in the West, the term *person* is used more or less synonymously with *human being*. We might therefore assume that asking what it means to be a person is the same as asking what it means to be human. But a little closer examination reveals some exceptions: someone in a permanent coma is still human, for example, but could be said to have lost some intrinsic part of his or her personhood. Certain animals, on the other hand, such as much-loved pets, might come close to being treated as persons by their owners, even if deep down the latter "know better." Further enquiry into the dominant logic in Western societies suggests a more or less widespread sense that to be a person is to be a self-contained, independent entity endowed with a set of inner mental or psychological capacities such as self-awareness, rationality, and responsibility. These criteria effectively constitute the individual as an autonomous being, the author of his or her own actions, an authentic self with a private identity, capable of having experiences that belong exclusively to that private self. This sovereign individual, self-governing and self-disciplining, is considered to have a separate and independent existence both temporally and spatially, with his or her own unique experiences as well as abilities, preferences, needs, and desires.

The commonsense Western view has largely taken it for granted that it is essentially because we are conscious, rational beings of this kind that we are able to enter into social relations with others. People are assumed to preexist the social relationships they enter into, giving rise to a conception of social relationships as a kind of supra-personal glue that binds individuals together, linking them up to form a larger unit—society—to which they are in some sense opposed but which mirrors their qualities of wholeness and enclosure at a larger scale. The processes by which people are drawn into social relations are often labeled "socialization" or "enculturation," revealing a related assumption that we begin life as essentially natural organisms, asocial and cultureless. There may be an implicit dualism at work here that opposes the body to the mind or soul as completely different kinds of substance and that tends to objectify "external" objects as existing entirely separately from the observer, implying a rigid distinction between subjects and objects. This further corresponds to the dualism of nature and culture: the body is basically seen as a biological organism, bounded by the skin and endowed with a more or less "given" or "natural" set of needs or drives that are met, controlled, or moderated by "culture," an artificial creation of joint human activity.

Processes of socialization or enculturation are correspondingly focused on cultivating the mind, comprising forms of learning conceived as primarily psychological rather than physiological. These are not absolute distinctions, but they do reflect general tendencies or habits of thought that stem from deeply rooted and widely shared assumptions about the underlying nature of reality: they constitute part of our shared understanding of what the world is like on the most fundamental level, or what kinds of things make up a world—what is sometimes referred to as an ontology.

Concepts of the person are deeply implicated in everyday practices, values, and social institutions ranging from morality and law to politics and religion. This was a point made forcefully by Durkheim (1973 [1898]), who pointed out the centrality of ideas and values surrounding the individual to the modern form of collective life. In the wake of industrialization and modernization, the notion of the abstract individual as the key locus of natural rights and moral values had become a key source of coherence in an increasingly secular society characterized by highly divergent lifestyles. Mauss (1983 [1938]) took this further by showing how this Western concept of the individual had a historical trajectory of its own, in which a range of influences, including ancient Greek moral philosophy, Roman law, and Christianity, all conspired to give shape to a concept of the person as an individuated self, separable from the particular role or social position he or she inhabited.

Since Mauss, a vast literature has grown up dedicated to exploring historical and cross-cultural variability in, and determinations of, the person or self.[1] Much of this literature has converged in drawing a somewhat stereotypical contrast between "Western" and "non-Western" forms of personhood. Generally speaking, the latter has been conceptualized as more or less the opposite of the bounded, autonomous, reflexive, and independent Western self; hence a proliferation of terms emphasizing its essentially "joined-up" rather than "individualized" qualities, as implied by descriptive labels such as "interdependent," "sociocentric," "dividual," "permeable," "multiple," "partible," or "detachable."[2] This may further correspond on a moral or ideological level to a contrast between the values of individualism and egalitarianism, on the one hand, and holism, on the other, the latter typically associated with forms of hierarchy and collectivism (e.g., Dumont 1972). Western social sciences are not immune to the same predispositions, and it has been suggested that their methodological focus on individuals as the basic units of social reality has hindered their ability to comprehend even individualistic societies (Dumont 1986: 11).

Forms of personhood are more divergent at the level of moral values and ideologies than in terms of actual, everyday experience of the self and of one's relations with others. In this latter sense, Western persons are undoubtedly more "relational" or "joined up," and less "individualistic," than the discourse of individualism would imply (see, e.g., Carsten 2004: 101–7). On the other hand, many of the features of individualism are to be found in a variety of non-Western societies. Scholars have long drawn attention to the fact that native Amazonian societies are structured in terms of symbolic idioms that relate to the construction of the individual or, more precisely, the fabrication of the body rather than the definition of groups and the transmission of goods (e.g., Seeger, Da Matta, and Viveiros de Castro 1979). In many areas of Amazonia there are no social groups that survive the lifetime of single individuals; the only social group is formed by the settlement, which has little continuity through time because its existence depends on the leader or headman and is constituted by his personal network of relationships (see Rivière 1984). The apparent individualism of some Amazonian peoples is thus in part the product of an atomistic social system; and yet these same peoples maintain an unmistakably strong orientation toward others, emphasizing the relational grounding of the self to a high degree. That we perceive these tendencies as contradictory, or their coexistence as paradoxical, calls into question some of the ontological assumptions that underpin much Western thinking about the person.

BEYOND PERSPECTIVES

A radical difference between Western and Amazonian concepts of the person arises from their divergent attitudes toward animals and other nonhuman beings. The significance of this difference was driven home by Descola (1992, 1996), who observed that nonhumans are often considered to possess a soul or spiritual principle and that it is therefore possible for humans to establish various kinds of personal relations with them, ranging from seduction or protection to forms of alliance and exchanges of services. These natural beings are thought to be endowed with human dispositions and emotions, the ability to talk, and a variety of other social attributes, including human forms of social organization, behaviors based on kinship and respect for certain norms of conduct (Descola 1992: 114). Descola drew the conclusion that these "animistic" systems of thought effectively invert the way Western "naturalism" deals with the differences between humans and nonhumans. As he later expressed it, if Western ontology proposes that humans and animals have similar bodies (all made up of the same basic elements) but very different minds or interiorities (only humans have higher-order consciousness), animistic ontologies propose the opposite: a fundamental discontinuity of bodies but a continuity of minds, shared by humans and nonhumans alike (Descola 2005).

This crucial insight forms the basis of what is now known as perspectivism. Especially as developed in a groundbreaking article by Viveiros

de Castro (1998), this theory derives much of its considerable explana-
tory power, and its striking elegance, from one key claim—that people
everywhere make some kind of distinction between what is "universal"
or "given" in the world and what is "particular" or "constructed" through
intentional action but that Westerners and Amazonians have almost
precisely opposed ideas about which is which. The most obvious example concerns the categories of nature and culture. Western thought posits a unitary nature, differently perceived or represented by the world's
many diverse cultures (hence the familiar notion of multiculturalism).
Amazonian ontology, by contrast, is "multinaturalist": it presumes a universal (human) culture but a multiplicity of natures.[3]

Though at first highly counterintuitive to a Westerner steeped in a
naturalistic ontology, such a formulation immediately helps us to make
sense of the claim that although all beings see themselves as human,
they do not see other kinds of beings as human but rather as nonhuman
predators or prey.[4] Animals are assumed to inhabit a cultural universe
more or less shared by everyone: they may dwell in longhouses, drink
manioc beer, have chiefs and shamans, marry exogamously, and so on.
We do not see any of this under normal waking conditions, because of the
limitations imposed by our own species-specific "nature," our (human)
body with its unique capacities, affordances, and dispositions. Where a
jaguar sees manioc beer, we see blood; a tapir's ceremonial house is for us
a salt lick. It is not merely that we see the same world in different ways:
in a multinaturalist ontology, different beings see different worlds in the
same way.

The implications of perspectivism for kinship and personhood have
tended to receive less attention from anthropologists than relations with
nonhumans, especially outside Amazonia, but they are no less significant. We typically assume consanguinity, or blood relatedness, to be
fixed at birth and relatively unproblematic; affines or in-laws, on the
other hand, are created through human intervention, specifically marriage. Thus anthropology has traditionally focused attention on marriage
patterns and their consequences while assuming that who or what counts
as a blood relation can be mostly taken for granted. Yet the evidence suggests that many Amazonian peoples see consanguinity as unstable and
in need of careful creation out of an assumed universal background of
real or potential affinity, which extends to include even enemies and nonhumans. This simple inversion of our own expectations helps to explain
why so many Amazonian social practices are focused on the body and its
fabrication, from everyday acts of feeding and nurturing to complex rites

of decoration and ornamentation. All living beings, nonhumans included, share the same generic soul, which sees only the same thing everywhere; bodies, on the other hand, are markers and instruments of difference. Conceived as bundles of capacities and affects as much as physical matter, it is the body that determines the world one apprehends.

Although grounded in the body, perspectives are not fixed or immutable. In fact, Amazonian social practice has been characterized precisely as an ongoing, essentially predatory "struggle between points of view" (Stolze Lima 2000: 48), in which all beings seek to impose their perspective on others while avoiding the attempts of those same others to do likewise. Fausto (2000, 2007) describes the Amazonian lived world as one in which different groups, human and nonhuman, living and dead, all seek to capture "others" and turn them into kin. Shamans and warriors seek to capture animals and enemy spirits, appropriating their names, songs, or souls as a way of ensuring the reproduction of the social group. At the same time, nonhumans try to capture humans by seducing or preying on them so as to transform them into members of their community. Such a formulation is especially useful for the way in which it brings concepts of power to the fore while making clear that they can no longer simply be associated with relations of coercion or control between humans. Instead, power is embedded in the relational matrix through which perspectives are transformed, especially relations of adoptive filiation, domestication, and "taming."

In this book I build on some of perspectivism's key insights, especially insofar as they confirm the need to firmly situate the study of sociality and personhood in a broader cosmological and ontological context. However, I also seek to moderate some of the theory's core assumptions and to move beyond it in certain ways. One of these concerns the emphasis on predation. Many Amazonian societies valorize hunting and warfare, while shamanic practice often partakes heavily in the symbolism of both these institutions. As Descola (1992: 94) put it, for the more warlike peoples especially "the capture and incorporation of persons, identities, bodies and substances form the touchstone of a cannibalistic social philosophy." Perspectivism builds on an established tradition of Amazonian scholarship that emphasizes the importance of predation as a key symbol or ideology, inscribing this directly into indigenous ontology. Subjectivity is determined by one's position within a relational matrix of predators and prey, and to be a true subject or agent means first and foremost to be a predator.[5]

An analytical emphasis on predation was an important step forward in recognizing the moral and ontological autonomy of Amazonian peoples, and it cautioned against idealistically projecting Western ethical values onto others. But it has also tended to privilege, and to generalize, masculine modes of relating to others in the contexts of hunting and warfare. An emphasis on the capture or appropriation from the outside of the elements needed for social reproduction, especially of souls or other vital forces through life-taking, has similarly meant downplaying the life-giving and other productive capabilities to be found within the group. Some of the most symbolically significant and sociologically productive forms of relationships established by Urarina are not with animals but with other nonhumans such as plants or material artifacts, often associated with feminine spheres of activity, and embedded in a relational ethics of care.

If the concept of predation is of limited utility in comprehending the Urarina lived world, this may be in part for historical reasons. The Urarina are a relatively peaceful people who nevertheless have a long history of subordination vis-à-vis powerful outsiders, to whom they see themselves as morally superior. They are understandably reluctant to accord full personhood to the powerful figure of the predator, and prefer to recognize the agency (not to mention humanity) of the subordinate party. Yet rather than simply identify as "prey," they instead seek out other ways of representing concepts of subjectivity and agency. While ideologies of predation are not entirely absent, this is far from the most important kind of relation in terms of the processes that constitute persons and groups.

The relationships of greatest significance in Urarina social life are instead often expressed through idioms of "companionship" or "fellowship," relations irreducible to kinship but more formal than friendship and typically grounded in certain forms of shared activity and structures of feeling. Often established with reference to the creation of new life and new persons, I suggest, the full realization of a sense of self is achieved through participation in the lives of others in the context of such companionships, which at the same time are the basis of Urarina social groups. They imply a sense of security and mutuality that is sometimes imagined as the intimate coexistence of fetus and placenta in the protective space of the womb, a founding state of proximity and mutual permeability that in some ways they seek to re-create.

In tracing through the implications of this argument, I call attention to the fact that although perspectivism challenges and relativizes many of the most deeply held ontological assumptions of Western thought, it does not challenge the assumption that the subject is ultimately a unitary point of view, even if an unstable one: it is essentially a perspective on the world, anchored in the individual. As in classical psychoanalysis, it is the supposedly formative qualities of a self–other opposition that is emphasized, understood primarily with reference to the visual field. A "self-image," for example, may arise when the self or ego sees itself reflected in the other, as though in a mirror.

Drawing on the Urarina material as well as Sloterdijk's (2011) theory of spheres, or spaces of coexistence, the alternative I propose is that a prior field of sensation informs the development of a self-image and that this field is constituted through intimate relations with others that are always already present, from our earliest moments of intrauterine existence. In place of the Western privileging of the visual field in the constitution of a sense of self, I shift emphasis to the acoustic domain. Rather than images, reflections, or perspectives—optical tropes that reinforce a self–other divide—I seek to show how it is above all within the psycho-acoustic field that subjects are called into being. This helps to foreground some of the broader ontological claims made, to the effect that human existence has a medial structure and that the subject is always situated in a shared field of protection and attention that logically and temporally precedes any isolation of a single point of view or subsequent polarization into the position of "predator" or "prey."

Urarina strive to achieve their personal autonomy and sense of self through a network of relationships far more varied than we would find in the so-called individualist West. Whether this is a hammock "singing" its lullaby to the baby who swings in it, a wife demanding cooperation from her captive tortoise, a shaman communicating with his powerful stone bowl, or simply the ongoing exchange of words and sounds that characterize all intimate relationships, selves are always connected to their alters within shared acoustic fields, and it is in this context too that they begin their process of differentiation. The Urarina subject is constantly under construction, less a "point of view" than an animated field of attachments and dependencies that always involves two or more. Yet simplistic contrasts between Western "individual" personhood and non-Western "relational" personhood run at right angles to what might better be described as a continual movement in which individual autonomy emerges from relations of mutual engagement and reciprocity but is then immediately directed at the reestablishment and re-creation of solidarity and connectedness, and in turn to the production of the autonomy of others. Partaking in the lives of others is not in conflict with the irreducibly individual and private dimensions of existence, or the experience of an inner life, but a condition for their emergence.

Such a focus on the intimate spaces of coexistence within which the contours of the self take shape further serves to highlight that what it is to be a person or self cannot be separated from the conceptions of the good that prevail in a particular milieu. As Londoño Sulkin (2005) has shown, standards of moral behavior may impose strong constraints on how the personhood of others is recognized or bestowed in Amazonia, tempering the perspectivist claim that all kinds of beings, human and nonhuman, are ontologically equivalent. I would emphasize that the particular understanding of morality that is of greatest relevance here is less that concerned with the content of obligation—with what it is right to do— than with what it is good to be and with the nature of the good life. In other words, the self exists in moral space, and understanding its sources, as Taylor (1989) makes clear, must incorporate an inquiry into how people seek to live the best possible life in accordance with their ideas of what makes life meaningful and fulfilling. The care of children along with trust in the relations of interdependency related to such care are primary moral concerns expressed by many Amazonian peoples (Overing 2003: 297), and my exploration of these themes emphasizes that the special importance placed by Urarina on patterns of care form part of a relational ethics rooted in ideas of mutuality, receptivity, and responsiveness.

In the following chapters I trace the path of development from the earliest moments of intrauterine existence through infancy and childhood to the cultivation of a gendered social and political identity to show how deeply intimate but asymmetrical attachments and dependencies shape Urarina experience and selfhood. These can, on occasion, extend beyond human society to include a variety of animals, plants, spirits, and material objects, raising questions about the position of humanity within a wider universe of potential subjectivities. This relative openness, or charitable disposition, as it were, to the personhood of nonhuman entities is such an important feature of many Amazonian societies because it points to radically different understandings of power, of the aims or ends of social life, and of the ontological importance of mutual coexistence as a precursor to the inner life of the individual. While issues of political subordination and relations to state power are not dealt with at any length here, we can reasonably assume that the early formation of subjectivity in conditions of intimate attachments and dependencies can condition one's subsequent incorporation into the social and political order (Butler 1997). By virtue of the nature of its own formation, bound to seek recognition under conditions not of its own making, the subject is rendered vulnerable to certain forms of exploitation or subjugation. As manifest in the most intimate spheres, power is rarely coercive, and largely expressed through vectors of caring, defending, seducing, or taming. These may in turn be thought of in terms of a broader matrix of subjectification, or subjection, implying the simultaneous subordination and forming of subjects. This process is clearly neither simple nor unidirectional, and the elicitation and manipulation of emotional attachments and desires are of paramount importance. A focus on the material and discursive practices of subjection, in this expanded sense, could shed new light on the complex relationship between autonomy and dependency, which I have already suggested lies at the heart of Amazonian sociality.

APPROACHING THE URARINA

This book is based on ethnographic fieldwork conducted between January 2005 and March 2007 in two communities of the upper Chambira River, which I call here San Pedro and Nueva Unión. Since their earliest appearances in seventeenth-century Spanish chronicles, and probably since their emergence as a distinct ethnic group, the Urarina have inhabited the middle and upper reaches of the Chambira River and its affluents in the region between the Pastaza and Tigre Rivers, now in the province and region of Loreto (map 1). Urarina communities may today also be found along the Uritoyacu and Corrientes Rivers, which like the Chambira flow into the Marañon River to form the headwaters of the Amazon.

The journey to these communities essentially begins in Iquitos, the regional capital and the largest city in the Peruvian rainforest. From here I would travel by passenger ferry southwestward up the Marañon for a day and a night, passing through hot, sparsely populated, low-lying rainforest, dotted along the way with predominantly riverine peasant, or *ribereño*, communities and a couple of small towns. There are also a number of Cocama communities along the lower Marañon; this group historically had close ties to the Urarina but were encouraged to deny their indigenous heritage for much of the twentieth century, until quite recently launching a project of cultural revitalization. On reaching the mouth of the Chambira, I would disembark the ferry and begin winding slowly up its dark, meandering waters by motorized dugout canoe, stopping overnight in villages along the way (figure 1). For the first day or two, the communities are predominantly mixed-descent mestizos who do not identify as indigenous, but beyond this are almost entirely Urarina.

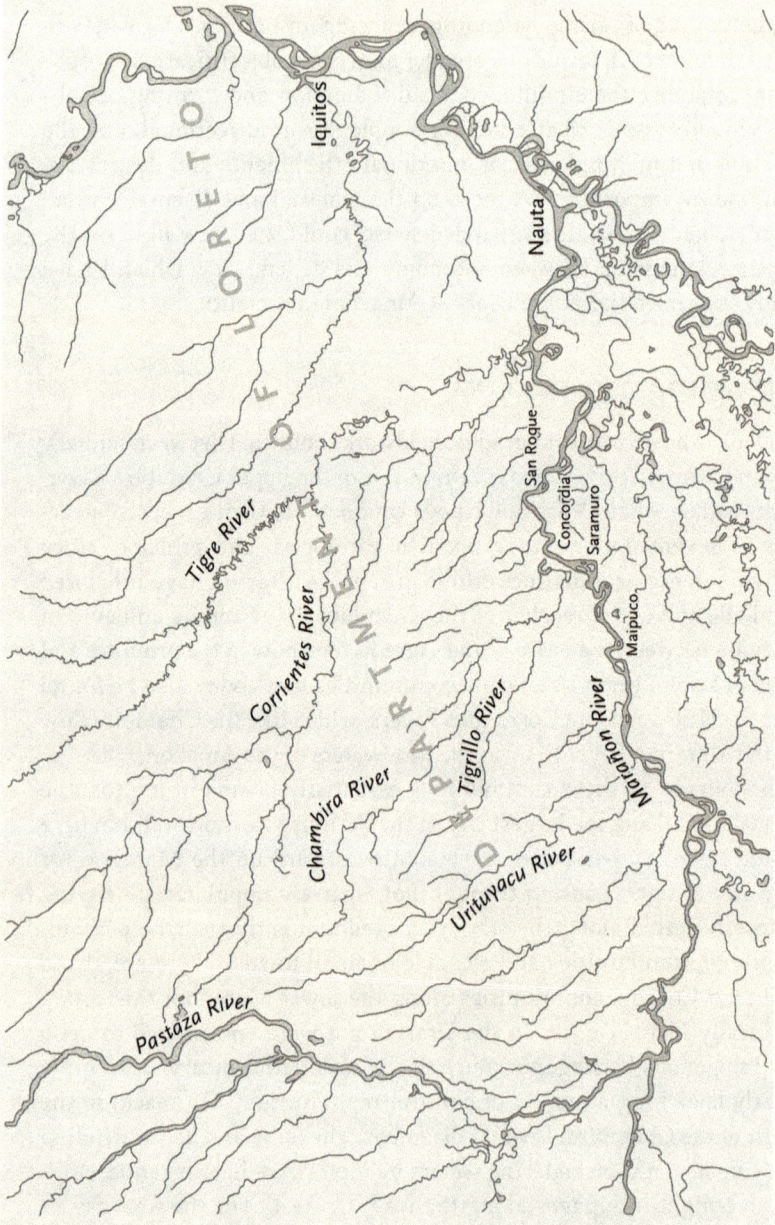

Map 1. Area inhabited by the Urarina.

Figure 1.   Preparing for a journey by canoe. Photograph by author.

The rivers are slow moving and sinuous in this low-lying, swampy land-scape, and liable to rise or fall several meters according to the season. As one progresses upriver toward the remoter headwaters of the Chambira, the river grows steadily shallower, and in the dry season especially one must be careful to avoid submerged branches and other hazards.

After around five days of traveling in this manner, one reaches the community of Nueva Unión; San Pedro is located a few hours farther upstream on a smaller tributary. Both communities are relatively small even by Urarina standards, comprising eight to ten houses and a school scattered around a central grassy plaza that doubles as a football field. The houses themselves are small and simple and made entirely of mate-rials sourced locally. Four hardwood columns support a pitched roof of thatched palm leaves; the floor comprises an elevated platform made from huacrapona trunks *(Iriartea deltoidea),* split open and joined together. The houses are otherwise entirely open, and the lack of walls is pleas-ant in the heat, especially at night, but makes privacy difficult. A simple hearth, comprising three combustible wooden poles arranged radially, with the cooking pot resting on their point of convergence, is usually located on bare ground just next to the house, sheltered by the overhanging leaves. People usually sit directly on the floor, though some men fashion low benches or utilize hammocks while resting during the day.

While most residents of a community are related to each other in some way or another, it is often possible to detect clusters of houses located closer together, reflecting extended family groups who tend to cooperate in common tasks and share food slightly more frequently with each other than with their more distant neighbors. Because postmarital residence is uxorilocal, with brideservice lasting at least several years, the houses in these clusters are often inhabited by a group of sisters and their in-marrying husbands. Urarina have no lineages, or any other kind of corporate group, and their social organization is relatively fluid. Many alliances are volatile and the social groupings that exist relatively unstable, with people coming and going as they choose, and mobility within and between communities remains high.

The economy is subsistence based, oriented to hunting, fishing, and swidden horticulture. A strong ethic of economic independence at the level of the nuclear family means that everyone is more or less equally competent in all the activities appropriate to their gender. Men still hunt with blowpipes on a regular basis but nowadays prefer to use shotguns if cartridges are available; less often, they hunt with dogs or set traps. Fishing is usually with hooked lines (done mostly by women) or spears (mostly by men), occasionally using poison made from crushed *huaca* leaves and released into shallow streams. Women assume primary responsibility for maintaining gardens once they have been cleared and planted, tasks with which men assist. Plantains and sweet manioc are the staple crops, though most gardens also contain smaller quantities of a variety of other cultigens, such as maize, papaya, and peanuts; these are supplemented by wild fruits gathered from the forest, especially from the ungurahui, aguaje, and pijuayo palms. Women generally spend much more time than men in the house during the day, engaged with cooking and child care, weaving, sewing clothes, or making string bags to exchange with fluvial traders. Many women also raise chickens, and men occasionally raise pigs, all exclusively for exchange.

The Urarina are a relatively large ethnolinguistic group by contemporary Amazonian standards, numbering somewhere around four thousand to six thousand, although exact numbers are difficult to determine because relatively few have identity documents or are covered in the national census. In the literature they have been variously referred to as Aracuies, Cingacuchuscas, Chambiras, and Shimacus, among other names, while Urarina themselves use the ethnonym *cacha*. As is common elsewhere in the region, this autonym essentially means "real people" or "true humans."[6] Other languages traditionally spoken in the vicinity of Urarina territory include Candoshi, Omurana, Iquito, Jebero, Cocama, and Yameo.[7] Although they have been erroneously accorded membership in a variety of ethnic and linguistic families since their first documentation in the literature, Urarina is today considered a linguistic isolate, unrelated to any other known language.

The Urarina language is used exclusively among Urarina themselves. Spanish is spoken only to outsiders, and then only by men. Most men are today reasonably competent speakers of Spanish, and a minority could be considered fully bilingual; women, however, generally do not speak Spanish. This is attributable in part to the pervasive gender segregation that characterizes Urarina society, and is indeed one of the most immediately distinctive features for an outside observer. It is generally considered inappropriate for a woman to converse with a man who is not her husband or close kin. Interaction with outsiders—especially with mestizos and other non-Urarina—is the exclusive province of men. Hence for both cultural and linguistic reasons the majority of my interactions were with men rather than women. Elderly widows were an exception to this rule (as they are to many constraints imposed on women generally), and I developed a certain rapport with a couple of older women, with whom I was able to converse in Urarina at a basic level and in Spanish with the help of a translator. For although I made a concerted effort to learn the Urarina language and, over time, developed a degree of competency in reading and writing,[8] I never learned to speak it well. This was due in no small measure to the complex verbal morphology, which proved particularly difficult to master.[9] As such, I spoke more Spanish than Urarina during my stay. When conversing with women, I often found it most convenient, and reliable, to record their responses to open-ended questions and then transcribe and translate them later. Hence although every effort was made to consider women's perspectives wherever possible, these constraints on the analysis of gender should be taken into consideration. I have little doubt that future work with women will reveal additional perspectives on Urarina society complementary to those elaborated here.

Because of the relative inaccessibility of these communities, visitors are relatively rare. Like many other Amazonian peoples, Urarina are understandably suspicious of outsiders and their intentions, and it took time and patience to build solid working relations of mutual trust. I eventually began to establish rewarding friendships with a small handful of men whose particularly insightful commentaries on a range of matters were of inestimable help in advancing my understandings. Their voices appear from time to time in these pages, and I have made an effort to stay faithful to their distinctive style of speech.

My greatest debt of all is to Lorenzo, without whose intellectual engagement with my project this book could not exist. At the time of my stay, Lorenzo was an aspiring and astute middle-aged man living with his second wife, their three small children, and his widowed mother. As an elected leader, or lieutenant governor *(teniente gobernador)*, of Nueva Unión, he thought constantly about how best to enhance its size and prosperity and was particularly interested in tapping into the resources of the state and its legal system to achieve his ends. While deeply interested in the stories and wisdom of the ancients, he was also a staunch advocate of progress, who regularly implored people to live in a disciplined, "organized," forward-looking manner. I came to admire greatly his resourcefulness, vision, and determination.

Jorge was a young man of roughly my own age who moved to Nueva Unión with his family while I was already residing there following a bitter dispute with his erstwhile neighbors farther upriver. He quickly became a good friend and indispensable assistant and translator. This was no doubt in part because of his own status as a relative outsider and newcomer to the community but also because he had spent a few years in his youth in the city of Iquitos and was comfortable speaking Spanish as well as relatively sensitive to, and understanding of, cultural differences. He also developed a reasonable comprehension of the aims of my project and helped me to explain these to others, alleviating suspicions about my motives. Jorge had two wives—not in itself unusual—but one of them was Lorenzo's mother-in-law. This was anomalous given Lorenzo's seniority in terms of age and was doubtless a source a tension between the two men, who did not often see eye to eye. Other valued companions in the field included Martín, one of the local Urarina schoolteachers who was also originally from another community; and Samuel, one of my nearest neighbors in Nueva Unión, whose tiny ramshackle house—in which I spent much time visiting—was always full of colorful pet birds, from tiny parakeets to imposing trumpeters. A congenial, middle-aged man living with his wife, mother-in-law, and four children, he was always happy to chat, ideally over a bowl of manioc beer prepared by his adolescent daughter.

One reason for including these people's individual voices where possible is to avoid giving the impression of a normativity or conformity that simply does not exist. Amazonian societies tend to be loosely and infor-

mally organized, with little emphasis on statuses or roles. They are relatively free of explicit or standardized normative codes and conventions,
and there is little by way of a tradition of exegesis. Even within the upper
Chambira area, I found that certain beliefs and practices tended to vary
from group to group, or even person to person.[10] This is another of the
ways in which Urarina society is quite individualistic, and there is often
a healthy difference of opinion to be found on a great number of matters.

This may be especially the case with shamanism, a cultural institution
of great importance in the everyday lives of many Urarina and which is
by its nature highly dependent on individual experience rather than the
standardized cultural transmission of ideas. Urarina shamanism is not a
restricted domain accessible only to initiates: any man willing to persevere may eventually be considered a *coaairi coera,* "drinker of psychotropics," by regularly consuming ample quantities over a long period of time
of decoctions prepared from ayahausca *(Banisteriopsis caapi)* or brugmansia, also known as angel's trumpet *(Brugmansia suavolens),* for the
only proper teacher is the spiritual presence of the plant itself, typically
referred to as its "mother" or "owner." For this reason, in this book the
term *shaman* generally refers to an experienced drinker of psychotropics
but not a separate category of person. In Nueva Unión and San Pedro,
most men of middle age or above were practicing shamans of one form
or another, who drank psychedelics on a regular basis for a diverse array
of ends. Although women do sometimes drink infusions of ayahuasca
or angel's trumpet, they rarely if ever persevere. Certain men seek to go
further by training to become a *benane,* or sorcerer, one credited with
the power to inflict harm on others by mystical means, as well as with
enhanced abilities to cure such harm. Such men are considered highly
dangerous, though they are also few and ever dwindling in number.

One of my earliest challenges, after my arrival, was adequately con-
veying, to my own satisfaction, the purpose of my stay. While I was graciously accepted into the community right from the outset, my attempts
to explain the anthropological endeavor were generally met with skep-
ticism or incomprehension. Finally Damian, the communal chief of San
Pedro, gave me a knowing look. "Ah, yes, now I see," he said, nodding his
head. "But if you really want to understand about us Urarina, how we live
and so on, we can't tell you all that. You have to drink ayahuasca, and
keep drinking and drinking and drinking. It will tell you everything, just
like it tells us everything." Though I did not expect the visions induced
by this powerful psychoactive infusion to substitute for patient partici-
pant observation, Damian's remark certainly brought home to me just

how seriously visionary experiences were taken. Anthropologists have long recognized that it is impossible to treat Amazonian ritual practices or cosmological ideas as separate from everyday social life, for these are deeply intertwined. As I have just mentioned, Urarina shamanism is far from a restricted domain of esoteric practice, of interest only to specialists. On the contrary, it comprises a kind of implicit background of shared meanings pervading a wide range of everyday tasks. In the case of infant and early child care, for example, shamanic ritual practices were often considered to be of great importance for ensuring a safe and healthy start to life. People's ideas about matters ranging from right conduct to the nature of the self were typically informed to some extent by religious and healing ceremonies involving the consumption of psychotropics. The resulting visions are deemed authoritative in a way that is difficult for us sometimes to comprehend, far surpassing the relatively unreliable sensory data obtained under normal waking conditions, where appearances are all too often deceiving. Yet such visionary experiences are just one important source of knowledge and of current practices and ideas; historical experiences are another and equally important one.

"THE ANCESTORS WERE ALREADY LEARNING"

Historical information on the Urarina is limited to a smattering of references in the accounts of early missionaries and traders. The first ethnographic portrait was made by Tessman (1930) in the course of his extensive travels through the Peruvian Amazon; his observations have since been supplemented by Castillo (1958, 1961), Ferrúa Carrasco and colleagues (1980), Kramer (1977, 1979), and, finally, Dean (2009), who offers a more extensive historical overview than can be accommodated here. My aim in the following is to enable an understanding of the Urarina as a distinct and unique group vis-à-vis their neighbors and to contextualize some of the salient features of Urarina culture by tracing them, where possible, to historical experiences of trade, warfare, missionization, and the gradual process of incorporation into Peruvian national society.

The Urarina were first contacted in the seventeenth century by Jesuit missionaries, who used the neighboring Cocama and Itucale peoples as guides and intermediaries. By the time the Jesuits entered the western Amazon in 1638, the exchange networks along the Marañon and Huallaga River systems were already under the control of the Tupian Cocama and Omagua, who had begun their migration up the Napo and Marañon some time prior to 1500. Due to their riverine base, superior technology, and warlike disposition, these groups came to play a critical and increasingly dominant role in the region, both trading with and raiding their neighbors. The aggressiveness of the Cocama, who were probably the Urarina's closest trading partners, intensified around the time of Jesuit contact, as a result of the European demand for slaves as well as the indigenous desire for European trade goods. Captives were taken from other groups to "ransom" for trade goods, and by 1640 the Cocama were regularly raiding the entire length of the Huallaga in search of iron tools, captives, and heads (Reeve 1993: 110–11). The decimating effects of disease epidemics contributed to the spiral of violence, and any death attributable to shamanic aggression might be met with retaliation. With their peaceful, even timid disposition, Urarina were likely victims of the raiding warfare into which earlier trade relationships deteriorated following Spanish contact.

The Cocama who assisted the Jesuits to "pacify" the Urarina had in turn been contacted and pacified by the Jevero, who, thanks to their access to European goods, were able to strengthen their position vis-à-vis others (Reeve 1993: 120). As was the pattern elsewhere in the region, proselytization and mission formation followed indigenous alliance networks, and each reinforced the other. The Jesuits eventually came to control regional exchange, and local populations were soon dependent on them for European trade goods, of which iron tools were the principal items. Trade came to center on the exploitation of salt and the exchange of blowgun-dart poison, both activities organized by the missionaries (Reeve 1993: 119). The mission town of San Xavier de Urarinas was founded on the banks of the Chambira in 1738, changing location twice before the Jesuits were expelled in 1767. By this time it had a population of six hundred persons and was considered one of the most established and potentially successful missions to fall under Franciscan jurisdiction (Kramer 1979: 12).

The Jesuit missionary Velasco wrote in the eighteenth century of the challenges faced by his colleagues in coming to terms with the characteristically fluid and independent way of life of the peoples who inhabited the Marañon and its tributaries.

> None of them had either small or large town. Divided entirely into separate tribes, with each tribe subdivided into small homesteads, each distant from the other, they were incapable of uniting themselves as a society. They found this abhorrent in the extreme because each family head wanted to be independent, and subject to his natural lord or prince only on the rarest of occasions. They readily offered

the missionaries friendship and peace; they promised to subject
themselves to their teachings and to receive the gospel, but to speak
to them about uniting together in settlements was to hit a sore point,
and achieving it was not just arduous, it was impossible.

(Velasco 1979 [1789]: 478)

Velasco further reported that the Urarina traditionally inhabited the
interfluvial areas, preferring travel through the jungle by foot to river
travel (Costales and Costales 1983: 124), and indeed the people I spoke to
also confirmed that their earliest ancestors did not fabricate, or travel in,
canoes. Dubbing them the "gypsies of the Marañón," Velasco observed
that they traveled overland in "flying squadrons," staying only as long in
an area as the duration of a particular fruit or hunt, constructing makeshift huts of leaves and branches.

Velasco's characterizations are revealing. They tell us that the Urarina
are relatively marginal to dominant political and economic structures,
that they prefer flight to confrontation, and that they have an ethos of
passive resistance. These features still structure their relations with outsiders today. The Urarina's peaceful, even submissive disposition contrasts sharply with their famously bellicose Tupian and Jivaroan neighbors. This did not escape the notice of the Franciscan historian Izaguirre
(2004: 615), who characterized the Urarina as a calm and pacifist people,
who received their first missionaries graciously and benevolently, to the
point of appearing obsequious and servile. The surrounding tribes, on
the other hand, would in such situations turn hostile and prepare to wage
war.

During my time in the field I recorded a number of myths and oral
histories dealing with the relations between the Urarina and their neighbors. Many of these concern the Candoshi or other hostile peoples whom
the Urarina refer to generically as *bacauha*. The stories often portray the
Urarina as the innocent victims of hostile raiding parties, typically in
search of captives and/or brides. Against tremendous odds, the Urarina
are forced to defend themselves through a combination of wile and brav-
ery. For example, in one story two Urarina women are kidnapped by a
Candoshi raiding party and taken back to their village, where they are
raised like pets. They are much admired by their new "owner" for their
obedience, though his children continually pester them and eye them
hungrily. They are fed all kinds of delicacies, especially pineapple, until
they grow tremendously fat. One day, they are sent to fetch firewood,
water, and maize to make a giant soup. It dawns on them that they are
themselves to be the main ingredient. Without letting on, they dutifully

begin dehusking rice and grinding maize for the soup. When they are sent to wash and scrub themselves well, they decide to flee. Luckily, they run into one of their uncles, who happens to be out in the forest, clearing a spot to build himself a small shelter. When they tell him their story, he gathers his companions and concocts a plan, and is finally successful in extracting revenge.

The term *bacauha* may be translated as "enemy" or "savage," and the people so designated are in many ways considered the diametric opposite of real people or true humans (cacha). Yet rather than simply define themselves as "prey" in relation to enemy "predators," Urarina tend to refuse or ignore the predatory mode of relation altogether, and typically spurn violence, cannibalism, and warfare as the concerns of barbarous, uncivilized "others." Even game animals are thought to be "given" to hunters by divine agents through acts of paternalistic kindness, in response to self-effacing requests. Yet if predation is not the primary model of interaction with the outside, there is nevertheless a distinctive ethos of "protection" or "defense," which figures as an encompassing value in Urarina notions of community and selfhood.

In some ways, notably their aversion to warfare, the Urarina might resemble the better-known Arawakan groups in their vicinity; yet they are quite dissimilar in certain other respects. The emphasis on genealogy and descent, refined agricultural techniques, and tendencies toward complex hierarchical polities that characterize the latter (Santos Granero 2005b) are all lacking among the Urarina. So too are the ritualized greetings characteristic of Arawak speakers, which "serve as reminders of a common humanity and peaceful ethos" (Hornborg 2005: 592). Urarina did not traditionally greet each other at all, and even today do so only occasionally, using forms directly copied from Spanish. That said, analysis of the kinship terminology does suggest a historical shift away from a two-line prescriptive system to a generational system, such that many cross-parallel distinctions are blurred, cousins are classified with siblings, and a certain exogamous ideology has come to the fore (see Walker 2009b). In other words, in place of an earlier marriage rule specifying a particular category of relative, there is now only a prohibition on marrying close kin, meaning that people seek spouses from ever further afield. This could be taken to reflect growing interest in long-term trade and a social system more accommodating of outsiders, which is at least comparable to the case of Arawakan groups such as the Matsiguenga or Piro (see, e.g., Henley 1996: 49–50). In addition, the cultural importance placed on relationships of trust, friendship, and love with both fellow humans and nonhumans, rather than exclusively corporeal idioms of shared substance, is in line with recent discussions of Matsiguenga and Amuesha sociality by Rosengren (2006) and Santos Granero (2007) respectively.

Urarina experience with missions was fairly moderate compared to that of many other groups, such as the Cocama and Cocamilla living farther downstream. Though they are broadly familiar with Christian idioms such as God and the Devil, sin, the Bible, and so on, it would be highly misleading to describe them as Christian. Nevertheless, the figure of the missionary or "priest" *(batiri,* from the Spanish *padre)* enjoys a special prominence in Urarina historical consciousness. Although long absent from the Chambira, priests are still almost wistfully spoken of as educators and benefactors, sources of gifts and important moral knowledge on how to lead a "civilized" life. The following story, told to me by a highly respected old man named Tivorcio, might be considered fairly typical.

> A long time ago, from the time of our creation, there was a priest. And the people got drunk, earlier, and the women had no shame, they used only tiny coverings that scarcely concealed their vaginas. That priest hardly weighed anything, like a bag of cotton wool. He made them learn to feel embarrassed, and speaking to them thus, he taught them. Before, the women would simply sit down on a fire log, without shame, hardly covering their vagina, and we could see it. Really. That's why the priest told them, that's no good, one must cover up, like this. When he spoke like this, the women learned, they learned to be embarrassed. When you get drunk, dance like this, he told them, that's how you dance, and with that the women learned everything. The men also learned. The men used to string up their penises out in the open, but then they started wearing clothing. They were already learning. That's how it's done for all us men.

Other accounts also lend credence to Izaguirre's depictions of the submissive welcome extended to Spanish missionaries, discussed earlier. But they reveal too a deeper level of anxieties and suspicions in people's attitudes to outsiders. Due to their "fear" or "ignorance" (not to mention a resistance to the sedentary lifestyles promoted by missionaries), the Urarina first contacted by these priests are said to have fled into the forest, terrified of being taken to the city as captives. Instead of receiving the gifts on offer, they invoked the wrath of their well-intentioned visitors. Such attitudes toward priests, both then and now, form part of broader interpretive structures that continue to inform constructions of some non-Urarina, including or especially divine beings. Complementary to perceptions of their Jivaroan and Candoshi enemies, certain other, no less powerful outsiders are here seen as benevolent, paternalistic providers of knowledge and other important gifts necessary for living well. Again somewhat reminiscent of the Amuesha case (Santos Granero 1991), power may be conjoined with love such that hierarchy is reconstructed as nurture and thereby legitimized—even if there is always a lingering degree of ambivalence.

After the expulsion of the Jesuits in 1767, the Marañon region was increasingly characterized by a nascent capitalism in which bosses and traders would exploit native labor in exchange for Western goods (Kramer 1979:13). Although rubber was not tapped along the Chambira itself, some Urarina were captured and relocated, and many others worked as debt peons for local patrones, periodically retreating into more inaccessible zones to avoid the perils of contact. By the middle of the twentieth century, the Urarina living on the Chambira River were in more or less continuous contact with whites. While continuing to derive income from extracted forest resources, the region entered a phase of commercial agriculture, characteristically dominated by "feudal" estates (San Roman 1975: 168–90). Some Urarina were bonded to such an estate located on the Marañon River at the mouth of the Chambira. With the gradual improvement of transportation facilities, especially air transport, the jungle region was further integrated into Peruvian national life. In the wake of this increased commercialization, a degree of competition emerged between a variety of entrepreneurs wishing to gain control of indigenous labor. In 1943 the Augustian priest Villarejo described the Urarina as being "submissive to whites" and quite willing to work for patrones or sell products to traders (Kramer 1979:16). These same patrones were nevertheless prone to threaten and even torture or imprison unwilling laborers, as confirmed by any number of collective memories and oral histories.

The name Shimacu was used commonly through the early twentieth century by neighboring peasant or ribereño communities, and it may still be heard today in the region, although Urarina themselves consider it derogatory. According to Dean (2009: 31), *Shimacu* derives etymologically from *cimarrón*, which in the Iberian Americas originally signified escaped feral livestock, then runaway Indian slave. There are echoes here of notions of "taming" or "domesticating" that are still quite important in Urarina culture, as well as the tendencies toward submissiveness and evasiveness that were first flagged by Velasco two centuries earlier. At least for some of their trade partners and neighbors, then, these tendencies had perhaps even come to define the Urarina as a group.

In 1960 a couple from the Summer Institute of Linguistics (SIL) began living and working with the Urarina, and have done so intermittently over the past several decades. The effects of this presence have been subtle and complex. In addition to being instrumental in introducing formal schooling, particularly literacy training, this husband and wife team helped to found the first Comunidad Nativa (Native Community)—the official landholding entity recognized by Peruvian law—setting an example that other communities soon followed. Although relatively few Urarina have "converted" to Christianity as a result of this missionary presence, at least so far as I could ascertain, it may have reinforced the importance of a number of apparently Christian themes already discernible within the "traditional" mythology and cosmology, which were presumably embedded in local idioms over the centuries following exposure to mission life. For example, one myth tells of how the son of God was sent to teach the Urarina how to lead a better life. Despite his ability to work miracles, such as turning tiny fish into big fish to feed the masses, the ancient Urarina refused to listen and ended up burying him in the sand.

In recent decades petroleum exploration has brought new migrants into the region and spurred the development of a local timber industry, as well as an increase in commercial agricultural production. Although lumbering is highly regarded by Urarina as a potentially lucrative enterprise, it is undertaken only intermittently, and always at the initiative of traders and private entrepreneurs (figure 2). During the period of my fieldwork, easily the most important commercial activity undertaken was the extraction of edible palm hearts, particularly from the *huasai* palm (*Euterpe precatoria*). Not consumed by Urarina, these are sold by traders to a cannery in Iquitos, as well as to local vendors. The Chambira is allegedly the largest single source of edible palm hearts in the Department of Loreto. Urarina exchange palm hearts and other forest products with mestizo traders under the system of *habilitación*. Desired goods such as shotgun cartridges, batteries, salt, or kerosene are advanced by itinerant fluvial traders on credit as they wind their way slowly upriver, incurring a debt that their Urarina clients must then work off, preferably by extracting the equivalent value of forest produce by the time the trader returns on his way downriver to Iquitos. Such transactions are of considerable ideological significance, rivaling hunting and gardening as bases for Urarina constructions of their cultural identity.

After being substantially reduced in number following contact, primarily as a result of disease, the Urarina population today is thriving.

Figure 2.   Rolling felled logs along a cleared path to the river. Photograph by author.

Despite their long and intensive history of contact, they have retained a strong cultural and ethnic identity. Although many Urarina are bilingual, all use the Urarina language exclusively among themselves, and even the majority of schoolteachers are native speakers drawn from other Urarina communities. Barring the occasional (unsubstantiated) rumor of some feared bacauha appearing in Urarina territory, contact with other indigenous groups is currently negligible. The Cocama, perhaps the group historically in closest contact, made a more or less conscious effort to erase their indigenous identity some decades ago, and most of the Urarina's other erstwhile trading partners, such as the Jebero, Omagua, Omurana, and Lamista, have more or less disappeared.

Social and political integration into the Peruvian nation has nevertheless been slow. State presence in the region is mostly limited to the locally elected lieutenant governors *(teniente gobernadores)*, on whom it confers nominal disciplinary power, a small primary health care outpost in the community of Nueva Esperanza, and modest funding for local schoolteachers. In the early 1990s the Fujimori government donated a number of aluminum dinghies to Urarina communities as part of its incentives to form Native Communities, effectively raising awareness of the potential benefits of political participation, although most of these have long since fallen into disrepair. The vast majority of Urarina living on the upper Chambira do not possess a national identity card (DNI), which is more than symbolic of their exclusion from national society; depriving them of suffrage, it effectively ensures their irrelevance to regional governments, which naturally prefer to focus their attentions on their voting constituency.

The continuing social isolation of the Urarina is due in large part to the geographic isolation of the Chambira River but also to Urarina people's deeply entrenched indifference to, and mistrust of, most forms of political organization. The Urarina were one of the last indigenous groups in Peru to form a representative organization, and the impetus to do so at all began as a mandate of the nongovernmental organization CEDIA (Centro para el Desarrollo del Indígena Amazónico), which has worked most intensively with Urarina communities along the Tigrillo, an affluent of the lower Chambira. The president and other officials of the indigenous organization, known as CURCHA (Consejo Urarina del Río Chambira), were drawn from these communities and supported financially by CEDIA, leading to a widespread sentiment, along the upper Chambira, that CURCHA is not representative of the Urarina people as a whole. In recent years the reach of CURCHA has been limited further by the increasing power of the Red Educativa, an institutional arm of the bilingual education program established by the SIL missionaries, though it remains to be seen whether this will develop into a rival ethnopolitical organization.

Urarina occupation of the Chambira basin is not entirely uniform; the lower stretches of the river are populated by mestizo communities; several live further upriver also. Where mestizos otherwise live in Urarina communities, usually after having married an Urarina woman, they tend to enjoy positions of influence. Many of the Urarina communities appear to cluster together into loosely endogamous units, defined by a higher density of matrimonial alliances within them than between them, and certain dialectical and other linguistic differences (e.g., forms of ritual discourse) are discernible. Mobility patterns are complex and not limited to uxorilocal residence patterns, but there is a certain territoriality that prompts people often to return to the general area of their birth. Several decades ago a group of Urarina crossed by land to the Corrientes River, where at least two sizable communities are now flourishing. In 2006 a small group of Urarina left the Chambira to join with a mestizo town on the banks of the Marañon, though it remains to be seen if the move will prove permanent. Migration patterns appear otherwise virtually non-existent. A very small handful of Urarina are known to have moved to Iquitos but in almost all cases are reported to have lost contact with their families entirely and renounced their former indigenous identity.

Nevertheless, the marks of change from the past half century or so are clear. For example, in place of the earlier system of debt bondage, based on strong hierarchical and occasionally coercive patron-client relationships, traders now have to compete against each other for native labor, potentially paving the way for the emergence of a market economy. Most people lead more sedentary lifestyles and live in larger communities than ever before, and this is associated with growing dependency on imported foodstuffs and manufactured goods. The majority of children attend school, even if literacy rates remain low, while resolutions to disputes or conflicts are today as likely to be sought through legal avenues as through traditional techniques of shamanic vengeance. Many people appear deeply ambivalent about these and other changes, and it is possible to discern two very distinct ethnohistorical discourses, one celebrating the ascendance of Urarina people into "civilization" from a state of ignorance and relative "savagery" and interminable feuding and another warning of an impending apocalypse as an unavoidable consequence of the gradual but tragic disappearance of the shamanic knowledge necessary for forestalling it. In a similar vein, material wealth in the form of watches, radios, outboard motors, and so on increasingly orients people's desires and structures their expectations. Yet these goods are also intimately associated with the devil, who is said to be their source and true "owner" and who punishes the souls of those who possess them in his celestial fire. In some other respects, however, life on the upper Chambira River continues much as it has since the times of the ancients, an assertion endlessly reiterated in the various genres of ritual discourse. Most of the inhabitants here remain perfectly content to continue making a living in the ways they know best: hunting the animals placed in the forest by the Creator, toiling in their gardens to reap the rewards of their labor, and so on; but above all by standing-leaned-together as real people must, seeking out that ever elusive balance between the various, sometimes contradictory ingredients indispensable for living well.

2. Vital Shields

Urarina dwellings are small and simple affairs. An overarching roof of thatched palm leaves shelters a raised stilt palm floor, but the dwelling remains otherwise open to the elements, allowing little by way of privacy. Walking past Lorenzo's house to the river one morning, my idle glance inside met with a familiar, homely sight. Lorenzo's wife, Renona, was seated on the floor with a leg stretched out in front of her, absently humming softly to her sleeping baby boy, who was tightly wrapped in blankets and barely visible inside a small, string hammock that arced gracefully back and forth through the air. By means of a long, taut string extending from the base of the hammock to a gap between her toes, a simple rocking of Renona's foot kept the hammock in constant, rapid motion and her hands free to sew her blouse with the bright red cloth I had recently given her. A large, heterogeneous bundle of gourds, dried seeds, and other items, affixed beneath the position of the baby's head, brushed softly against the floor as it passed through the bottom of its trajectory, producing a gentle rattling sound in a steady, rhythmic fashion. The tune Renona was humming, in the form of a bilabial trill, was instantly recognizable to me as the "lullaby" always sung to infants throughout Urarina territory. The baby stirred in his sleep, and she switched to a sung version, improvising the lyrics from a stock of familiar themes and formulaic expressions.

All young women learn this valued art of returning infants to sleep, the condition in which they are considered to be best protected from the dangerous and harmful world beyond the hammock. Sleep is also the state in which infants are thought to be most readily shaped and influenced by the many songs, remedies, and artifacts that parents and other relatives dutifully provide. Urarina people maintain that a newborn baby enters the world in a highly vulnerable and ambiguous state of existence and that continual intervention is required in order to form and fortify its body, protect it from disease, and ensure its successful transition into the condition of fully human, social personhood. The material and discursive practices discussed in this chapter reveal much about the ways in which parents, and others, strive to cultivate valued physical and mental capacities in infants, even as they sleep, and highlight how the foundations of personal autonomy and agency are seen to lie within intimate relations of nurturance and dependency.

These same practices of infant care also implicate local theories of reality. In particular, they raise questions about the nature of matter or physical substance and its relationship to subjective meanings and intentions. The Western notion that "thing" and "concept" are ontologically separate has been challenged on several fronts in recent years.[1] In the Urarina lived world, to be sure, the songs and chants that accompany a newborn baby's emergence from the birth hut are in many ways as physically real and tangible as its gifts of body ornaments and artifacts, and all are essential to the process of making persons. It is not simply the case that words are objectlike, for artifacts such as the hammock and its rattle come closely to resemble a powerful form of song. Exploring these themes leads us to reflect on weaving and singing as analogous forms of action as well as conceptual paradigms for the general creative process through which bodies, and artifacts, are carefully and skillfully brought into being.

EMERGENCE

The birth of a healthy child nearly always brings joy to the life of a community, but is neither a singular nor a decisive event. The passage through the birth canal from the womb is but one brief moment in the painstaking process of forging a new person—a process that began many months before and will it is hoped last for years to come. There is a moment that has a perhaps even greater existential significance: the infant's "emergence" from the warm and secluded space of the birth hut. Known as the *jata,* this is a small, purpose-built enclosure made from palm leaves or, on occasion, from assorted blankets and fabrics, often constructed by the husband as a temporary adjunct or annex to the couple's own house and sheltered by the same roof. It is a protective space, existing no longer than the ten or so days for which it is required, intended to shield a newborn baby from the many harmful elements in the surrounding environment to which it is considered especially vulnerable. Like the menstrual huts in which pubescent girls are secluded at the onset of menarche, also known as jata, it is also a liminal space for both the containment of polluting blood and the safe transition from one physicosocial status to another.

Following a birth, mother and child dwell together inside the birth hut for a period of up to ten days, at least until the remnant stub of umbilical cord drops off from the child's navel. During this time, the midwife (*michuera*) and other female kin assist the mother as much as possible with her various needs and duties. This includes ensuring a steady supply of food, water, and firewood for the small fire that burns slowly but continually inside, for the purpose of keeping the baby warm and snug at all times. The tightly woven palm leaves (or blankets) have no windows or large openings, and the atmosphere inside the tiny space—warm, dark, safe, and enclosed—is reminiscent of the womb from which the child has recently arrived. The construction and use of the jata may be seen as a way of delaying an infant's potentially painful exposure to the relatively harsh climate outside the comfortable, intrauterine world to which it has grown accustomed, prolonging an otherwise overly abrupt transition from a state of contained suspension in amniotic fluids into the cold, open air.

Emergence from the birth hut is in some ways a kind of "second birth," which confers social legitimacy on the newborn.[2] The event takes place at dawn, following the performance by the father or a more senior male relative, of a lengthy cycle of ritual songs known as the child emergence chant (*canaanai mitu baau*). This may last up to several hours, and "blesses" a small mixture of achiote and a type of piri-piri grown especially for this purpose, used subsequently to paint the infant and its newly prepared hammock prior to their entry into the world. Like other chants in the genre known as *baau*, the emergence chant is generally performed by men and appears to be transmitted patrilineally. Baau are highly specialized, and usually their intended purpose is to cure illness or malaise in babies and young children held to be of malicious or mystical origin (*uunaatiha*). A typical baau invokes a series of beings held to be immune to the type of harm being treated, with the aim of incorporating or appropriating this resistive quality into the target and thence into the child. The kapok baau, for example, invokes a number of birds said to nest in the branches of the kapok tree (*Ceiba pentandra*), emphasizing their resilience. In this way baau chants often reflect prominent ecological and interspecies associations.

Often performed sotto voce, alone or in the company of close kin, the baau always has a target object that it "blesses" (often a small amount of plantain soup to be subsequently consumed by the child). Breath is particularly important in the performance of baau, and short, sharp exhalations with lips slightly pursed, marked in my transcriptions as "pshew!," punctuate and divide the verses. Such sharp breaths are held to be essential to the efficacy of the chant, for they are associated with the putative entry of the words into the substance being blessed. Lorenzo explained it to me using an analogy he knew I would readily appreciate: "It is just like how you mix sugar into your coffee." Others told me it worked rather like gossip, the power simply "spreading out" everywhere within the patient.

In the predawn cold on the morning of Nujuari's emergence, Lorenzo sat calmly next to the birth hut with his hands cupped tightly around a small gourd, held right next to his mouth as he sang the emergence chant. His unusually sweet, hushed, and melodic singing voice seemed well suited, I thought, to the delicate existence of the child sleeping peacefully inside the hut a few feet away. As he reached the end of each stanza, a sharp exhalation of breath—pshew!—marked the decisive moment at which the full force of the words entered into the mixture. As if to emphasize their stubborn physicality, he held one hand over the top of the bowl at all times, preventing any possible escape before the breathy words themselves were properly absorbed, even as he rested from time to time to chat casually with Renona or me. The song itself consisted largely of repetitive intonations of key words and expressions, mostly centering on the baby nearby, who is represented here (as in all baau songs) as *aino calabi*, "son of aino,"[3] or as *ujuari*, "green" or "unripe"—an expression often used for very small children, roughly until the time they learn to walk, and representing the period during which they are considered most vulnerable and defenseless. The song makes repeated references to the process of painting the child with the achiote mixture, in particular, the chest area *(ranisijie)* extending from the center of the collarbone to the bottom of the rib cage. The term evokes the principal load-bearing columns of a house *(anisijia)*, and has a similar role as one's foundation or "support." All food and drink must pass through the ranisijie in the digestive process, and it is here that an affliction or illness is most likely to take hold.

caa aino calabi nijianaco que	This newborn son of aino
rai acarera coinainaritiin	Painting his vital breath with achiote
chabana neein ne baitenachara	That which is never forgotten
cana necoacuna jiniichaain necoacunaquica	Created together with our creation

inoaera nichane rai necoerejete	Inoaera's child
rai acarera que	With his vital breath
aino calabi ne nujuaricho acarera	Unripe son of aino's vital breath
ranisijie coinaina coinainaritiin ne	Painting the chest with achiote
ca lauri coiane que	With our group's achoite
aino calabi coinainari coinainaritiin ne	Painting the son of aino with achiote
chabana baitein	Never forgetting
chabana chanenachara	That to which nothing ever befalls
cana necoacuna jiniichaain necoacunaquica	Created together with our creation

As the song progresses, a plethora of beings, real and mythical, contemporary and ancient, human and nonhuman, are invoked in turn, each noteworthy for a particular desirable property or form of knowledge, especially immunity to illness or harm. Lorenzo's version of the emergence chant invoked, at one point, three species of turtle in succession, all considered to have copious quantities of vital breath: the quality, he later explained to me, that enables them to live underwater and that makes them so resilient, long-lived, and difficult to kill.

chabana nitanacanaachara	That to whom nothing ever befalls
caa tariacha	This yellow-spotted river turtle[4]
tariacha nichane	Yellow-spotted river turtle
cana counujene ucuane nii asaaun	Deep inside our rivers
ca lauri ne counujene ucuane	Deep inside our group's river basin
necoanacotecoquica tariacha nichane	The yellow-spotted river turtle goes to dwell
chabana cana lauri cabelara que enecotaera que necocunaiteein ne	Never ill from our world's terrors and afflictions
chabana baitein ne	Never being forgotten
baitenacanaachara	That which is never forgotten
tariacha necoerejeteco rai acarera que	Offspring of the yellow-spotted river turtle's vital breath
aino calabi nujuaricho rai coianena acarera mitu que	Painting the unripe son of aino's vital breath with achiote at his emergence
ca aino calabi ne coinainaritoco coinainaritiin ne	Painting this son of aino with achiote
nujuaricho acarera bujuainaa bujuainaritiin	Defending the unripe one's vital breath
aino calabi ranisijie que ca lauri ne enecotaera que nii bujuainaa bujuainaritiin ne	Defending the son of aino's chest against the afflictions of our world
Pshew!	[Blows]

A wide variety of other beings were invoked by Lorenzo throughout the course of his chant that morning, including the sun and moon (prefaced by the term for "father-in-law"), the anaconda, the giant celestial jaguar, and a handful of quasi-mythical ancestral figures known as the "thunder-people" *(araracuru)*. Depicted as ancient and brought into existence jointly with the Urarina people, these beings are noteworthy for their vital energy and presumed immunity—and that of their offspring—to accidents and misfortune.

The diseases or afflictions *(enecotaera)* of particular concern to parents like Lorenzo are those of "our group" or "our world" *(cana lauri)*, as distinct from those afflicting people elsewhere. As my neighbor Jorge put it, "People along the Chambira suffer from different diseases than the people in Iquitos." Local concepts of sickness and health are discussed in more detail in chapter 6, but it is worth noting here that Urarina generally distinguish between, on the one hand, "their" afflictions, particularly the various forms of mystical harm (uunaatiha) and sorcery *(saatiha)* associated with the local landscape's diverse inhabitants (sometimes referred to in the chant as "frightening dangers," *elunai*, or "terrors," *cabelara*), and, on the other, diseases such as influenza, smallpox, and measles, which are understood to have their origins in the city. The chant aims to defend the child from the former by "shielding" *(bujuatiha)* the chest area. This term can mean to shield, to block or impede, or to erect a barrier. Jorge offered the example of building a crib for a child who has recently learned to crawl, in order that it doesn't wander off or fall from the edge of the (unwalled) house. In other words, we could say that the chant thus aims to prevent illnesses from passing into the body by assembling various properties of resistance to harm, of diverse origin, into a unified "vital shield" that is given concrete expression in the achiote used to paint the child and its hammock.

As soon as the infant emerges from the jata, in sum, this is immediately replaced by a new kind of virtual, protective space within which it may safely dwell. Yet there also remains a strong sense in which it is the child's own identity that is symbolically transformed by the song's performative force. Through its repetitive juxtapositions, the song has the apparent effect of gradually building up a new, compound identity for the child by means of a controlled incorporation of alterity. This is less a form of "magic predation" (cf. Severi 2002) than an alignment and orchestration, through ritual, of distinct but fragmented perspectives (Oakdale 2005). There is no sense of adversity here, and the enunciator himself is not referred to or mentioned. It is to the words themselves, rather than their narrator, that agency is attributed. I would suggest that the chant problematizes and blurs the boundaries between participants in order to effect a process of integration through which the child's identity is gradually established as diffuse and multiple. The vital shield constructed for the child is somehow not entirely separate from itself—and yet not fully identical with it either.

This ambiguity—neither fully "self" nor fully "other"—is in fact a recurring motif in Urarina thought and praxis. In this chant, the focal quality of vital breath (acarera) is more than once juxtaposed or otherwise associated with the child's *corii*, which I have chosen to translate as "shadow-soul."

catanaca enoto ne	Father-in-law sun
rai bacauhino acarera neein	His anaconda is vital breath
rai corii acarera que	With the vital breath of his shadow soul
rai aino calabi nujuaricho	His unripe son of aino
acarera coinaina coinainaritiin ne	Painting vital breath with achiote
Pshew!	[Blows]

Urarina postulate that all humans, and possibly a number of other beings, possess two types of soul, the corii, or shadow-soul mentioned above, and the *suujue*, "heart-soul." Whereas the latter is closely bound up in notions of hardness, interiority, and the "heart" (*suujua*) as the seat of thought and emotion, the shadow-soul is associated with reflections, doubles, and companions. At death, the shadow-soul is said by some to return to the place where the placenta was carefully buried just after birth, from whence they travel together to the sky, rather as though birth was the moment of their separation or bifurcation. This essential pairing or coupling is precisely what is thought to establish an animated, protective space: a shielded and controlled environment, perhaps akin to an immune system. Vital breath inflates and animates this space, like a bubble, just as in the chant the sudden burst of breath at the end of each stanza is the decisive moment in which enters the full force of the words intoned. In all this, the canaanai mitu baau prefigures the operation of the infant accessories, and especially the hammock, with which the child is simultaneously equipped.

DELEGATIONS OF CARE

A baby always has to have its things. Otherwise it would die. It's necessary to give it all its things when it emerges from the birth hut. When its umbilical cord drops off, we can hand them over. That very instant it should have them all. One must give it clothes, too—otherwise it will die. One must care for it. If we don't hand over its clothes, it might get struck by diseases. That's how it's been since the time of our ancestors. That's how we were created, that's how we care for our babies.

Rosa spoke to me as she gently rocked her granddaughter's hammock, with newly worked strands of palm fibers draped across her lap. I had been asking about the palm fiber bands that cut gently into the girl's soft flesh, fabrication of which—as Rosa made clear—is part of a mother's essential duties. Along with bracelets, anklets, and leg bands, these so-called infant accessories (*canaanai rucuele*) include a belt, necklace, and wrist talisman, all made from either cotton or palm fibers, to which other materials may later be added. While these do have a certain visual appeal (and are typically referred to in Spanish as *adornos*, "ornaments"), they are also considered vital to an infant's well-being. In various ways, the infant accessories are intended to "nurture" and "care for" (*beraiha*) the infant. In fact, the verb *beraiha* may mean either "to care for" or "to give food to," and in the routine course of Urarina social life the latter is indeed the quintessential expression of the former. Although the accessories are not thought literally to feed the baby, a commonly cited rationale for the use of the belt, anklets, and bracelets was quite simply "so the baby will grow fat." When asked to elaborate, Lorenzo speculated that the bands "retain the blood of the food," thereby causing the baby "to fatten up faster." Blood and food are considered more or less interchangeable substances, and the correctly placed accessories are presumed to assist in controlling and regulating the flow of substances within the infant's body. The bodies of infants are notoriously "leaky" in their natural state, and the belt, legbands, anklets, and bracelets help to contain the fluids within, enabling its proper growth and physical development.

The necklace (*riria*) is similarly intended to play a caring, protective role: strung with seeds or glass beads, interlaced with the roots of a piri-piri plant, it is said to shield its wearer against a particular type of mystical harm (*janai*) to which babies are thought particularly susceptible. The wrist talisman (*chaje*) is a bulky collection of dried seeds and animal teeth attached to the end of a short length of string and fastened to a bracelet. This produces a rattling sound when it moves, much like the hammock's rattle (discussed below), known as the "baby lullaby" (*canaanai joororoa*). This too is associated with the maternal role; as Lorenzo put it, "A mother has to give music to her baby, so it can sleep." Making such rattles—like making the other accessories—allows her to delegate this and other caregiving tasks to a series of artifacts in which her maternal love is invested or "enfolded" (Latour 1996).

Care and support are in fact integral features of "ornaments" or "accessories" of all kinds. Calabash trees are adorned with animal skulls in the hope that the gourds they produce will be bigger, fatter, and harder. Bracelets are often put on pets as part of their domestication and incorporation into the household. All women wear elaborate necklaces of glass beads, and these too are known both as her "accessories" *(rucuele)* and her "throat protection" or "throat support" *(raro bujua)*. People draw analogies to the way the principal load-bearing columns of a house "support" its roof. Houses too should be generously equipped with accessories, the *loreri corujele*, which include such quotidian miscellany as woven fans and ceramic jars, as well as the skulls of game animals tucked into the thatched leaves of the roof. One man told me, "Without them, the house has no power. It's as though it were abandoned. Someone who has died can be buried, and he will not have his accessories . . . whereas we, those who are living, don't want to copy the dead." The accessories are signs of life, and essential to it. They are always personalized and inalienable, made to be kept rather than exchanged, for in a way accessories are seen to share in the existence of their owners. This is perhaps especially the case for personal accoutrements such as clothing, body ornaments, and jewelry, and it would be virtually unthinkable to transfer, lend, or sell these for any reason. At death, such belongings are buried with their deceased owner, or left by his or her grave for the recently disengaged shadow-soul to "play" with, safeguarding against its restlessness or discontent.

Their important protective function notwithstanding, baby accessories, people were often keen to emphasize, are used quite simply because the babies themselves want to wear them and would otherwise be discontented. Hence a mother adorns her baby with a necklace similar to her own "because the baby wants to wear one" or "wants to be like its mother" and "would cry without it." The rationale for the wrist talisman is even more explicitly related to the infant's own subjective well-being: it is a toy with which "it is always playing" and without which it would quickly become irritable and afflicted. Like miniature companions and caretakers, the infant accessories give expression to an important sentiment that people are most content when accompanied and protected within intimate spaces, enclosed, supported, and maintained. As it happens, these themes also figure prominently in the soothing songs carefully tailored to lull infants to sleep.

LULLABIES

Come on, go to sleep, little Nujuari!	chajaocha siniura Nujuari laojoiricha
Why don't you want to sleep, little Nujuari?	chanutera ne bana sini Nujuari laojoiri
Why do you cry, little Nujuari?	chanute chanatoi Nujuarira laojoiri
Come on, go to sleep, little Nujuari	chajaocha siniura Nujuari laojoiri
Because the floodwaters have covered over your placenta, maybe that's why you're crying from pity	iicha misicha jooca tabanaa najanotera nicoisichoicha
Come on, go to sleep, child	chajaocha siniicha canaanai
That's why you drank banana drink, so you sleep, little child	nii coata te acau coin siniicha canaanai laojoiri
That's why you drank banana drink	niira coata te jarera coicha

Urarina women, like Renona, spend a lot of their time singing lullabies to sleeping (or nearly sleeping) infants. Yet, as noted earlier, the capacity to dream makes sleep far from a passive, predictable state of being. Like the altered states of consciousness that shamans induce through the consumption of psychotropic substances such as ayahuasca and brugmansia, sleep heightens one's awareness to many events and happenings in the spirit world that are not normally perceptible. This is thought to be especially the case for babies, who naturally possess a special sensitivity to such invisible fluctuations. This can make sleep difficult or even dangerous; an inability to sleep is taken as a sign of affliction, or worse, sorcery. Martín, the young Urarina schoolteacher at Nueva Unión, once told me, "Sometimes, when people are about to arrive at the village, or a peccary is near, my baby doesn't want to sleep. It doesn't feel like sleeping, because the peccary annoys him a lot." Lorenzo similarly emphasized that his own baby was especially reluctant to sleep when people were about to arrive at the community by boat. "They make him dream of them, and that wakes him up," he explained. Partly due to this heightened sensitivity, coaxing babies into sleep is a specialized and sophisticated task and a parental duty of considerable importance. "A mother has to give music to her baby, so it can sleep," I was told.

Lullabies constitute a distinctive and unique vocal genre, performed exclusively by women. Men claim total ignorance of the genre and are reluctant even to imitate it, on the stated grounds that they "don't listen" or "don't pay attention" when their wives and others are singing. Although the melody does not vary, the words are personalized and addressed directly to the individual child and its present circumstances. Imploring the latter to sleep with a combination of threats and enticements, the lullabies often suggest that the child go off to reunite with the mother or father, who has recently departed for the garden or forest. This is possible thanks to the hammock, referred to in the songs as the infant's own dugout canoe, in which it should sit or lie in order to safely travel through the world of dreams.

Consider further the lullaby sung by Renona to her youngest son, Nujuari:

chajaocha baba sacuniu canaanai	Come on, follow Daddy, child
nedain nete chanatoriqui canaanai	If you stay you will cry, child
baba coaraniu canaanaiche	Go and see Daddy, child
chajaera laulautoracha canaanai	Come on, go in canoe, child
chajaocha laulautiin siniura canaanaicha	Come on, go lying down and sleep, child
chajaocha tijitijico canaanai	Go along swinging, child
aiyate amua cui ne baba	So Daddy can go hunting
baba caijie cuniu	Follow behind Daddy
ayate amua cua baba sacuniu baba	Daddy went hunting, follow Daddy
turuane tene iichotache mama	Mummy will scold you when she arrives
inae baba jourichaje elo canaanai	The rain closes in on Daddy
cotihaniu canaanai	Go and call him
inae baba setejiriaje elocha canaanai	The rain is going to soak him, child
baba que tacaain cotihaniu	Meeting Daddy, go and call him
chajaocha baba que tacaniu	Come on, go and meet Daddy
chajaecha baba corianeniu aiyania ne nerinaae baba coriaranu	Come on, go and accompany Daddy, or he will have no companion
chajaecha baba sacuniu ne nia coriaranu ne te	Come on, go and follow Daddy, or he will have no companion
baba casareen anocai	A ghoul will scare Daddy
corianeniu canaanai	Go and accompany him, child
baba achano ruhacaniu canaanai	Go carry Daddy his lunchpack, child
chajaecha baba achano ruhacaniu canaanai	Come on, carry Daddy his lunchpack, child
aiyneeine te neein chanatoi ne ii ra cotaicheen ne baba	If not, if you cry, Daddy will scold you

Unlike the child emergence chant (and other discourse in the baau genre), the lullaby is addressed directly to the infant, in its potential capacity as a person or subject. By means of the hammock "canoe," young Nujuari is implored to go and follow his father, who has gone hunting in the forest, and to be his "companion" (*coriara*). Such companionship would be beneficial for them both, for Nujuari's father has gone alone and is likely to suffer the discomfort of a soaking by the rain "closing" on him, not to mention the approach of the ghoulish souls of the deceased. Threats and punishments are just as liberally inserted in the lullabies to provoke sleep as are incentives, and there are also ample warnings of future crying and threats of scolding by the mother or father. Rosa's lullabies, for example, often included overt threats that the whites or mestizos would come and carry her granddaughter away if she continued to resist falling asleep.

chajao tijicho ii raauruine aansaiuru	Come on, lie down, the mestizos will take you
chajaochara mama caije cuuniu canaanai	Come on, go after Mummy, child

The snippet of Renona's lullaby that opened this section offered a possible reason for the affliction preventing young Nujuari from sleeping, namely, that he is crying out of pity, and even "wants to die," because rising waters have inundated the site where he was born and where his placenta is still buried. Indeed, several people confirmed to me that a child will cry inconsolably when estranged from its placenta and/or umbilical cord. The continuing connection between the two also bears on the fabrication and use of the baby hammock itself, a highly personalized and important artifact that issues specialized lullabies of its own.

THE SIGNIFYING RATTLE

The fabrication and use of the baby hammock are among the most important of all parental interventions. When not in the arms of its mother or sleeping in her bed at night, an infant spends almost all its time in the hammock, under constant supervision. There are no baby slings or other carrying devices, and a mother will usually choose to leave her child at home with another caretaker rather than risk taking it with her on her daily round.

The mother weaves the hammock from palm fibers (*Astrocaryum chambira*) just prior to leaving the birth hut. At the moment of emergence the infant is transferred immediately into the hammock, which, like the infant itself, has been painted with achiote as part of the emergence ceremony. The weaving can comfortably be completed within a day, and is often begun and finished the day prior to emergence. The weave is a looser version of that used for the fabrication of string bags that resembles netting; a baby inside can certainly give the appearance of having been "caught" in a net.

The wooden end poles (*cocoatauha*) of the hammocks are made from the branches of the calabash tree, the fruits of which are used to make bowls and gourds of all sizes for domestic use. These trees are planted in the community and continually pruned back such that the trunk grows thick and sturdy; the tree's short stature often belies its age. This practice is said to produce bigger and more abundant fruit. As already noted, these trees are also heavily adorned with animal skulls, sometimes referred to as its "fertilizer" (*abono*) and said to stimulate and enhance the fruit's "hardness." The hammock is similarly said to help "harden" and "thicken" the infant, an ongoing task discussed further below.

When it is being used, one end of the hammock is usually tied to the slender trunk of an alauhijia tree,[5] which has been carefully cut from the forest and "planted" in the house by driving it through a gap in the floor. This tree is unusual for several reasons. It grows only in forest clearings, also called alauhijia and to which it stands in metonymic relation.[6] Urarina refer to such clearings as "ghoul's gardens" (*anocai ocoana*) or "jaguar's gardens" (*janolari ocoana*), after their supposed producers and "owners." I was cautioned that jaguars "like to wander around there" and that women were particularly afraid of them. But it is not these extraordinary origins in and of themselves that make the tree such a popular choice for baby hammocks; rather, people seem to like this tree because "it never rots or deteriorates."

The bulk of the hammock's rattle (*torara*) comprises a number of different species of dried, hollow gourds and seeds, each carefully pierced at one end and threaded into large bundles on twine woven from the frond spears of the chambira palm. These tend to knock or brush against each other or the floor when the hammock is swung by the caretaker. Up to a dozen different varieties of seeds and gourds may be present on a rattle, artfully strung together in homogeneous bunches. The noise they produce, said to please and placate the infant, is a nonverbal equivalent of the lullabies sung by caregivers, referred to by the same term, *jororoa*, and regarded as equally soothing and sleep-inducing.

The rattle promotes more than just sleep, however, for attached to the seeds and gourds is a diverse and often extensive collection of animal parts, such as bones, teeth, claws, beaks, and tails, collected from many different species of birds, primates, reptiles, and other creatures. These are woven together with the remnants of foreign goods, including empty bottles, disposable razors, plastic spools, mirror frames, and sewing kits. While certainly impressive on aesthetic grounds, most of these items are more or less explicitly associated with some useful quality to be instilled in the developing infant. The shoulder bone of the sloth, for example, an animal said rarely to defecate, is attached to build resistance to diarrhea. The tongue of a songbird might be added to develop the child's vocal abilities, or coati teeth to transmit this animal's ability to find honey and avoid snakebite. Snail shells might be tied to the rattle "so the baby's ear doesn't grow too big," while tiny glass vaccination bottles wrapped in colorful cotton jackets, collected from the visits of local health workers, continue to build resistance to measles or smallpox. Many of these items are gender-specific; spent shotgun shells, for example, always collected from kills, not misses, promote hunting ability in a boy, while empty cigarette lighters assist the rapid acquisition of a taste for tobacco. Packets of needles might be affixed to a girl's rattle "so she will know how to sew—so she doesn't grow up useless," and plastic combs so her well-brushed hair will remain free from lice. A single rattle may boast dozens of such components, the only limitation being the mother's enthusiasm for the task. I was told, "Sometimes the mother attaches lots of ornaments, because she loves her child a lot, and wants it to grow well."

The majority of the qualities transmitted in this way are thought of as a form of embodied knowledge, which it is the parents' duty to inculcate in their child. Apropos of the Amazonian Cashinahua but equally valid for the Urarina, McCallum (1996: 347) wrote that "the body is construed as an individual entity constituted—in indigenous terms, 'grown'—through knowledge. This knowledge is imparted, in a variety of material, spiritual, and linguistic ways, by people who have acquired it from others, and as such it is weighty with resonances of gender, kinship, and morality." The acquisition of such knowledge, while closely linked to notions of "memory" and "experience," need not pass through any "mental faculty." Bodily growth and mental and emotional development are all inseparably linked, just as abstract qualities and mental states are typically expressed in and through tangible, concrete bodies and other substances.

The conceptual logic that governs these processes of transfer, which recalls the Frazerian notion of contagious magic, is commonplace throughout Amazonia and by no means restricted, in Urarina society, to the context of the rattle. Hence dogs are sometimes fed wasps' nests to make them fiercer, or their tongues rubbed repeatedly with those of songbirds to make them bark louder and more often. Animal skulls are placed in the branches of certain trees in order that the gourds they produce be similarly hard and durable. Coati tooth necklaces are worn to help their wearer develop the ability to find honey, while shamans sleep on jaguar skins to appropriate the predatory qualities of this feared but esteemed animal. Sometimes the transfer of properties is undesirable and involuntary: prefabricated cigarettes rolled in white paper are thought to turn one's hair white and are therefore avoided, particularly by boys, whose susceptibility is thought to be greater. Lizard bones are carefully disposed of so dogs will not find and eat them, lest they subsequently be bitten by a snake. Similar premises may underlie more complex chains of causation. I once heard it said that the reason the ungura-hui palm *(Jessenia bataua)* fruits collected by old Manuel always turned out to be hard and difficult to peel was because his mother used to hit him with a palm fiber fan when he was a child.

There is a frequent emphasis in such notions of controlled or uncontrolled transfer on physical contact between the source object and the person to whom the quality is transmitted, generally through eating or direct and prolonged contact with the skin. Yet many of the relevant qualities associated with a particular object are nevertheless neither immediately apparent nor actually present in it. Whereas a tapir skull might be placed in a tree to promote the hardness of the fruits produced, the shoulder bone of the two-toed sloth—an item very often attached to hammock rattles—might count hardness and whiteness among its more salient properties, yet is intended to transmit neither of these but rather a skill or behavioral quality of the animal itself, namely, continence, which the bone anchors or indexes.[7] Such qualities would not suggest themselves to someone unfamiliar with the ethology of the two-toed sloth, or to someone unfamiliar with the meaning and typical functioning of the rattle itself as a cultural artifact. Similarly, given the ambiguity surrounding some such items, the properties (if any) it is intended to transmit may be evident only to someone familiar with its source or origin. Nevertheless, for a typical Urarina observer, the purpose or rationale of most items on the rattle could readily be inferred with high probability of success provided their origins can be identified, because many meanings are more or less conventionalized and invoke widely shared notions of desirable forms of knowledge.

A mother does not always actively seek items for her rattle but often receives them as gifts from female kin or encounters them fortuitously in the house, garden, or forest in the course of her daily routine. Often simply items discarded by others, many acquire meaning and value only through association or juxtaposition with the other objects on the rattle. In a different context, or on their own, the various bones, beaks, and so on would generally be regarded as inert and worthless, and the forms of knowledge they subsequently index would probably not suggest themselves. The items making up the rattle, in short, not only offer information to a typical adult observer but also constitute a structured system of signs: of differences, oppositions, and contrasts. Assembling the rattle effectively involves a physical manipulation of indexes, a kind of inscribing practice partially analogous to writing, preparing a message for the desired transmission of knowledge and experience in the form of information.

The rattle taken as a whole therefore signifies the complex series of personal skills, knowledge, and qualities most desired by a mother for her offspring, and recognizable as such, or "readable," by anyone liable to enter into its vicinity. From such a vantage point, we might consider it the material instantiation of a local model of personhood. By enacting or bringing forth a series of values surrounding a desirable way of being, according to a reasonably well-defined system of conventional practice, the rattle is also highly normative. Its "meaning" inevitably reflects a balance between the norms and values held by the mother as an individual and those socially constructed or prevalent in society at large through the mother's ability to select particular items and not others, and even to assign them new meanings, as final interpretive authority is always invested in her. In other words, the rattle's construction amounts to an early assertion of the person the child will be. This has particular consequences for the developing infant: from the Urarina point of view, the infant develops both physically and psychologically in accordance with the values given concrete expression in the rattle, which serves as a kind of scaffolding for this process. Yet if the rattle may be "read" by an Urarina adult, this is not the case for the baby to whom it belongs, who does not read it but hears it.

ENTANGLED STATES

"Do you want to go traveling in your hammock?" Rosa's tiny granddaughter, who had recently begun standing on her own, was still too young to speak. Yet to my surprise, she appeared to understand the question perfectly well. "Brrrrrr!" she sang, imitating the distinctive, vibrating sounds of the lullaby when produced as a bilabial trill. The girl was promptly lifted into her hammock by her mother, who was about to head off to the garden, and instructed curtly to go to sleep, and to "go wandering" (*tijiaco*). After tucking her in, the long cord was handed over to Rosa, who, hardly pausing for a moment in her task of making a string bag, began idly rocking the hammock to and fro, singing softly while she worked (figure 3).

Figure 3.   A grandmother watches over a baby in its hammock. Photograph by author.

While the transmission of qualities generally requires either oral consumption or direct physical contact to be deemed efficacious, the rattle does neither. It is attached beneath the position of the baby's head, out of reach and out of sight. The transmission can occur only through the sounds that it is the intended function of the rattle to produce, as the physical indices are reconstituted in sound when the hammock is set in motion by a caregiver. Sounds, physical properties, abstract values, and mental states are not clearly distinguishable in Urarina ontology. By lulling the baby to sleep, the rattle establishes the necessary conditions of its own reception. On one level, the narrative content of these sounds is a wordless lullaby; on another, its performative force works to build up the child's body as a compound of qualities, experiences, and knowledge of diverse origin. We might suggest that from an Urarina perspective the rattle induces the child to accept the identity implied in its composition, the first stage of an ongoing process of interpellation. The rattle's call particularizes and humanizes the baby's body, which is still considered too ambiguous by its parents and caregivers.

The role or identity offered in this way is always gendered. The items chosen to adorn the rattle are often gender-specific, reflecting behavioral norms and the wider gender division of labor in Urarina society. Again, this reflects a future ideal rather than a present actuality. When born, babies are essentially genderless; thus clothing and ornaments pertaining to either sex are used arbitrarily by a mother until around two to three years of age. The hammock's message is thus also an early but integral part of wider social practices of gendering, both material and discursive in nature. Ideas surrounding the hammock suggest that the sexed body itself has a history, starting from a state of relative undifferentiation, and always comes into being through directed social practices.

The hammocks are like caretakers or carers as well as companions of the baby, and this protective function is epitomized in the sonic transmission of resistance to diseases. I was told that the hammock is not only the baby's companion (coriara) but also "like its cojoaaorain," the avian caretaker or spiritual guardian of game animals. One man defined the cojoaaorain as "one who communicates with you in order to care for your life . . . for your defense."

The hammock certainly seems much more than an artifact to the infant, and I wish to suggest that its power and status relies in large measure on a conceptual assimilation to a more overtly organic kind of entity. In many ways, the hammock is like a "transitional object" (Winnicott 1971), in that it partially takes the place of the mother-child bond and is instrumental in the development of relative independence. The infant's disposition toward the hammock does appear to be characterized by a kind of attachment, an affective bond responsible for behaviors that seek out proximity. As noted earlier, such an attachment is recognized and promoted by mothers, whose first answer when asked why they supply accessories to their babies will usually refer to the fact that the baby itself "likes them," "wants to wear them," and would be unhappy without them. The fact that they themselves wear similar ornaments is also deemed significant, for "all babies want to match their mothers."

I first became aware of this intense emotional bond when I once callously, and ultimately unsuccessfully, attempted to purchase a hammock still in use. "That hammock's owner is going to cry and cry tonight!" warned my traveling companion, who quickly managed to dissuade me. A child estranged from its hammock is liable to protest and cry inconsolably, even more than if separated from its mother. Jorge once told me, "Whenever I go on a journey, I always have to take my son's hammock along, even if the canoe is full. I can't leave it behind, otherwise he cries nonstop. He'll just cry and cry from sorrow." Separation of this kind causes such distress that a specialized incantation *(cojiotaa)*, such as the following, is required to minimize the affliction.

inae nedaa ii amaa quiche	Your hammock has stayed behind, little boy
coa nee chanatoha	Don't be crying
baiha te inae turuine chabana te turua ca nete	Later, whenever we arrive here
inae cuanai amuriquin laulaueriquin	Lying inside [your canoe] you will go
ii casco cuanai quiche	In your dugout, little boy
coa ne baiha coisiha nedai ii casco	Don't be crying later, your hammock has stayed behind
ii casco laecaaente ratirini cana nenaja	You've left your dugout docked in the port at our place
coa ne baiha coisiha chanatoha ne baiha quiche	Don't be crying later, little boy
inae nedai ii casco	Your hammock has stayed behind
inae turuine te cuanai amuriquin jelaijen	When you arrive you'll travel inside [it] just the same [as before]
cana amunajau te jaiti niaca quiche	We're still journeying, little boy
coa ne baiha chanatoha nedai ne te ii casco	Your hammock has stayed behind, don't be crying later
cosinotoanajau te nedani cousinia coina te ratirini mama	It's leaky, Mama left it behind to mend when she arrives

In this incantation, delivered in a hushed voice, at breakneck pace, the hammock again features as the child's personal canoe, in which it journeys through an invisible landscape: an image that recalls the use of canoes as coffins for burying the dead. While certainly suggestive of travel (whether through the real, spirit, or dream world), the figure of the canoe is at least as important for its evocation of a state of enclosure and containment, more specifically, I would suggest, the state of containment that pertains to intrauterine life. This is, in fact, the state to which death is considered in many ways a return; at this time, the shadow-soul (corii) is said to return to the placenta, which was carefully buried by the mother in the same hole into which the baby was born. This enables the identification of its family and birthplace, establishing a localized continuity between the womb and the afterlife.[8] A shadow-soul unable to find its umbilical cord and placenta is condemned to eternal wandering and discontent.

The role of the hammock as a second, extrauterine womb is given concrete expression through the attachment to the rattle of the baby's own umbilical cord. Carefully wrapped up within a tiny, colorful cotton sack as soon as it falls from the navel, it is positioned alongside a variety of other "toys," mostly tiny pieces of wood carved by the mother, with which the baby's shadow-soul is said to "play." The location of these toys behind the baby's head, out of sight and well out of reach, reinforces that this play is not conceived in a strictly physical sense. Linguistically indistinct from the placenta *(misi)*, the umbilical cord is treated with great respect by adults. It cannot be touched or removed from the hammock by anyone but the child itself, who will ideally dispose of or "lose" it in the course of playing.

One stated reason for the careful and purposive treatment of the placenta after birth is that any accidental contact with another person, animal, or spirit is considered troubling and even potentially lethal for the infant, with whom it maintains an enduring connection. A child is said to cry inconsolably when estranged from its placenta and umbilical cord, and Renona's lullaby proposed as the cause of young Nujuari's afflictions the fact that rising floodwaters had temporarily inundated the land where his placenta was buried. The hammock must similarly be kept close and carefully protected against accidental contact with alterity. When not in use it is untied and laid carefully on the floor of the house, and preferably kept by the baby's side, ostensibly because the shadow-soul of a deceased child is liable to come and lie in the hammock, swinging and playing. "There's no trusting the spirits," as Lorenzo once put it.[9] Thus deposed from its rightful place, the child is said quickly to suffer from vomiting, diarrhea, and fever, symptoms that further manifest or epitomize lack of containment.

A variety of other ideas and practices further reinforce this conceptual assimilation between the gentle, nurturing companionship offered by the hammock to the baby and that offered by the placenta inside the womb. The canaanai mitu baau used to prepare the hammock for use refers to the child's shadow-soul growing in the hammock "as in the womb," and the weave used for the hammock, which is a looser version of that used for the fabrication of string bags, together with the extensive collection of hollow seeds, gourds, and empty bottles attached to the hammock all further suggest and reinforce these relations of "carrying" and "containment." There are no fragments or pieces used here, and one might speculate whether the gourds are in a sense symbolically pregnant. A baby in a hammock is always tightly wrapped in blankets and is fully contained in a protective and nurturing space that facilitates growth, much like the womb. Safely inside, it dwells in a sonic universe circumscribed by the sounds of the rattle and is insulated physically and symbolically from the outside world. The rapid swinging motion, which ideally extends to near-horizontal, subdues the child by resisting and ultimately overriding its tentative exercise of agency. A baby in a hammock is rarely spoken to, outside the lullaby and in this subordinate, ideally sleeping, dependent state is considered best protected and most receptive to the formative messages that inaugurate it as person and subject.

Urarina recognize that the hammock, like the placenta, becomes an integral part of both the mother and child, and cannot be unambiguously interpreted as belonging to either. The relationship between all three is, in this sense, also metonymic. Much like the placenta, the hammock binds a baby to its mother and mediates between them. As many lullabies make clear, its use is a means of prolonging their union. Over time, a baby's "vitality" or "vital breath" is said to permeate the hammock, a kind of "ensoulment" through which each becomes an extension of the other. An outgrown hammock (unlike the rattle's individual components) is never thrown away or reused by other children but simply guarded carefully by the mother until it deteriorates.

The material configuration of the baby in its hammock stands in clear contrast to a typical Western cradle, in which toys and other interesting objects are placed above the infant, in its line of sight and often within grasp, as passive objects or patients for it to examine and manipulate as an agent. The situation here is rather the reverse; the baby occupies a passive position in relation to the hammock, whose rapid swinging motions resist and ultimately override its own tentative exercise of agency. It is tempting to suggest that it is ultimately the latter that "plays" with the former. The rattle's sounds, emanating from behind the infant's head, resist the objectification of their source. I suggest that the hammock is not yet an "object" for the infant, who is not yet a "subject"; their state of mutual entanglement at first transcends this polarity, even as it is one of the principal means for bringing it into existence.

WEAVING ARTIFACTS AND INFANTS

Renona wove Nujuari's hammock and other infant accessories from palm fibers just a day before Lorenzo's performance of the emergence chant. She had been collecting items for the rattle for many months, perhaps even before she became pregnant. Many items were not actively sought out but happened upon by chance in the course of her daily activities. Others were gifts from close female kin, taken from rattles their own children had outgrown, and others still came from Lorenzo himself. All the items were slowly and painstakingly threaded together on palm fiber twine and assembled into large bundles, which were then drawn into a single bundle. The end result is always a rather motley assembly of individual items that nevertheless come together to manifest a kind of unity and harmony. The selection of particular items, it seems, is partly a matter of adhering to cultural conventions and partly a kind of bricolage: any item found lying about can be put to novel use in the rattle, recruited into a project that bears no relation to its original purpose or function. Lévi-Strauss (1972) famously used the concept of bricolage to describe the characteristic patterns of a certain kind of intellectual activity, namely, mythopoesis. I want to suggest that the rattle is roughly equivalent to a particular form of discourse, although not that of mythology; instead, it instantiates something like a physical, material version of the emergence chant. Each may be seen as a broadly analogous way of building up vital shields or protective spaces within which new personal and bodily identities may be safely elaborated.

Recall that the emergence chant essentially comprises repetitive juxtapositions of key words and expressions that work toward a clear goal that seems to be, in a performative sense, the controlled incorporation of relationships that characterize various "others." A number of beings are invoked in turn, each associated with some desirable property or form of knowledge to be appropriated and instilled in the target. At the same time, the achiote mixture blessed by the chant is supposed to physically "shield" the child once painted onto its skin. If the chant describes or even brings about some form of interaction with beings such as turtles, jaguars, and the sun—"touching" them, as Martín once put it—it does so in a highly controlled manner. Just about any other form of contact, up to and including a parent laying eyes on one accidentally while walking in the forest, would be considered highly dangerous. These beings are not directly communicated with, in their potential capacity as persons or subjects, but evoked as constellations or inventories of behaviors, skills, and properties, from which one is singled out as especially relevant. Despite the chant's self-referential qualities, the relationship between the enunciator and the child target is never directly referred to. The individuality and differentiation of the participants is minimized in order to effect a transfer of qualities across personal boundaries, establishing the hammock's and the child's identities as loosely symmetrical but compound and diffuse.

The fabrication of the hammock itself draws on a similar set of procedures. Many of the rattle's components derive from animals that if seen or encountered in their entirety (whether alive or dead) would be considered extremely dangerous to a newborn baby, capable of inducing grievous harm by mystical means. In normal circumstances, even an animal part such as a bone, beak, or talon is thought to contain or anchor residual elements of that animal's agency and subjectivity and is therefore dangerous. For this reason discarded animal bones are never thrown on the fire after eating, for the flames are said to force out the animal's heart-soul (suujue), prompting it to warn off the approach of its living animal "companions," thereby making themselves available to a hunter. But in place of an ensemble of remnant, lingering subjectivities of this nature, the hammock is considered to possess a single vegetal soul (neeura), the type common to life-forms such as trees. This transformation is effected through the labor process of the mother, which neutralizes and homogenizes this diverse soul matter, deindividuating (or "dividuating") the identities of each item while retaining and enhancing its indexical relationship with a particular quality or skill. It incorporates the items into a unique artifact that is thought to insulate and protect the infant while manifesting a diffuse, unthreatening form of subjectivity.

In short, the hammock constitutes something like a material instantiation of the baau genre of ritual communication. The technical processes that give rise to it are equivalent to those that underwrite the performative force of the chant that subsequently blesses and prepares it for use. Both the rattle and the baau are in turn homologous to the putative action of the hammock on the baby.[10] The hammock's rattle comprises a carefully arranged juxtaposition of indexes that are reconstituted in sound when the hammock is set in motion by the caregiver. If the narrative content of these sounds is a wordless lullaby, its performative force builds up the body as a compound of qualities of diverse origin.

Such actions support the claim, increasingly recognized as widespread in Amazonia, that bodies themselves are artifact-like: as Fernando Santos Granero (2009: 7) has expressed it, persons "are not born as such, but must be intentionally manufactured or shaped through the input of a variety of substances and affects provided by parents and kin." (see also Londoño Sulkin 2005). He further suggests that in Amerindian ontologies "it is craftsmanship rather than childbearing which provides the model for all creative acts," and thus people and objects share the same "symbolic frame of fabrication" (Santos Granero 2009: 6; cf. Van Velthem 2003:119). I would like to suggest that at least in the Urarina case the particular mode of craftsmanship in question is weaving.

The fabricated, artifactual body brought forth by the hammock is not a unique, self-contained entity but the precipitate of a multitude of integral relationships, an enchainment of both human and nonhuman others. The rattle is equally an apparatus for the construction of kin relations, in a cultural milieu in which genealogy is ascribed relatively little importance. Each rattle contains items used previously in the formation of other children, which are then either redeployed by mothers on their younger siblings or passed on to her sisters and other close kin. All their respective children are thus related by virtue of the fact that their bodies are composed from similar sources: just as each rattle comprises traces of all the other rattles used not only by the mother but also by her extended family in the hammocks of other children, so too the baby's body comes to reflect or refract pieces of the bodies of all those children with whom it shares some kinship relation.

The production of kinship through intentional acts of nurture places us squarely back in the domain of women's practice. The power of the hammock, or baau, derives from the agency of its maker (or enunciator), which it indexes, together with the fluxes of properties set in place through the assembly (or invocation) of the relevant items into a safe, harmonious whole. The majority of women's labor is directed at similar ends: the quintessentially female tasks of cooking and above all weaving involve such a patterned integration of diverse elements. Weaving is absolutely central to Urarina female identity, and the associated technical knowledge helps to legitimize the authority of older women.

Women themselves play this integrative role in the uxorilocal structure of Urarina society, incorporating in-marrying men into the household. It is largely through their intentional acts of feeding and nurture that such men, typically from an initial social-structural position as outsiders, are transformed into relatives and coresidents, consolidating the domestic unit. The newborn, too, must be incorporated—a task greatly assisted by the hammock—and this furthers the husband's own incorporation, progressively turning him into a consanguine.

If weaving epitomizes the incorporative activity by which the hammock and the infant each come into being, it may be partly because a significant feature of weaving, as Ingold (2000: 344–45) has observed, is how form emerges, not through the application of force from without, or the imposition of a preexistent conceptual design, but through gradually being built up out of a pattern of rhythmic movement. This takes place in a field of forces that "is neither internal to the material nor internal to the practitioner (hence external to the material); rather, it cuts across the emergent interface between them" (342). In the case of a woven basket, for example, there is no surface that is transformed or worked on; rather, the weaving itself produces "a peculiar kind of surface" in which each successive loop of fiber is alternately inside and outside, so far as the surface of the basket is concerned. Strictly speaking, this surface has no "inside" or "outside."

The rattle is similarly not the product of conscious design but rather emerges in the course of a mother's everyday activities, as she comes across or is given objects that she then creatively redeploys for novel uses, incorporating them into the hammock. There is a certain degree of contingency or chance at work here, and the fabrication of the hammock is at once a way of working through her own ideas about the kind of person she hopes her child will become. The notion that persons are not made or grown but *woven* is also asserted by Urarina themselves, in the context of a well-known myth in which a woman weaves children from cotton for her surprised husband as an ingenious way of giving birth without suffering. The fabrication of the hammock entails a transfer of responsibility for the ongoing performance of baau incantations, considered so essential to the care of infants, to a material artifact capable of producing them with just a minimal investment of kinetic energy—somewhat reminiscent of a pianola or player piano, whose pneumatic mechanism produces preprogrammed music via perforated paper rolls. These entanglements of matter and meaning, of sound and substance, are a recurring theme in Urarina social life and essential to the practices that call forth new persons.

The hammock also perpetuates a distinctly female form of agency, working to continually reproduce and consolidate the authority of women in the domestic realms of bodily and child care. Men rarely touch, let alone swing, a hammock and claim ignorance of the procedures for its construction and use, not to mention the origin or significance of its constituent parts, deferring all questions on the matter to their wives. Yet it is the relationship between the hammock and the child that is of greatest importance: to the latter, the hammock is simultaneously companion, caretaker, and shield. It enables the child to dwell accompanied within a protective and nurturing space, inside which it begins to emerge as a unique human being out of a backdrop of relatedness to near and distant others. Yet this process is only just beginning; and even once the hammock is finally outgrown, the pursuit of such shared spaces of protection and care continues.

3. Conceiving the Conjugal Body

Buuno's first marriage lasted just three days. It began in high spirits when Anita, on a brief visit to the community, passed the night in his bed after a drinking party and remained there the next morning. Though already twice divorced, Anita had no children, and the young couple was clearly happy with the union, as was Buuno's father, Sere, who immediately offered his daughter to Anita's brother. But when the father of the bride learned of these events by two-way radio, he made some swift inquiries into Buuno's character. It was duly reported that the lad was a poor hunter, and the marriage was rejected on the grounds that Buuno was *nijiaoajeri*, unskilled and lazy, literally, "to be discarded." Sere in turn immediately retracted his offer of his daughter's hand. Not long afterward, Anita returned home.

Like all marriages, Buuno's began entirely free of ceremony or ritual, requiring nothing but public recognition of cohabitation. Many marriages begin as trysts or clandestine liaisons that subsequently become public; just as often they begin as casual suggestions or propositions by close relatives of the bride or groom. Yet despite the informality with which many marriages begin, making them last is difficult; in the early stages especially the relationship is fraught and prone to dissolution. A debilitating shyness at the outset can take weeks to overcome, and many factors may lead to breakdown. Only with the birth of a child does the marriage begin to stabilize, and a couple with two or more children is likely to remain together. In this chapter I argue that the reasons for this have much to do with how marriage and childbirth are viewed, not as singular or discrete events, but as complementary facets of a single, ongoing process through which persons and tightly knit social groups jointly come into being.

Other Amazonian ethnography has successfully demonstrated how commensality, or eating together with others, can produce "communities of substance," social groups based on the consubstantiality of individual bodies.[1] The theory of perspectivism offers a handy explanation of why this should be so: because perspectives are grounded in the body (rather than, say, the mind or soul), this is necessarily the site from which identity and difference emerge. Categories of identity, whether personal, social, or cosmological, are accordingly frequently expressed through bodily idioms such as food practices or body decoration. My goal here is to take a different tack—to describe the way procreation, childbirth, and the emergence of proto-subjectivity in infants form the basis for constructions of marriage and ritual co-parenthood. Associated with the newborn's heart-soul and shadow-soul, respectively, these are spiritually charged forms of companionship in which the emphasis is less on shared bodily substance than on intersubjective involvement and emotional attachment. Examination of these two intimate relationships points to the medial, distributed quality of subjectivity and its basis in care and mutual belonging, closely associated with the evocation of benevolent, protective impulses in others as a key avenue for expressions of agency.

I begin with a discussion of the powerful emotion of shame or embarrassment experienced by new and potential spouses and the asymmetrical processes of "taming" and "domestication" through which this can be overcome. This amounts to bringing under control an initially threatening experience of openness to the other, gradually replacing fear and vulnerability with a sense of security, trust, and codependency. I show how the marriage is conceived through an idiom of mutual defense but is finally consolidated only after the birth of a child. Of particular importance is the infant's progressive hardening and finally ensoulment, a process that is intrinsically linked to the successful performance by both parents of the couvade, which further unites them in a shared project. At the same time, severing the child's umbilical cord is the occasion for the construction of ritual co-parenthood, leading to the emergence of the shadow-soul as the placenta's ethereal replacement and the basis of subsequent companionships. The creation of new persons and the creation of intimate social groupings are therefore largely the same process.

DOMESTICATING HUSBANDS, TAMING WIVES

Bucu was a young man in his early twenties who had recently married and started a small, independent settlement a few bends downriver from

San Pedro, where I was living at the time. In the course of a drinking party one afternoon in San Pedro, Bucu suggested to Doinita, his classificatory brother and several years his junior, that he marry the younger sister of Bucu's mother-in-law, who was living with him at the time. As the young girl's father had died, she was effectively in Bucu's care. Though he had never laid eyes on her, Doinita could see no objection and promptly accepted. Still a teenager, he had for some time been making valuable contributions to the household economy through his hunting prowess. The following day, Doinita packed up his few belongings and the two men set off together downstream. A little over two weeks later, Doinita returned by canoe to visit his family. Trying to make conversation, I casually asked how his new wife was faring. "I have no idea," Doinita replied with a nonchalant shrug. "She's never spoken to me." As he was soon to enter his third week of married life, I was taken aback. He explained that she was still too "ashamed" *(necoejiha)* to speak to him and confessed that he, too, was mostly too ashamed to speak to her. His few feeble attempts to strike up conversation had been defeated with resolute silence. This lack of communication was, he agreed, rather inconvenient at times if not downright frustrating. He revealed that she had nonetheless handed to him the occasional bowl of banana drink, albeit wordlessly and with eyes averted: an act of some significance. Though they had been sleeping in the same mosquito net, the marriage was, Doinita admitted resignedly, still to be consummated.

If the transition to married life is not marked by formal ceremony, neither is it entirely free from convention. Doinita's experience, it turned out, was not unusual. Carapa soon confirmed for me that when he got married he, too, did not speak to his wife, for "a whole month." Chaburo claimed that many couples begin speaking only after a week or so, though they may have sexual intercourse after just three days. Many men I spoke to insisted not only on the inevitability but also on the desirability of an extended initial period of mutual "shame" or "embarrassment" (necoejiha)—which can take the form of a kind of institutionalized avoidance—and seemed to regard it as one of the most important prerequisites for a lasting marriage. Many credited their own period of shame with a key role in the durability of their present marriages. Sere explained the rationale as follows:

> When we first get married to a woman, we are ashamed. Because we are ashamed, we can't converse with the women. We can't talk at all for four days, and then, after five days, with a little bit of shame, we can talk. When she herself begins to talk slowly, we can talk slowly

as well. Then after six days we can talk with our wives. When we are first married we are ashamed, we cannot speak the day after getting married, only after two or three or however many days, for she is ashamed of us, and we too are ashamed of her. Being ashamed like this when we marry a woman, we can live together peacefully. Some men when they first get married to a woman speak to her. When he speaks to her, the day after getting married, the woman no longer wants him. And because she no longer wants him, they can live together for maybe a year, and then the man is already bored. When the woman speaks to the man before he speaks to her, she gets bored with her husband and wants another man. That's why, when some men get married because the woman herself has sought him out, without her being ashamed, when she sees another man, she wants him too, and she tires of her husband.

The shame or embarrassment that marks the onset of marriage, and takes the form of temporary avoidance, is consistent with the demonstration of mutual respect, modesty, and propriety. Its duration varied in practice from a few days to a few weeks and was overcome in a slow, cautious, circumspect manner. Although the shame is demonstrated by both partners, it is viewed as an essentially feminine trait, and it is women who especially need to be "tamed." Carapa thought it should ideally be the woman who initiates conversation, which she will do "when she is ready." Demonstrating shame is part of a broader series of strategies used by both sexes to ensure lasting fidelity on the part of their partner. A woman thought too forward in initiating a marriage will be suspected of a casual attitude toward men, deemed most improper, and a propensity to initiate illicit affairs. She should instead be gradually and gently lured into the marriage, or at least seen as such. Jorge put it this way: "When a woman seeks out a man herself, later on she'll want to seek out another man, just the same. That's why I don't give the woman lots of things right at the outset, but over time, little by little."

The giving of gifts referred to here is an important part of the taming process, as it is of marriage in general. When wooing a girl, I was told, the most important phrase to use is *ii belairichaani*, meaning "I will love you." But this love is rather different from that between lovers, whether married or not. The latter is often described as *itajeriha*, "to mutually love each other," where love is figured primarily as desire. *Belaiha*, "to love" (or perhaps "to care for lovingly"), is of a different nature, for it implies the state of generalized reciprocity only achievable through marriage. *Belaiha* also means "to give as a gift," and such gifts, whether meat, industrial goods, or something else, are figured as the material instantiation of love, through concrete acts of giving.

If shame and avoidance are to some extent deliberate and institutionalized, they are nevertheless grounded in a strongly felt emotion that is effectively the product of years of socialization. Casual interaction between the sexes is strictly limited, and girls in particular are taught to shy from any interaction with men. Learning to act demurely is part of the process of becoming female, and I was often struck by the difference in behavior between a girl of around four or five years of age, who is not yet really considered "gendered," and one just a few years older. The latter but not the former, for example, will know to turn her back to any male nonkin who is casually passing by, whether on foot or in canoe, and to refuse any form of interaction unless absolutely necessary. If required to talk, she will do so without turning to face her interlocutor. Such behavior is strongly linked to a sense of sexual propriety: simply making eye contact with such a man is considered suggestive of openness to a sexual encounter. Sere spoke as follows about the women of San Pedro:

> When visitors arrive, from San Marcos, or Nueva Unión, or Copal, or wherever, the women flee inside and conceal themselves even more. But some women are not ashamed. Without being ashamed, some women desire the mestizos. They only desire the mestizos, and among Urarina themselves they are ashamed. Although they are ashamed among Urarina, once mestizos arrive: "Ha! !Ha! Haa! Ha! Ha! Haa!" They pretend to be ashamed, these women. When a man arrives who lives far away, they hang up a woven sleeping mat and hide themselves behind it. And there inside they hide. What must they be thinking, those women? They must be thinking, "Maybe he'll desire me." Perhaps they think like that, and perhaps that's why, when a man arrives, they sit and hide like that, and don't get up from there.

Sere's comments reveal a sense that the display of shame may be less than fully transparent. As I understand his reasoning, women may act ostensibly to "protect" themselves from predatory males, although in signaling their moral rectitude and femininity, and indeed awareness of their desirability, they may be using strategies to attract attention as potential spouses. To speak of women as aiming or needing to protect or "shield" themselves from men is commonplace and may be considered in this context part of a broader assimilation of women and game animals in male discourse. Many women are considered, prior to or at the outset of marriage, to be *uraaeca*, "wild" or "clever." With continual guidance and much hard work by her husband, she will eventually become *eratiha*, "tame" or "meek." In the context of hunting, animals deemed uraaeca are those that flee from the hunter, thwarting his attempts at appropriation. The term incorporates a sense of shyness or reticence. "Tame" animals, in contrast, are those that do not flee immediately but instead offer themselves up to the hunter, as they should. A jaguar, which would not be expected to flee in fear on sighting a human, would not be classed as uraaeca, "wild," nor could it ever be thought "tame"; it transcends these categories. Jorge explained, "A women who is 'tame' is a woman you can approach without her running away, one you can joke around with."

Given their immediate amenability to taming, it would appear that many women, at least, identify less as the "prey" of men than as potential pets—the captured offspring of game animals, particularly vulnerable once loosened from their parents' protective grasps, ready to be trained, protected, and loved. It should be stressed that this role is far from a strictly subservient one, or bereft of agency. Pets in general are entirely expected to maintain a sense of their own willfulness and personality. The deliberate demonstration of "shame," especially as a strategy of seduction as described by Sere, could be seen in this light. Although a wife would not explicitly be designated a "pet" *(iri)* of her husband, the taming of wives through matrimony is referred to as *irilaa*, "to raise" or "to tame," a process whose primary objects are otherwise pets and orphans.[2] It is always men who speak explicitly of the need to tame women in marriage, particularly if to a young girl, whose first marriage may be a fearful and distressing affair. Despite the norm of uxorilocality, it requires a painful separation of sorts from her mother, who nonetheless gives continual advice and encouragement. Lele, a girl of around fourteen and married for less than six months when I met her, obviously preferred to spend all her time with her mother rather than with her husband, whom she often left sitting alone in the small house he had built adjacent to that of his in-laws. Her mother would gently push on her the responsibilities of being a wife, encouraging her to go over and spend time with him, instructing her to take him manioc beer before he sets off to work, and the like, thereby assisting in the task of gradually reconfiguring her emotional attachments within this expanded web of dependencies.

Let us consider now another aspect of shame that relates to its inherently intersubjective quality. As a form of self-consciousness, shame is intrinsically linked to the presence of the other. It arises when we pass judgment on ourselves as objects, stepping outside of ourselves for a moment, all too aware of how we are being perceived by another person. This is, in a way, a heightened form of awareness. As Sartre (1969: 221) writes, "Shame . . . realizes an intimate relation of myself to myself.

Through shame I have discovered an aspect of my being." In other words, shame is grounded in an act of recognition. It evidences a kind of openness to the other but also an essential vulnerability. It is associated with fear of the other's judgment and, more broadly, of emotional harm.

This might help to explain why, in contrast to the case of either pets or orphans, male attitudes toward women can be particularly fraught and precarious. This is put down to the latter's *colareba*, "fearfulness," a kind of force of repulsion associated with terror and that which induces it. The experience of colareba is associated with two prototypical encounters. The first is the colareba of an anaconda, which fills one with such fear that one is physically incapable of moving any closer. The second is the fear that may grip a man when he approaches a woman he fancies, an uncontrollable nervousness or timidity that some say physically prevents them from approaching someone they nevertheless desire and wish to seduce. The position of women, to be sure, is scarcely one of powerlessness, or free of ambivalence.

Fearfulness, like shame, may be a way of mediating a sudden experience of resonance with the other, preventing or forestalling a troubling loss of autonomy or identity. Shame allows the experience of openness to unfold gradually and respectfully, at the correct tempo. Fright at the prospects of mutual dissolubility are overcome through the taming process, which reestablishes feelings of security and codependency that ultimately have their roots in prenatal experience. The condition of standing-leaned-together, epitomized in marriage, requires just the right mix of autonomy and dependency, and balance here is essential: neither pole must lean too heavily, or too quickly.

Men, too, are transformed through marriage. *Coriaa* is a term used exclusively in this context and means roughly "to domesticate" or "to change." People usually translated *coriua* into Spanish as *amansar* (to tame); however, it is clearly not synonymous with *irilaa*. It pertains more explicitly to the household, into which incoming men are progressively incorporated; the performance of couvade, discussed further below, is especially significant here. A man who recognizes his growing sense of conjugal responsibility or duty might admit, *inae canu coriaa*, "she has domesticated me." In a sense, this is an unsurprising outcome of any ostensibly unidirectional taming process: witness the well-known ability of pets everywhere to reciprocally "train" and even "tame" their owners. Coriaa may nevertheless explicitly be conceived as something mutual and symmetrical; namely, *itacoriaauru*, "together they each domesticated the other." The trepidation and the sense of timing in marriage are integral to this process.

An important dimension of seduction and taming is love magic. This is used only by men, at least to the best of my knowledge, and often makes use of the sunbittern *(Eurypyga helias)*, a small bird often spotted while one is traveling along small streams by canoe, and renowned for being strikingly "tame." People were happy to demonstrate the pleasing, purring sound it makes while fluffing up its wings in a clearly adorable and perceptibly flirtatious fashion. One well-known love charm requires a man to seek out a sunbittern, setting out at dawn without consuming food or drink. On encountering it in the forest, he must shoot and then bury the bird where it fell to the ground, leaving it for a week or so before returning to extract its thigh bone. Fasting is mandatory from the moment of its death, and manioc beer and banana drink are especially to be avoided. Kept in absolute secrecy, the bone is carefully placed inside the tube of a roll of thread. From a well-chosen vantage point the suitor looks through the tube at his chosen girl, who may feel that someone is "whistling" or "kissing" her. From that moment she will be enamored of him, gazing on him fondly and offering mashed banana drink, ready for his next advance, without the faintest idea of what just befell her.

The steadfast devotion aimed at in most love magic is just one of several desirable qualities a man hopes to inculcate in his wife. *Jaonacaaitoha*, for example, is a well-regarded trait subsuming diligence and initiative: a woman "who likes to go and fetch firewood," for example, or who "likes to prepare manioc beer even though her husband hasn't instructed her to and offers it to guests without being told." A related trait, similarly quintessentially female and expressly desired by men, is *raunojoetoha*, "to offer widely." Of course, claims made for the desirability of such traits could also be considered part of a disingenuous male discourse, for by systematically shifting responsibility for food sharing to their wives men are better able to avoid allegations of stinginess. But it might also be rendered as a form of social intelligence or savvy, an aptitude for offering wisely, as much as widely, antithetical to wildness insofar as it indexes social responsibility and forthrightness. Little by little, the processes of taming and domestication ideally continue until the couple achieves a state of mutuality, contentedness, and relative tranquillity.

SOUL MATES

A young woman in her mid-twenties, Runura always seemed more than willing to express her contentment with Lorenzo, her first and, to date, only husband, who was considerably older and had several children by a previous marriage. When I invited her one day to elaborate on the reasons for her satisfaction, she replied:

> I'm living well now; nothing befalls us. We are living well because I have my sons, to whom nothing happens, because I'm with my husband. Even when he's drunk, he doesn't do anything to me— that's why I'm content. Whatever must have happened with his [ex-] wife, earlier? How she must have wronged this man, who sought me out. Now I'm with three sons, I'm living contentedly. In this way, I can't leave him and he can't leave me. Even if he travels far away, to the city, nothing happens, and I do no wrong here either. I wait peacefully, and I receive him well. He works properly, this man. I've always lived peacefully with this man. That other woman who he separated from, on the contrary, she must have been with another man. I prepare my manioc beer for him, and he invites his neighbors. I also invite my companions, and we drink among women. Thus I work peacefully. He has maintained me with his work, provided my clothes . . . that's why I wait for him when he travels far away, even though I'm very hungry, and my children are also very hungry. When we die, we can be very sad, we can cry . . . I can invite my ritual co-father, my ritual co-mother, all of my companions . . . When my husband dies, and when I die, my shadow-soul [corii] will follow him.

Runura's short monologue reveals a number of important ideas surrounding marriage that were amply supported in further conversations with Runura and others. Her sense of "living well" *(raotojoeein ichaoha)* was clearly bound up in the nature of her relatively good family life and what that entailed, centering first on her three sons, whom she credited as largely responsible for her general contentedness as well as the strength of the marriage itself. Children—sons and daughters equally—are central to people's perceptions of the value and durability of a marriage, a point to which I return below. In addition to providing her with sons, Lorenzo maintained them all with his hard work. Ample provision of food (especially meat) and foreign goods (especially clothing) featured prominently in the accounts of all women to whom I spoke at any length on this topic. These were judged to be reciprocated above all with manioc beer, which is instrumental in integrating the family into the life of the wider community. Of some note here is Runura's view of the marriage as a permanent affair, extending beyond death to the time her shadow-soul (corii) will eventually be reunited with that of her husband.

Runura's mother-in-law, Bajaro, emphasized slightly different aspects of her former marriage to Urerejeri (Lorenzo's deceased father), and yet the way in which a notion of companionship underwrote its positive elements was strikingly similar. "When my husband lived, the father of my children, he went out walking taking his blowpipe and darts, and brought back squirrel monkeys, red squirrels, all that is found in the forest, and I always accompanied him," she told me. "My husband was very satisfactory, he always provided food for his children. Sometimes, when he went to fetch manioc, we went together, to weed and pull out manioc together. I worked together with my husband, I sweated, we labored together and suffered together, I didn't stay in my house." Although both Runura and Bajaro emphasized a strong sense of reciprocity, it was the fact of participating together in daily tasks, not merely the complementarity or commutability of the products of their labor, that made this marriage a happy one (figure 4).

An expression that perhaps comes close to epitomizing notions of the "ideal" marriage is *jiniiquiin itaque suujua nacateein*, typically glossed in Spanish as "mutual respect" (e.g., "respectan entre ellos") but that literally translates as "together they each defend the heart of the other." *Acatiha* means both "defend" and "forgive"; used in conjunction with *suujua*, the heart, as the invisible seat of thought and emotion, it implies fidelity and the security of a tranquil union in which each partner may honestly report that "we are peaceful together" *(raotojoeein te itaihaniaca).* The construal of marriage as a form of mutual defense or protection helps to explain a pervading fear of singleness as a uniquely vulnerable and unnatural condition. This extends to an abiding concern for the fates of widows and widowers. Bajaro told me that her former husband, Urerejeri, on his deathbed repeatedly expressed his anxiety that she would "suffer" after his departure and that people "would want to mistreat her." Lorenzo nodded gravely when I asked him about this, saying, "Yes, [bad] things always happen to widows ... The people steal from them, or are stingy with their food ... those savages *[taebuinae]* always mistreat them, together with those who have no father and no mother." Such comments reflect the widespread opinion that marriage is a way of protecting the interests of the spouses in a way that is difficult if not impossible otherwise.

The overt mutuality and codependency of married life coexists alongside a discourse and public practice of male supremacy. Men unswervingly portray themselves as the sole decision makers in any important matter and the initiator of any new project. In sharp contrast to their usual treatment of peers, husbands routinely command their wives in an abrupt and authoritative manner, especially in front of other men. Despite the norm of uxorilocality, women are portrayed (and indeed por-

Figure 4.   A husband and wife mend their canoe together. Photograph by author.

tray themselves) as objects or assets that are exchanged in marriage, and the severe restrictions on women's mobility further impedes their relative autonomy. Yet to what extent this gender asymmetry represents genuine inequality is difficult to ascertain; some women, for example, appear oblivious to their husbands' demands, and tactics of passive resistance seem relatively common. People of both sexes would probably deny that women are subordinate in the sense of being "controlled," and even though it is not uncommon to hear a man referred to as the "owner" *(nerora)* of his wife, one man considered that the latter is not "really" owned, pointing to the fact that a woman can always separate from her husband if she wants to and can easily remarry.

If the question of inequality is difficult to resolve definitively, it should be noted that gender segregation is patently strong and a salient principle of social organization. Marriage requires a woman to drastically curtail interactions with all other men, "out of respect for her husband." Even her relations with her brothers are now marked by great circumspection, and in the public sphere segregation is the norm; even a husband and wife will rarely sit or talk together when in the company of others. For dancing at drinking parties this protocol is relaxed, although men are still expected to first request permission to dance with the wife of another. In spite of this stringent segregation, or perhaps even because of it, infidelity is ubiquitous. I had the distinct impression that many people carried out clandestine affairs and were quite attached to these romantic liaisons. Yet these relationships remain of quite different import and emotional tenor from marriages. One reason for this is that the latter are explicitly oriented to, and structured by, procreation and childrearing.

A THEORY OF PROCREATION

Cries and general commotion roused me from my reverie one hot afternoon and brought me swiftly to the makeshift enclosure of faded, rose-colored blankets near the entrance of Antonio's house. Stooping to fit under the low roof, I glimpsed the glistening tiny baby girl lying on a soft bed of leaves in a pit dug near the hearth, where a small fire was smoldering. Rejoana was mostly hidden from view behind her mosquito net, but I could see her legs stretched out straight on either side of the pit. Before long virtually everyone in the community was present and talking animatedly—all except for Antonio, the father, who, strangely, was nowhere to be seen. As Rejoana's mother instructed a small child to fetch some warm water, conversation turned to a single topic: who would cut the umbilical cord? I realized that the baby was indeed still attached to its placenta, which had already been delivered and was lying beside it and which seemed to be gently throbbing from the blood still circulating through its veins, giving it a uncannily lifelike appearance. Questions flew back and forth, and I heard my own name mentioned a couple of times. Then a voice came from within the mosquito net, which I realized was that of Antonio himself. Peering through the mesh, I saw his legs pressed against his wife's and realized he had been sitting right behind her the whole time, as though to demonstrate the collaborative nature of the event. He and his wife had decided that Ensanjoan, Rejoana's female cross-cousin, would cut the cord. She did so swiftly and efficiently, as the baby was lifted up by its maternal grandmother and gently wrapped in blankets. Like everyone else, I was so distracted by this new animated presence in our midst that I momentarily forgot about its erstwhile companion, left behind, for now, in its blanket of leaves. With the main excitement over, the crowd began to disperse.

One reason childbirth is such an important event in the life of a community is that it inevitably reconfigures a number of wider relationships within the residential group. The most important of these is between husband and wife. The positioning of the father right behind the mother during the birth gives physical expression to the idea that birth is a joint process in which both parents participate; the expression *canaanai siri*, "to be pregnant" (lit., "to have child"), can be said of either expectant parent. An examination of the practice of couvade helps us to understand why this is so, but first it is necessary to examine a series of ideas surrounding procreation itself.

The standard Urarina theory of conception holds that semen (*ujue*), and semen alone, creates and builds the fetus inside the womb. Semen is said to derive from digested food, particularly soup and manioc beer, and is also referred to as "men's milk."[3] As elsewhere in Amazonia, repeated acts of sexual intercourse are said to build the fetus and make it stronger; although at least one person also claimed that a single act of intercourse can be sufficient to conceive if the woman's body is "ready." Inside the womb the fetus is gradually fabricated as a solid body from liquid materials: its human form arises through the coagulation of blood and the concrescence of solid from liquid. Young and old women are thought to become pregnant equally easily.

Partible paternity, or multiple biological co-fathers, is admitted as a possibility but seems to be accorded little significance, despite widespread marital infidelity. In contrast to other theories of procreation, such as those of the Ye'kwana or Yanomami, that posit that all men who have sexual relations with a woman since the birth of her last child contribute to the formation of the next one (Alès 2002), conception is here a more decisive event in which additional semen can add on to, or be incorporated in, a fetus once a woman has already become pregnant. The scenario of partible paternity most often recounted to me—the paradigmatic case, as it were—involved a woman being pregnant by her husband and then having clandestine relations with another man, whose semen mixes with that of the husband. The resulting child, recognized to have two (or more) genitors, is known as *unosi*, from the word for "leech" (*uuno*), presumably making reference to the parasitic nature of its early growth in the womb. A baby born to only one father, in contrast, is *nejesinaje*, "pure." Usually a cuckolded husband whose wife becomes pregnant in his absence will still be said to have contributed to the formation of the fetus, and social paternity is always ascribed solely to the husband. Although partible paternity is certainly a relevant factor when considering the significance of paramours, biological or secondary co-fathers (unlike ritual co-fathers) do not generally recognize their children, and I have not heard of them participating in couvade restrictions or of assuming any responsibility for the upbringing and maintenance of either the child or the mother.

If queried about the relative contributions to a newborn baby of the father and mother, an Urarina will reply that it is entirely the father who, with his semen, is responsible for the formation of the child, regardless of whether the latter is male or female. It is the father who supplies the fetus's individuality. There is a sense in which it is he who determines the child's sex, for it is said that a man who eats excessive quantities of snails (*erori lauina*) will give birth to only girls. Lorenzo confided that his own mother used to constantly reprimand him for eating them when he was a boy. He nevertheless felt that an overall balance in the sexes of one's offspring was not only desirable, but highly probable, and claimed that if three sons result from a man's first marriage he will surely produce three daughters in the next.

As distinct marriages imply distinct women, there would seem here to be a hint of ambivalence surrounding the women's role and the notion of the fetus as built from masculine substance alone. Nevertheless, there is no overt acknowledgment of a female component to the fetus itself, at least initially, and the mother is conceived as first and foremost the receptacle for its growth. Over time, however, her blood is acknowledged to mix with the substance provided by the father, and this too contributes to the formation of the fetus. Correspondingly, descent, to the extent it is reckoned at all, is bilineal, and the idiom of shared blood (*coichana*) is often used when speaking of the bilateral kindred (*arai*). Although there is a sense in which nonuterine siblings, or those sharing only a father, are slightly less closely related than uterine siblings with different fathers, both are said to share blood in equal measure.

Jorge claimed that a child receives its "blood, bones, . . . eyes, head, everything" from the father, whereas the mother contributes "only blood." When I pointed out that I had only recently overheard people comment on physical resemblances between Sena's wife and her baby girl, he qualified his statement, acknowledging that such observations are indeed sometimes made but primarily in the case of skills, such as weaving ability. Comments on parent-child resemblances seem equally likely to be based on physical characteristics (e.g., a son "pulls out the face of his father," *inaca meri rocoha*) as on behavioral qualities (e.g., a son "has the manner of his father," *inaca ichao tocoania*, lit., "like the father's life"). Widespread claims that boys take after their father and girls take after their mother may refer primarily to the latter, but it is also true that no strong division is made between the "biological" transmission of substance and the social conditions of upbringing. This essential complementarity, albeit one founded on structural asymmetry, is given further expression through the institution of the couvade.

FROM COAGULATION TO ENSOULMENT

A woman who becomes pregnant (*ausurinitia;* also *canaanai siriha,* lit., "to have child") is soon subject to a series of dietary and other prohibitions. Because the husband is also subject to many of these—especially after the birth of the child—they form part of what is known in the literature as the couvade. Dietary avoidances are largely structured around the potential transfer of undesirable qualities; hence yellow-footed tortoises (*Geochelone denticulata*), lesser anteaters (*Tamandua tetradactyl*), and other "slow moving" animals are avoided with the stated aim that the birth proceed "swiftly" and free of suffering, while the electric eel (*Macana* sp.) and rainbow wolf fish (*Erythrinus* sp.), said to "rot quickly," should be avoided lest the fetus similarly rot and miscarry. Activities considered potentially dangerous are also strictly avoided, from carrying heavy loads to the fabrication of mastate bark (*Poulsenia armata*) sleeping mats. A woman who cuts a mastate tree is said subsequently to feel pains in her womb, such that it would be necessary to intone the appropriate chant (*torori baau*) to save her life and that of the fetus. Pregnant women are known to have cravings, which should be satisfied by their husbands on the grounds that "the baby inside wants to feed well." A husband should also not mistreat or beat his wife, and particular care must be taken to ensure the baby is well lined up in the womb, not askew. A month or so prior to the anticipated birth he may drink psychotropics to see if the birth will go smoothly and to request Our Creator for assistance in this regard.

Following the birth, couvade restrictions are observed by both parents. These proscribe aspects of the diet and the scope of activity (in particular, sexual activity) of each. Although the precise nature and duration of the restrictions may vary considerably, particularly where they concern matters of diet, in almost all instances the consequences of infractions are borne by the baby, in the form of illness or underdevelopment. Both parents are forbidden many of their routine domestic duties, from fetching water and firewood to hunting in the forest. I was told a mother should not bathe in the river for a month, or make manioc beer for two months (said to cause harm to the stomach), and a father should not play football lest his baby's stomach "grow swollen." Neither parent should bathe in the river until the baby's umbilical cord falls, for otherwise it will "rot." For at least a couple of weeks after the birth, both parents are advised against leaving the house at all unless absolutely necessary, for fear they might "look at," or otherwise come into contact with, any of the many species of animals or trees considered particularly dangerous to a newborn baby. Such contact is held to induce a form of mystical harm (*buunaatiha*), whose common symptoms include swelling of the stomach and fever, curable only by the appropriate baau chant. There are literally dozens of distinct baau tailored to each of the many possible sources of harm. A few months after the birth of his baby girl, Antonio told me he did not want to fell a *sacarena* tree (possibly *Thevetia peruviana*), lest her hair fall out and her skin rot and putrefy. Even the father's being in the sun is enough to induce fever, as Buchilote informed me one day had befallen his own newborn baby. He had spent much of the previous day in direct sun and admitted to me that his wife was furious, to the point of having informed him that if their baby died he would be "burying it by himself," without her help. This extreme vulnerability of a newborn baby through the activities of parents lasts at least until it is four or five months of age.

Anthropological analyses of the couvade date to the beginnings of the discipline. After reviewing (and rejecting) earlier attempts to define it as a rite of passage or as concerned primarily with the legitimation of paternity, the thrust of Rivière's (1974) contribution was to situate the institution within the broader problematic of body-soul dualism. Drawing on Gudeman's (1971) interpretation of *compadrazgo* (co-parenthood), Rivière (1974: 431) argued that the couvade was similarly about the spiritual, as opposed to physical, creation of a new person; the central problem, as he saw it, was how the body and the soul, created independently, "come together" in the newborn or "coalesce to form an independent individual." Rival (1998) later insisted that the Huaorani couvade should be understood as the rite of a couple, in which both mother and father participate, though with differing implications for each. Extending and typifying the practices of sharing that defined residential groups, it consolidated the domestic unit and, properly viewed against the backdrop of uxorilocal postmarital residence, incorporated incoming men as consubstantial kin. A further twist was added by Vilaça (2002), who saw the alimentary restrictions of the couvade as a means of forging a distinctly human body, in contraposition to those of animals, with whom potentially transformative contact must be avoided.[4]

The consequences of not adhering to couvade restrictions are understood to be physical and material as much as spiritual. In many cases they involve what people describe as the "rotting" of body parts, their apparent atrophy or putrefaction, a notion that explicitly countervails against hardness and connotes an excessive liquidity. Similar consequences befall those who break the injunction on sexual intercourse, which of all the couvade restrictions is the one ascribed greatest importance by Urarina themselves.[5] Some advised that the couple should ideally abstain for up to six months following the birth but subsequently admitted that in practice the length of time was often somewhat less. Lorenzo's comments were revealing: "Well . . . when the parents reach four months, if they can't bear it any more, they can give a few kisses . . . yes, some only make it to five months, others up to six months."

The drastic consequences of premature and inapt sexual commerce are well understood by everyone: the baby will grow feeble and thin. Referred to thenceforth as *itosaje,* such a child is said to be unable to stand or even crawl and will also be prone to chronic diarrhea, black in color. The sight of a child who has not learned to walk by the time it grows to a certain size, perhaps at one to two years of age, inevitably attracts speculation and gossip concerning its parents' irresponsibility.

The expression of the consequences of violating couvade restrictions in terms of such direct harm to the baby is reinforced in the aforementioned myth of Our Creator's Envoy, referred to as the origin of the injunction on postpartum sexual intercourse, which it proclaims to be ten months. In the story's final episode, Adam's wife fabricates a child from cotton. She warns her husband not to harm the child (itosaje) by insisting on sexual relations, but he doesn't heed her instructions, and the child collapses, incapable of walking. The problem seems to be largely one of exclusivity: he should not be "making another baby" (*cocoalateein,* lit., "to give [the child] a younger sibling") while the first is still growing or still sitting (rather than walking).

This in turn highlights the quasi-material connection between the parents and the newborn. To explore this further, let us consider briefly the couvade violation chant *(itosaje baau),* widely considered the most potent (if not the only) curative for the affliction caused by breaking the couvade restrictions, and of some interest at least for the additional insights it furnishes into the institution itself. The chant is performed on an ongoing and regular basis until the child recovers but may also be used as a preventive measure by parents unable or unwilling to adhere with due diligence to their imposed celibacy. Its central narrative dimension is the invocation of a series of birds noted for the ability of their off-spring to walk from the moment the eggs hatch. These birds, particularly the marbled wood quail *(Odentophorus guianensis),* are also used as representations of ritual co-parents in drinking songs. In fact, birds figure prominently in the symbolism of virtually all accounts in mythology and ritual language concerning birth and companionship. The first few lines of the version I recorded ran as follows:

itosaje que	*itosaje* harm
colarene colarane que colarena	Tiny round reddish
chabana ne bacohara bacohara	Never break, break
aloonri ne ranisijie	Chest of the undulated tinamou[6]
necoucoujuatia que	Defending
aino calabi ranisijie	Chest of offspring of *aino*
bujuaina bujuaina	Shielding, shielding
rululuritiin	Rubbing down
aloonri ne ranisijie	Chest of the undulated tinamou
necoucoujuatia qui ne	Defending thus
bajari ne ranisijie necoucujua	Defending the tinamou's[7] chest
soseri ne ranisijie necoucoujuatia que	Defending the *soseri*'s[8] chest

The chant begins by relating the condition of itosaje to the state of being "split" or "broken" *(bacoha),* an expression often used with regard to the "broken" feet *(tijia bacoha)* of a child sufficiently mature to walk but still unable to do so. The condition is much later in the chant related to the likely cause: the penis looking or "poking around" *(toraraa)* inside the womb or vagina in unsanctioned sexual commerce, much as one might furtively or surreptitiously "poke around" inside someone else's belongings while the owner is distracted. Building on recurring notions of an integral and quasi-material bond between an infant and its parents, a series of connections is evoked between the strength or vital energy required to learn to walk (a milestone on the road to personal autonomy of singular cultural importance), bodily "hardness," and notions of containment, specifically, the shoring up of semen in the father and the unpenetrated closure of the womb. There are also overtones here of those recurring notions concerning dependency (in this case on the parents) as a condition of autonomy.

As with most discourse in the baau genre, the notion of defense or protection, conceived particularly as a form of shielding, enjoys special prominence. Jorge offered an interesting everyday example of *bujuatiha,* "to shield" or "to put behind," by referring to the way women cover up or "shield" their newborn baby with cloth or blankets, preventing curious visitors from looking at it. While professing doubts as to the real purpose of this apparently common practice, he suspected it was perhaps intended to thwart malicious gossip imputing that the infant bore little resemblance to the husband and thereby questioning his paternity. The shielding effected by the chant is of course similarly directed at guarding against the consequences of illegitimate sexual activity. Sharing a common root is *necoucoujuatiha*, a ritualized version of *necouhatiha*, "to protect oneself." Jorge's example from everyday speech was again illuminating: "For example, I desire a young, single girl, and I am always 'annoying' her, but she doesn't want me. Then I have a child with my wife, and she comes to cut its umbilical cord, and bathe it well. I might say to her, '*necoucujuatiha te aansai*,' meaning you are defending yourself, saving yourself, you are making yourself my ritual co-mother, and now I can't do anything with you!" Once again it is here an unsanctioned sexual activity or lack of containment that necessitates adequate protection.

Much of the performative force of the chant is conceived in terms of physical actions, such as "rubbing down" (*rululuhin*). This is a healing technique, often performed under the influence of ayahuasca or brugmansia, in which the healer rubs or massages his hands downward along the arm, stomach, or other nominated part of the patient in order to calm the affliction. The chant simultaneously aims to "dye" (*lomoha*) the blood and inner part of the infant's body, particularly the stomach, in much the same way as palm fibers are dyed prior to their incorporation into a weaving project. In this way the child's blood "returns" or "goes back" (*necauhina*) to its normal state. As Jorge put it, "The chant is entering the baby's body, and removing the affliction, and the baby is becoming happy, because his body is being cured." This happiness is supposed to manifest itself as a "singing for joy" (*acurunaa*), an activity associated particularly with birds such as the *catataoha* (possibly *Daptrius americanus*), said to sing with joy when the weather is fine. The connection between fine weather and individual health is developed further below.

A mother resumes most of her principal daily chores, such as fetching water from the river and gathering firewood, at the cessation of her postpartum bleeding, said by some to last up to a month. Known as *canaanai baca*, "baby juice," this substance is associated with the infant itself and sharply distinguished from menstrual blood and the menstrual cycle, though both are marked by similarly severe injunctions against any form of activity (including walking), and their cessation may similarly be hastened by consuming the right infusion of piri-piri (*Cyperus articulatus*).

In addition to being the occasion for the easing of certain couvade restrictions, the cessation of bleeding is a transitional point marked by a small ceremony, which I shall designate *fledging.* From the moment of birth, the infant's feces is diligently collected, where possible, by the mother and guarded in a special basket *(curaori)* woven from leaves of the ungurahui palm *(Oenocarpus bataua)* employing a technique similar to that used for the thatched roofs of houses. When bleeding has ceased, the full curaori basket is taken to the forest and left tied to the trunk of a hog plum tree *(Spondias mombin),* a species distinguished by its extraordinary resilience.[9]

The task is usually performed by the father, accompanied by the mother and, with her, the feces' tiny owner (nerora). Walking a small distance behind her husband, the mother carries a large gourd full of ashes, collected from the fireplace in the birth annex, with which the baby was kept warm. These are scattered along the trail through the forest. While walking, the father or mother, or both, intones the *canaanai ujue cojiotaa:*

jojona bede te aocoe	The child of the sungrebe[10] flies from the nest
jojona calaohi te aocoe	The son of the sungrebe flies from the nest
chariji bana uunatenachara	That which is never ensorcelled
jojona calaohi te aocoe	The son of the sungrebe flies from the nest
uunatenachara nacuari calaohi te aocoe	The son of the water turkey[11] which is never ensorcelled flies from the nest
chariji bana uunateen naojoaenachara	That which is never being ensorcelled thus
nacuari calaohi te aocoe	The son of the water turkey flies from the nest
uunatenachara necouri calaohi te aocoe	The tiger heron[12] which is never ensorcelled flies from the nest
chariji bana uunateen naojoaenachara	That which is never being ensorcelled thus
necouri calaohi te aocoe	The son of the tiger heron flies from the nest
jojona calaohi te aocoe	The son of the sungrebe flies from the nest
nenatenachara necouri calaohi te aocoe	The son of the tiger heron which is never ensorcelled flies from the nest
uunatenachara chabatasi calaohi te aocoe	The son of the kingfisher[13] is never ensorcelled as it flies from the nest
uunatenachara chabatasi calaohi te aocoe	The son of the kingfisher is never ensorcelled as it flies from the nest

The cojiotaa, as a genre of ritual discourse, differs markedly from the baau in many regards, including content, delivery, and performative force.

Generally speaking, the cojiotaa is used to achieve a specific end or practical purpose but never to heal illness. The *elo cojiotaa*, perhaps the most widely used exemplar, is deployed to avoid or postpone an imminent rain shower while one is away from the house. Others might be used to make crops grow in greater abundance, to make fish poison more effective, or to increase the strength of manioc beer. Like the baau chants, cojiotaa draw on extensive webs of analogies and associations in effecting a process of transformation. Unlike the baau, however, there is no incorporation of qualities from external sources or third parties, and they are addressed directly to a listener, who is usually the intended target of the desired change. As such, the performative aspect of these two genres is quite different. Unlike the baau, cojiotaa construe both the enunciator and the listener(s) as individualized subjects and agents. The *fanara cojiotaa*, for example, is addressed directly to the plantain tree and may be figured as a kind of imperative—a direct instruction or command. Instead of breathy exhalations, they are punctuated by sharp cries to get someone's attention, rather like shouting, "Oi!" Cojiotaa are less restricted to the mature and elderly and are as likely to be performed by women as by men.

In the particular case of the canaanai ujue cojiotaa transcribed above, there is nevertheless a certain similarity to the baau genre, namely, the apparent recourse to a principle of analogic transfer. This takes precedence over the particular species chosen, which is again liable to vary at the discretion of the enunciator. *Aocoa*, the verb of central importance here, means "to fly" but exclusively in the context of a bird's first, tentative flights from the nest, when its feathers have only recently grown. The ritual disposal of the feces is thus conceived as a kind of fledging: an act of nurture leading to a new, partial independence. As in the canaanai mitu baau, biological substances (achiote, mother's milk, feces) anchor processes of analogic transfer, through which an emerging person is configured in relation to heterogeneous "others" and to the natural environment. The almost metaphysical attachment of a newborn to its feces echoes that which binds it to the placenta; it further emphasizes the "leaky" nature of proto-personhood and the paramount importance of containment.

An additional specimen of ritual discourse, known as the *enua suujui cojiotaa*, is sometimes employed some three months after emergence from the birth hut. The baby is held firmly by the parent during the performance, with a leg on either side of one of the main load-bearing columns (anesijia) of the house, against which its hands and feet are gently rubbed. Similar beings are invoked as in the mitu baau, with the addition here of Catiri, who figures in many myths and is often equated with the son of Our Creator (*Cana Coaaunera calaohi*), and sometimes with Our Creator himself.

ton ton ton ton ton	Ton! Ton! Ton! Ton! Ton!
chabana baitenachara catiri necoerejetera mituera	The emerged offspring of Catiri never dies
ton ton ton ton ton	Ton! Ton! Ton! Ton! Ton!
chabana baitenacharara enoto coranuna bedetera mituera	The emerged child of the sun's maiden daughter never dies
ton ton ton ton ton	Ton! Ton! Ton! Ton! Ton!
chabana baitenachara atene necoerejete	The emerged offspring of the moon never dies
coranuna necoerejetetera mituera	Emerged offspring of its maiden daughter
ton ton ton ton ton	Ton! Ton! Ton! Ton! Ton!
chabana baitenachara inoaera bede najano mituera	The emerged newborn child of Inoaera never dies

Though clearly directed at an appropriation of the hardness, symptomatic of resilience, of house columns, the enua suujui cojiotaa can only be fully understood in the broader context of local theories of personhood. It represents a culmination of a process that began with the body's formation by the concrescence of liquids into solids: a consolidation or soft coagulation of blood and semen. From this liquid or semiliquid state the child is built up in the womb, hardening and coalescing in a process of gradual solidification that continues well after birth. The final stages of this process, which arguably never ends, is not merely a hard body, but what is perhaps the ultimate expression or *emanation* of hardness: the heart-soul (suujue). In Urarina thought and language, this is strongly correlated with the hard interior of trees (*suujui*), and represents not only the interior dimension of the person, but its hardest dimension, the culmination of hardness and an expression of the distance traveled from the primordial liquid state.[14]

The practice of the couvade, together with other institutions surrounding birth, must be understood in this light. To represent the soul as being "placed" in the body, as many writers have done, would be misleading in the Urarina case: it would be to misread the relation between the two by imposing a static substance dualism over what might more accurately be represented as a dynamic theory of emergent properties. Notions of the heart-soul later detaching from the body during serious illness or shamanic performances need not contradict this original process of emergence. The heart-soul solidifies the person as it individualizes it, seal-ing it off from its environs, a mark of individuation and impermeability and an antifluid that controls against corporeal leakage. The practices of couvade and ritual performances such as those outlined above are only preliminary steps in the sealing of a body, which, still without its own definite soul, remains porous, permeable, and malleable. This state is not without its advantages, however, particularly for parents with an active interest in molding their child outside the womb, for example, through use of the baby hammock.

Through their joint participation in the task of creating, and then "hardening" and "ensouling" the body of their offspring, the relation-ship between husband and wife is progressively consolidated. This is expressed in various ways, ranging from notions of mutual respect and protection to the unification of their shadow-souls after death. They are effectively joined through the body of their offspring, and the more this third body is sealed, individuated, and particularized—a process expressed locally through the idiom of the heart-soul—the more closely bound up with each other the parents become. This is a continuation of the taming process, discussed earlier, which began with a heightened form of self-awareness arising from an openness to the gaze of the other, experienced as shame. Such openness does not disappear but is cultivated and deepened, even as the initial feelings of vulnerability gradually give way to more positive experiences of mutual belonging. This recalls the primordial state of dependency and coexistence within the protective space of the womb, for such is the basis of subjectivity. Yet there is an additional and equally important step to be taken in the formation of the new person that centers on its separation from the placenta. In addition to initiating the child's induction into society, this is an event that ensures that childbirth inevitably extends its influence beyond the conjugal unit.

THE BIRTH OF SHADOWS

The procedures for giving birth, including the construction of the birth hut, birth hole, and infant accessories, and by implication the couvade itself, are said to have been imparted to humans by the black-capped capuchin monkey (*Cebus apella*). Prior to this time the husband had to cut his wife open with a bamboo sword to extract the baby, killing her in the process. According to a well-known myth dealing with this subject, a regretful husband leaves his pregnant wife alone in the forest while he seeks out some suitable bamboo. The capuchin monkey approaches

and teaches her the correct techniques, including the importance of couvade restrictions, such as the husband refraining from hunting. A version of this myth has been attested for the Huaorani by Rival (1998), who
wished to draw attention to the fact that the concern expressed for the
fate of the wife is the converse of the principal concern embodied in the
couvade (and of which the injunction on hunting by the father, described
in the myth, is a component). But first I wish to discuss in greater detail
a slightly different aspect of the Urarina version, namely, the indispens-
ability of the birth paraphernalia and technical procedures, especially the
significance of the act of "setting up" *(michua)* the baby and cutting the
umbilical cord. This requires a further step back to assess the broader
significance of birth itself and its mythological resonances.

I will start with another well-known myth, which tells of the simultaneous origins of manioc, terrestrial water, and daybreak. Here is the text
in its entirety.

> A long time ago, the sky was dark. Because the sky was dark, and
> our days were dark, the ancient people felled the mother of manioc.
> When they felled it, they called for Hummingbird. "Hummingbird,
> you who move so fast, pass over the top of this lupuna tree, and carry
> this boiled manioc over to the other side." Saying this, they sent
> Hummingbird. But Big Hummingbird could not go, so they called
> for Little Hummingbird. They boiled manioc, and when it was still a
> little hot, they sent Little Hummingbird over to the other side. When
> he arrived, at that moment, they said, "Now we can fell the tree, it
> is not good for us, it is much too dark, let's fell it, so it can become
> dawn, so it will be day, so there will be daybreak over here." Speaking
> like this they sent Hummingbird. When they had felled it, when
> that lupuna tree had fallen over, it turned into a river, this Marañon
> River, and Iquitos. Turning into a river, all its branches turned into
> tributaries. All the branches of the kapok turned into tributaries, all
> in immense rivers running in their respective directions. All of the
> rivers were made from the kapok branches, it is said. That's how Our
> Creator created all that he did. He created it like this because it was
> going to be better. Because that's what Our Father said, that's how
> Our Creator made our rivers for us. The trunk of the kapok turned
> into the Marañon, and its branches turned into the tributaries. That's
> what the ancient people used to say. And when day broke over here on
> this side, the people were pulling out the roots of the kapok tree, and
> making manioc beer, and that's how manioc came into being. Because
> that kapok is the mother of manioc, and that's why the ancient people
> planted it. Up until the present day there is manioc, for making
> manioc beer, for fermenting and becoming strong. Manioc is the

branch of kapok, it is said. That's how Our Father created us. He gave us everything, our houses, and created the plants, and just like that we are all real people. That's why all the rivers, all the tributaries, are lupuna, the Marañon River, all the rivers that flow direct. When day broke, when the kapok tree fell, everything became river, and that's how it stays up until today.

The absolute centrality of manioc, particularly manioc beer, in defining the institution of ritual co-parenthood as a companionship between adults is discussed further below. According to most informants, the principal subject (and proper title) of this myth is "the creation of manioc" or "the mother of manioc." Yet such claims confront the curious paradox that manioc must have been present in some form at the very outset, as it was given to Hummingbird to carry. This is in fact far from unusual in Urarina mythology: gardens, canoes, and maize, for example, all exist at the outset of the stories ostensibly relating the circumstances of their "creation." This suggests that the myths are either allegorical in import (which seems likely) or that Amazonian notions of creation are fundamentally different from our own, a possibility to which I shall return. Leaving aside for the moment its presence at the beginning of the story, manioc appears in this myth as the transformation, or offshoot, of the kapok tree, its "mother" *(neba)*. This could be read as a tale of domestication, of an uncontrolled forest tree into a controlled (or controllable) garden staple, achievement of which requires the appropriate knowledge. When I asked Jorge why the people sent Hummingbird over the top of the tree to the other side, he speculated, "Perhaps they were sending the manioc to where God is, so that God takes pity on them, telling them that the roots of the kapok is manioc." But there remains the mystery of why dawn, or daybreak, is associated with this transformation.

Fortunately, the semantics of the original Urarina text are denser and invite a richer reading. The central verb *janoha*, "to clear up" (in the sense of dawn or daybreak) also means "to give birth."[15] An expression in the original text such as *nijianoaine*, "in order to have daybreak," thus also has the possible meaning "in order to have birth." That a native speaker would connect these meanings is clear, for when translating the myth I asked Jorge to supply an additional example of the quotidian use of *nijianoaine*, which he had just translated into Spanish as "so as to have daybreak" *(para que amanezca)*. Of a woman suffering during labor, he offered, one might say, *"mucu te nijianoaina,"* "grab her so as to give birth." The relation between kapok and manioc (which realizes its destiny, mixed with water from the rivers and female saliva, in the form of beer), figured as one of domestication and filiation, thus also provides an allegorical frame for the conceptualization of birth itself.

From the verb *janoha* is derived *janonaa*, "day," a term that also carries a broader sense of time as a sequence of days, perhaps time in general, and particularly its relation to the weather (not unlike the Spanish *tiempo*). This is the origin of the expression *cana cojoanona*, literally, "our days":[16] a fundamental cosmological concept that implies a sense of both epoch and world and that must be understood in the context of an apocalyptic eschatology according to which the world is destined for inevitable catastrophic collapse. As discussed in chapter 6, this is signaled above all by the gradual deterioration of the weather from a state of clarity (fine and sunny) through increasing rain and cold to permanent darkness—in short, death. Yet the end of the world, even if ultimately inevitable, is also deferrable through shamanic action. The deferral of the apocalypse is effectively the promotion (and de facto creation) of day and daylight and hence of time in general. It is directed at "making light" and the reproduction of life in the form of forest animals. In this sense shamanism is closely allied with feminine procreative power, which is not to say that shamans are themselves symbolically "female" but rather the power harnessed by the shaman, through his alliances with the mother of ayahuasca and brugmansia and with Our Creator, is effectively a male version of female reproductive energies.[17] Both are held to be necessary to the creation and support of life.

The richer significance of the myth now starts to unfold. Prior to Hummingbird's intervention, the kapok tree stood tall but barren, in a world that was dry, dark, and essentially timeless. Its conversion into manioc and thence into beer is a parable of birth and the triumph of fertility, marking the onset not only of cycles of individual and cosmic rebirth, but of the full and proper flowing of fluids through the cosmos. The myth of the cosmic deluge arguably deals with the same theme. The event of birth has, of course, long been considered to be closely associated with flood myths generally: according to Dundes (1988: 1), the flood myth is "a cosmogonic projection of salient details of human birth insofar as every infant is delivered from a 'flood' of amniotic fluid." For the nascent person, the event of birth marks a defining and irreversible transition in the circulation of fluids, as the maternal blood exchanged via the placenta is replaced by exchanges of mother's milk, food, and finally manioc beer. The direct transfer of blood in the womb, which is arguably a paradigm for the construction of consanguinity in its narrowest possible grade, is replaced by the consumption of other fluids that similarly work to forge the affective ties that bind together members of a community.

The act of cutting the umbilical cord must be assessed in this light. At first glance it would appear that the act is symbolic of the separation of the infant from its mother. As anyone who has witnessed a birth well knows, however, this is not precisely true: the newborn is severed from its placenta, the entity with which it has cohabited in the intimacy and shared space of the womb for the past several months. As proposed earlier, it is as though in this original state of suspension in fluids, defined by the incessant interchange of blood between mother and child, the placenta acts not only as mediator and source of nourishment but also as shadowy "first companion"; its severance opens up a space to be filled by future replacements, the first of which is of course the hammock. In this way the infant's capacity for sociality, which has its origins in the womb, is gently and very gradually redirected away from the realm of the non-human and toward its fellow humans.

Not without justification is the placenta treated with some reverence after birth, as an entity that, after its careful burial by the midwife, or michuera, should come into contact with no one but the newborn. Because of an enduring connection to the child that supervenes physical separation, any accidental contact with an animal or harmful spirit is said to result in illness. Only at the moment of death is a person said at last to be reunited with his or her lost partner and companion. Such postmortem unification is also, of course, precisely what happens to the shadow-souls of spouses, and marriage is implicitly represented as a transformation of this primordial, perduring relation. Although never explicitly formulated to me in such terms, I would suggest that the shadow-soul comes into existence at the moment the placenta is severed from the infant, as its lingering, shadowy trace, serving to recast this absence or empty space as a newfound capacity for relatedness. What appears as the infant's individual loss is a necessary stage in the re-creation of society and its own transformation into a social being.

RITUAL KINSHIP AND MULTIPLE FILIATION

I have argued that the heart-soul is thought to emerge through the joint action of the parents, especially via the performance of couvade and related rites, who are thereby conjoined in intimate and indissoluble companionship. They are related less by any direct sharing of bodily substance than by the medium of this third body, for whose creation they are responsible and whose individuation the heart-soul epitomizes. Cutting the umbilical cord is similarly an act of individuation in the first instance, and the ritual co-parents formed in this way are also brought together in intimate companionship with the parents through the medium of the child. This is concurrent with the creation of the shadow-soul, associated above all with the capacity for those same intimate relationships uniting husbands, wives, and ritual co-parents. It is this latter relationship that I now wish to explore further.

The Urarina ritual kinship system is a variant of the compadrazgo, although I suspect that certain elements predate missionization and other forms of postconquest contact. I will set aside for the moment such questions of origins in order better to concentrate on its present mode of operation, some aspects of which are widely distributed throughout Latin America. The institution known as compadrazgo has been reported in the literature since Tylor (1861: 250–51) and has been subject to a number of interpretations.[18] Of particular interest here is Gudeman's (1971) attempt to locate it within the Christian conception of human nature as inherently dual. The two dimensions or aspects of the person, spiritual and natural (or cultural and biological), are entrusted to different sets of persons, such that the "Birth Set" (comprising mother, father, and child) is to the "Baptismal Set" (comprising minister, sponsor, and child) as the natural is to the spiritual. It was on this basis that Rivière (1974) drew an analogy with the couvade, as similarly concerned with the "spiritual," as opposed to natural, creation of the person. Yet Rivière also drew attention to what he saw as an important difference: whereas the compadrazgo is modeled on the family and the relationships within it, in the couvade the model is a physiological one, such that "all or part of the processes of pregnancy, parturition and nurture serve as a model for the spiritual creation" (433). While I am fundamentally in agreement with Rivière's perception that both institutions represent related approaches to a similar, overarching problem, I suspect that this distinction, too, may be overdrawn.

A mother will usually choose her midwife some time prior to giving birth. In many cases the mother and father will together decide on another married couple to be their ritual co-parents, though in every instance the mother will independently approach her nominated co-mother and the father his nominated co-father. The parents usually invite others to assist at the birth and become co-parents, but it is not unheard of to offer one's services. Urarina are clear that ritual co-parenthood is a relation that is ideally established with nonkin, or someone "not of the same blood." Jorge told me:

> When my son Aroldo was born, I called to my mother to help. But she said to me, "No, how am I going to touch your blood! Better to seek out another to cut the umbilical cord." And I didn't want her to do it either. So I went looking for another old woman. How can someone be both things, grandmother and godmother? That's no good. I'm the blood of my mother, that's why it's no good. The godmother should be of other blood.

The one who severs the umbilical cord is also known as *necoereje dadaera*, "toucher of offspring." Physical contact with blood while assisting with a birth and cutting an umbilical cord, blood that is a mixture of the two parents, seems central to the way the relationship is conceptualized. Yet the relationship is moral as much as physical, and agreeing to assist at a birth is no trivial matter. Meroahori recalled for me an episode that occurred when he lived on the Tigrillo River involving a girl who purportedly became pregnant by her own father.

> When this girl was about to give birth, no one wanted to cut the umbilical cord. Everyone, male and female, refused it. As a result, the girl ended up giving birth alone in the forest. She left the baby there, and returned to the village. Later, her neighbors went out searching, and finally found it, abandoned and well covered with leaves. Though just a few hours old, the baby spoke to them in a clear voice: "Damn! My mother is evil, a real sinner *[osati]*; those who don't know Our Creator, those who conceive children with their own fathers, will bring about the end of the world, and will be punished in the celestial fire."

A child and those responsible for cutting the umbilical will thenceforth address each other as *camichua* and *camichuera* respectively. Although the relationship never formally terminates, the terms are generally employed only until adulthood. The obligations of co-parents toward the children at whose birth they have assisted are relatively minor, and very vaguely defined. Lorenzo admitted he felt particular responsibility for ensuring the continued health and well-being of Wilder, his *michua*, or godchild, and would heal him whenever he fell ill. Others, however, could cite no particular responsibility, and the relationship is thought of more in terms of mutual affection than obligation. The relationship parallels that between a name giver *(cabaichera)* and name receiver *(cabaichae)*, which is instituted through the bestowal either of a psychotropic name from a state of psychedelic trance or of a Spanish name from a state of alcohol-induced drunkenness (see chapter 5). Taken together, these provide a system for reckoning relatedness complementary to that supplied by the kinship terminology, and are bound up in a kind of complementary filiation.

Even more important in terms of transformations effected in attitudes and behaviors are the relationships of ritual kinship instituted horizontally, as it were, between parents and their co-parents. In the case of ritual co-parenthood arising from the cutting of an umbilical cord, two couples are typically involved. Up to four distinct relationships are therefore instituted through a single act, the tenor of which differs considerably according to whether or not they are between people of the same sex. The relationship between opposite-sex co-parents is marked by solemn respect and, to an extent, avoidance. Sexual relations in particular are strictly forbidden. In many instances, the two are already classificatory brother and sister. It could therefore be said that the relationship itself is modeled on, or analogous to, the brother-sister sibling relation.

The affective dimension of the relation between same-sex co-parents is quite different. It is similarly characterized by an avowed mutual respect but at the same time, and somewhat paradoxically, often involves a great deal of joking, especially between males. This takes place despite assertions that "you shouldn't joke with your co-fathers" and can lead to an intriguing form of humor. For example, Jarano (whose name also refers to a species of fish) was often addressed by Buchilote, in an obviously jocular manner, as *coonfa peje*, "fish co-father."[19] When I asked why, he explained, "Jarano is a fish, that's why. I say coonfa to him in order to show him respect. You always have to respect your co-fathers, and they have to respect you too. You shouldn't joke with them. They can help you joke with someone else though, they have the right to defend you." The "defense" referred to here pertains to the exchange of banter and gentle teasing that takes place during many drinking bouts and especially collective working parties (minga). Often a third party—ideally a co-father—will step in on behalf of the "insulted" and hit back at his teaser with some form of joking counterattack. In practice, however, co-fathers often end up exchanging teasing banter themselves. This can also take the form of pranks or practical jokes. Several times I was told the story—usually between fits of laughter—of a man who dared to play a practical joke on Don Arturo, one of the more powerful (and feared) of the Chambira's itinerant traders, whom he had earlier made his co-father.

Although people sometimes make co-parents from total outsiders, such as itinerant traders, the greatest numbers of such bonds are formed with same-sex, same-generation affines. Co-residents, especially in-marrying men, tend to make themselves into co-fathers in an almost systematic manner, as part of a unification process whereby the entire residential group is progressively transformed into something resembling a bilateral kindred. Linguistically, ritual co-parenthood overrides affinity: affines made into co-parents subsequently address each other only as the latter. I was told, for example, that even if he so desired a man could not continue to use "cadaa" (brother-in-law) to address someone who is now also his coonfa or confaire (co-father).

The importance of the co-parent relationship in terms of offering a new term of address can hardly be overestimated, for it is primarily in such terms that it is conceptualized and spoken about. When Jorge first came to live in the community of Nueva Unión, he was surprised at how many of the men, all previously brothers-in-law, had already managed to make themselves co-fathers. He naturally felt somewhat excluded. "All of them are family there, hey," he said to me. "All the time you hear, 'co-father,' 'co-father,' 'co-father.' Hopefully next year I'll baptize their sons so I can say co-father, too."

The popularity of the co-parent relation is in part attributable to this possibility for avoiding same-sex affine vocatives. Lorenzo told me:

> Earlier, co-mothers [comadres] used to say *cadaqui* [sister-in-law] to each other. This wasn't because they didn't have co-mothers but rather because they didn't know how to say *comaire*. My mother always liked to say *comaire* to her co-mothers, but my grandfather would correct her, saying, "No, you don't say *comaire*, just *cadaqui*, nothing more!"

Lorenzo claimed his mother was taught the term by her own mother, who was Cocama, not Urarina, and she continued to use it in spite of her father's protests. Her preference is unsurprising given the widespread aversion to using same-generation affinal address terms, possibly reflecting a slightly negative valuation of this relationship. Hence although *cadaqui* is still regularly used by some women, many others (for whom comaire is not yet an option) choose an alternate form for both address and reference, such as *ichaso sinijera* or *ichaso comasai* (my brother's wife), or simply use their names. Shortly after I arrived in Nueva Unión, when I was still trying to discern the relationships between each inhabitant, I asked Shebaco (whom I later learned was married to Lorenzo's sister), "Your what [i.e., type of relation] is Lorenzo?" "He isn't my anything," replied Shebaco—before conceding, after a long pause, "Well, he's my brother-in-law."

Whether for convenience, lack of alternatives, or deliberate strategy, co-parents are very occasionally made from consanguines. Generally speaking, the latter would continue to address each other with the consanguineal address term rather than as co-parent. For example, Lorenzo baptized the son of his brother Ernesto, whose wife subsequently addressed Lorenzo as "co-father" *(confairiana)*, and Lorenzo in turn addressed her as "co-mother" *(comairiana)*. However, Ernesto and Lorenzo continued to address each other simply as "brother" *(ichaso)*. "Ernesto cannot call me 'confaire,' because we're brothers," Lorenzo explained.

There are nevertheless certain contexts in which co-parenthood is of greater ideological significance than consanguinity, particularly when the importance of mutual respect is at issue. In the only such case I was aware of, Rosa cut the umbilical cord of her daughter Rosalia's baby girl, turning this mother-daughter pair into co-mothers. I once happened to record an especially heated and drunken argument between the two during a drinking party, which descended at one stage into physical violence. Rosa venomously rebuked her daughter's lack of respect:

> You are forsaken by Our Creator! When your child was born, I cut its umbilical cord—and you fail to recognize this! I am your co-mother and you don't recognize it! You are the forsaken one, you lead the life of a savage beast! If you really don't recognize me as your co-mother, let's see you hit me! If you really don't know that I have touched your blood, let's see you hit me!

In the context of this exchange of insults, it was Rosalia's failure to show respect to her as co-mother (rather than as mother) that Rosa, and others to whom I later spoke, found most reprehensible.

Alongside the respect that ideally characterizes the ritual co-parent relation is an intensification of cooperation and mutual care. For men, this takes the form of mutual "defense" against aggressive joking during drinking parties and joint participation in certain productive activities such as hunting. Female ritual co-parents are also prototypical "companions" who are likely to undertake certain activities together, such as fishing. The affective dimension of the relationship is even more explicitly construed in terms of mutual support and nurture. In the following song, sung during manioc beer drinking parties, the singer depicts herself as an orphan, "pretty" but "wandering around" helplessly.

aiyaya aiyaya	Oh yeah
ujuateje neucaan	I'm an orphan
amuemujue	Wandering around
caoatoha inatiin te	So pretty nevertheless

ujuateje neucaan	I'm an orphan
amuemujue	Wandering around
caririjieen amuemujue	Just like this I wander around
dojiaracaan ne canucha ajeiton	I'm drunk on manioc beer
caratirin chujiara	Like this they're leaving me
canucha ne ajeiton	I'm the drunk one
ajeitocoaunra canuicha comaire	I'm the only drunk one, co-mother!
chajaote necoatijiae	Come on, let's dance
necoatijiaecaa comaire	Let's dance, co-mother!
ichorojoecaan ne ajeton	I'm drunk on the force of manioc beer
ichorojoe dojiara necaune	With this force of manioc beer
najeente tijiara nedojiaen nedojiaen	Just like this, inebriated, inebriated
cana ratiriin chujiara	They've really left us
cana joerateurera	Those who raised us
canucha ne ajeiton comaire	I'm really drunk, co-mother!
Aiyayaya	Oh yeah

The tone of this and other songs is humorous but also designed to evoke nurturing feelings in the listener and co-mother—in short, the benevolent disposition and sense of togetherness that ideally characterize this relationship. The singer achieves this in part by identifying with the subject position of "orphan," inviting her listener to take pity on her. An orphan, *ujuateje*, was defined for me by Jorge as "one whose mother and father have died, and who lives abandoned and wanders everywhere." Such a predicament, of course, immediately induces pity in others. Orphans figure prominently in Urarina mythology and discourse and are still quite common today, despite peaceful relations with neighboring groups and (presumably) an improved mortality rate. The orphans living in San Pedro and Nueva Unión were all under the care of siblings of one of their deceased parents.

The term used to refer to the process of "taming" pets or wives, iri-laa, is also used for raising orphans, a relatively common conflation in Amazonia. Like the pet, the orphan is a familiar symbol that often emerges in the context of warfare. Yet in contrast to some other Amazonian peoples,[20] the Urarina do not position themselves in such schemes as the master or adoptive father but rather as the pet or orphan. In one myth, two Urarina women are abducted and held captive in a *bacauha* (Jivaro or Candoshi) village, and constantly referred to as "pets" (iri) by their captors and new "owners" (*erora*), who try to fatten them up in order to eat them. The women stubbornly resist, remaining "wild" (*uraetoha*), until their uncle finally arrives and defeats the entire enemy group.

Within these latter groups, too, people are reported to sing songs in which they strategically position themselves in similar ways to achieve certain ends. Taylor (1983, 2001) has discussed the role of "pet-position songs" among the Jivaro, typically addressed to spouses in order to evoke sentiments of affectionate compassion. Feelings of tenderness and pity are closely and explicitly linked in these societies; their evocation by a wife, at the correct moment, is evidently considered an effective means of averting or disarming a husband's anger. Surrallés (2003) also describes a genre of Candoshi songs in which the (female) singer describes herself, in a humorous and self-deprecating way, as a pet or orphan in need of love and care from her brother or husband. If the paradigm of "familiar-ization" indeed lies at the conceptual core of all affective relations among the latter, as Surrallés asserts (2003: 98), the direction in which it pro-ceeds cannot be determined merely by the participants' relative quotients of power or agency.[21] Just who is the "agent" and who is the "patient" in each case is far from straightforward, and these qualities are not readily reduced to single individuals.

In Urarina thought, the position of orphan or pet is certainly an ambivalent one but also a far from powerless one: in no way does a mas-ter or predator alone possess agency. Eliciting a nurturing or benevo-lent disposition in others by deliberately assuming a demure, relatively helpless or subordinate position is a common and widespread strategy for achieving one's goals. Although apparently symbolically feminine in nature, it is employed not only by women, and indeed it is central to many forms of shamanic action. That the singer of the above songs is typically female might thus reinforce a sense in which processes of familiarization are themselves often or even always gendered in nature. The distinctly feminine trait of shame or embarrassment, demonstrated by both spouses at the beginning of marriage, is also the default attitude assumed by all Urarina vis-à-vis outsiders today, including or especially itinerant traders. If Urarina identify themselves as the captured "pets" of the Jivaro in myth (and to a lesser extent as their conquered "prey"), this further implies a gendering of intergroup relationships given the struc-tural closeness of women and game animals.

In the context of the above drinking song, the figure of the orphan also serves to highlight an analogy between the asymmetrical relations of taming that characterize marriage and same-sex ritual co-parenthood. In fact, and considering also the importance placed on nurture, care, and mutual defense, I would venture that if opposite-sex ritual co-parenthood evokes the brother-sister sibling relation, same-sex ritual co-parenthood evokes the husband-wife matrimonial alliance. In both cases the construction of ritual kinship could be considered exemplary of the distinctly Amazonian penchant for transforming and domesticating a potentially dangerous affinity. Yet the end product of this process is not necessarily consanguinity, despite the importance of "touching blood" and the like. What is sought, it seems, is a kind of proximity rather than identity, founded in irreducible difference.[22] To the extent that the relationship is grounded in or expressed through the body, it is not shared "substance" per se that is deemed important but more ethereal or spiritual aspects of the person, such as the shadow-soul. The conjugal union, for Urarina, is not a one-flesh union. The marriage clearly maintains the separate identities of the spouses as they undertake a common project. Spouses are simultaneously separate persons and united partners. Conjugality is nevertheless marked by a centripetal movement, revolving around an axis defined as two standing in relation and receiving its ultimate expression in the heart-soul of the newborn. We might say, with respect to the latter, that the conjugal body eventually gives rise to a conjugal soul.

From one angle, the couvade may be described as a form of "spiritual nurturing" (Rivière 1974: 430), a ritual relating to the spiritual creation of a newborn child. Yet this need not be seen as opposing the view that the couvade is a means by which a man lays claim to being a child's father. To treat these functions as alternatives between which one should choose is to overlook a crucial fact about Amazonian sociality, namely, that the reproduction of persons may be inseparable from the reproduction of social groups. This process extends well beyond the construction of consanguinity as consubstantiality, implicating spiritual and affective dimensions of the person that are constitutively intersubjective and irreducible to the body. While bodily transformation plays an important role, as perspectivism would predict, it is the augmentation of the infant's subjectivity via processes of ensoulment that is the basis of the newfound solidarity between the two parents, on the one hand, and two sets of co-parents, on the other. The creation of new life is what consolidates and confirms the matrimonial alliance, although both are ongoing processes, and full conjugality does not precede parenthood for the two are inseparable.

4.   Mutuality and Autonomy

From the earliest appearance in the womb through to a restful state of receptivity in the protective space of the hammock, the creation and early growth of a new person is at every moment wedded to a broader process of socialization and the formation or consolidation of companionships between spouses, ritual co-parents, and others in the infant's innermost social circle. As discussed in the previous two chapters, this process often hinges on implicit ideas about the nature of subjectivity and materiality, usually revealed through practices involving the bodies of infants and related discourse surrounding the heart-soul and shadow-soul. This chapter introduces into the discussion a moral dimension, examining both what it means to be a moral person and how moral behavior is inculcated in infants; the latter does not proceed through an internalization of norms but rather through habitual practices that become a constitutive part of personal identity, inseparable from the experience of an autonomous self. I seek to keep squarely in focus the composition and coming into being of persons while furthering the analysis of how Urarina represent and resolve the apparent tensions between dependency and autonomy, hierarchy and equality, and society and the individual.

The gendering of personal identity is a key component of the transition from childhood to adulthood and centers on techniques for the acquisition of embodied forms of knowledge. Significantly, the source of many of the skills acquired is largely external, not only to the person, but also to human society broadly construed. Beginning with the baby hammock and related accessories, parenting and caregiving practices reveal a sense that the developing self continues to enfold a variety of ecological relations and capacities, which coalesce to form a person's embodied identity. My development of this theme here resonates with McCallum's

(1996: 348) observation that the Amazonian Cashinahua treat the body as "continuously fabricated out of the environment by the agency of others." Similarly, Overing (2003: 299) has proposed that the Piaroa view of human capacities is "radically externalist" in that "the forces for selfhood are on the most part dangerous, and have their origin external to the self." This is contrasted with the Western notion of self, held to be "radically interiorised from the start" (299). Urarina manage both "external" and "internal" views of the self, however, and a key problematic throughout this chapter is how these relate to personal development and everyday social life.

As children pass through a transition point known as "the thickening," gentle parental encouragement gives way to disciplinary measures and punishments, and the emergence of a moral conscience. Urarina discussions of moral behavior gravitate around appropriate forms of sharing, particularly of food, and this necessarily forms part of the analysis. I argue that the imperative to distribute food widely stems in part from humanity's existential condition of subjection to divine authority and benevolence. The understandings of subjectivity and agency that structure this condition, and their relation to voluntary subordination, in turn underwrite Urarina sharing patterns, which occupy a nebulous middle ground between unsolicited or reciprocal giving and giving "on demand." Focusing on linguistic semantics as well as observations of typical behavior, I argue that the asymmetrical relationship between givers and receivers echoes and generalizes the elicitation of pity in the drinking songs of ritual co-parents. This leads to a discussion of how individual autonomy is prioritized in a social environment characterized by mutuality and phenomenological immediacy, which further highlight the origins of personal identity in an array of relationships with both near and distant others. In the final section of this chapter, I return to Urarina concepts of the heart-soul and shadow-soul and suggest that these offer complementary perspectives on the nature of human experience, as both uniquely alone and always lived in the company of others.

THE THICKENING

A newborn baby may be referred to as *lareequi*, "small, round, and red," or alternately as *nujuari*, "green" or "unripe," both terms emphasizing its general condition of vulnerability. This is a time in which the baby is simply encouraged to sleep, protected and nurtured within its hammock, while parental interventions, as described in the previous chapters, are generally aimed directly at the morphology of the body. When the baby finally begins to outgrow the hammock, the parents intensify their efforts to shape and form the infant and its developing dispositions. The child now enters a phase of growth known as *nelerijia,* literally, "it is thickening up," a term used to describe the growth of trees as their trunks "thicken" over time. This is also the phase in which children are gendered: very young children are essentially genderless, dressed indifferently in the clothes of either sex, equally adorned with beads and necklaces. Parental interventions are still required, though with steadily decreasing frequency, until the children reach social maturity: first menstruation for a girl; the ability to hunt and maintain a garden for a boy.

Training an infant to walk begins early, with an emphasis on learning to sit independently. Throughout the first few months of life, infants are incessantly propped up on people's laps and then on mats; as soon as they begin to fall, they are righted again by their caregiver, until either party tires (figure 5). Of course, sitting and communicating in face-to-face scenarios are of great importance in the Urarina social environment, as they are in most other small-scale societies.[1] But it is really walking, rather than sitting and looking at others, that is the ultimate goal.[2] Learning to walk is a milestone on the path to autonomy of singular significance: much more than weaning, which often extends indefinitely, and until well after all the mother's milk has dried up. A child's first steps are also accorded greater recognition and importance by adults than its first words, which may seem surprising given the very strong emphasis placed on vocal artistry in Amazonian cultures.[3] Although quantitative data is lacking, I believe that the average Urarina baby learns to walk unaided much earlier than its Western counterpart, if only because it is so intensively encouraged.[4]

Learning to walk is assisted by the use of a specialized aid, constructed by the father. This is essentially a guided track, extending from one end of the house to the other and comprising four equidistant, parallel poles along which glides a wooden cube by means of hoops affixed to each corner. The baby is inserted into the cube, and, unable to sit or fall over, it slowly makes its way along the track, from one end to the other, where it is turned and faced the other way. As a child becomes increasingly mobile, makeshift walls may be built around the perimeter of the house floor to prevent accidental falls to the ground below. Otherwise, an infant is usually allowed to crawl or walk wherever it pleases, and only if it is faced with immediate danger would a parent intervene.

Herbal medicines *(coi)* are also prepared to speed the learning pro-

Figure 5.   Boys encourage their baby sister to stand upright. Photograph by author.

cess, a task often assumed by a coresident grandmother. She will prepare a decoction of the necessary plants,[5] which she has cultivated in her own patch of house garden. This is fed repeatedly to the baby at around six months of age. A series of dietary restrictions are simultaneously assumed by the mother until such time as the baby learns to walk. The child itself does not diet; on the contrary, it is fed as many eggs and ground peanuts and as much maize and animal fat as possible, especially when it is on the verge of walking. Eating well is considered as important for mental or emotional well-being as for physical well-being, and the lack of good food is closely associated with tiredness and unhappiness. The infant may also be fed preparations for "growing fat," and there is a variety of piri-piri, *ledene cobiri,* cultivated specifically for this task. Although the mother does not herself drink, she is said also to grow fat, again highlighting the physical connection thought to obtain between parent and child.

Once an infant has learned to "waddle" *(maremaruha),* it is continually encouraged to do so through incessant instructions to carry out trivial errands. These typically involve fetching some small object from one relative, seated a few meters away, and then delivering it to another. The toddler waddles back and forth across the floor, from mother to grandmother to aunt to sister, on such Sisyphean tasks until it tires. More than mere practice in walking—though they are also that—these errands are a form of training for the important role of messenger and go-between. Almost any delivery or receipt of goods from one household to another is made by children; it is their labor that keeps the wheels of the sharing economy turning. Even more indispensable is their role in making requests of others, especially where there is a chance that those requests could legitimately be denied: for example, the innards or another cut of raw meat from a recently slain animal (when a shared meal will likely later be offered) or the loan of items such as shotguns or kerosene. Using a child safeguards against the considerable embarrassment caused to all parties in the event that the request is refused, and there is less pressure to capitulate to the request if it is made by a child. Indeed, the choice to send a child in the first place is already something of an admission of its potential deniability.

Similarly, a wife wanting to speak to a husband busy drinking manioc beer in the house of another will not go and speak to him directly but send a child to pass on a message or instruct him to return to the house to speak to her. As children are not entirely immune to the potential embarrassment of a denied request, even apart from the inconvenience to them, training them to be unquestioning in their acceptance of such a task is important. Hence from the youngest age possible children come to accept such errands, immediately and without question, as being part of the fabric of who they are in relation to others and as underpinning their love and acceptance by those around them.

A related exercise, of no lesser importance, involves the constant ferrying of food from one relative to another within the household. A bit of roasted banana here, a small bowl of soup there; it is not long before one can observe the same toddler on being given any piece of food or a bowl of drink automatically taking it over to a relative and offering it to them. The obliging adult will duly receive the food, perhaps making some pretense at having a sip or a nibble before handing it back again. Pleased with the interaction, which becomes almost a game of sorts, the child delivers the food to another family member and the process is repeated.

We can now see why it is walking, rather than talking, that is the developmental milestone par excellence and the focus of the most intense concern and interventions of caregivers. Speech is first and foremost a technique for maintaining or even augmenting the infant's attachment to the mother: a kind of transposition of the umbilical cord into the aural domain, as it were, in order to ensure the continued provision of care and nurture. Walking, by contrast, develops separation from caregivers and is the grounds of physical and psychological autonomy. Yet it is not the independent assertion of will, or the ability to pursue individual desires and interests, that is celebrated by adults. Rather, it is the ability to establish or affirm connectedness to others through intentional acts of sharing: in short, the infant's newfound capacity for social agency. Developmental theorists have pointed to infant locomotion as a key catalyst for change in a number of other domains of development unrelated to motor skills, leading to a kind of "cognitive revolution" (Gibson 1988). More important from an Urarina perspective, however, is that walking fundamentally changes infants' social interactions. This is especially true insofar as these interactions involve objects, for walking upright frees the hands for carrying. Instead of waiting for adults to come to them to share objects, infants are now able to transport objects to caregivers in order to share them. This would explain why the skills of walking and sharing are intrinsically linked from the very outset, as mutually complementary expressions of autonomy.

In accordance with this aspect of their development, children learn at an extremely young age to "help" their parents, or at least to act in concert with them, well before they are capable of making any tangible contribution to the household. This appears to take priority over the formation of and participation in age-based peer groups. A baby girl, barely able to walk, will be seated by her mother's side and given a knife with which she will happily set about cutting discarded vegetable scraps and other refuse. A year or two later, the mother will expect her daughter to accompany her in the garden, weeding and planting, and the two will set about it together even if the child is still largely incapable of the necessary physical coordination to be of any real use.

It is not difficult to recognize the overwhelming effect of this incessant training in running errands, helping others, and, above all, sharing food and other possessions as a matter of course. Children receive recognition and validation as persons as and when they involve themselves in activities directed outward from themselves, toward the satisfaction, not of their own individual needs and desires, but those of the household as a whole. Expressions of individual will are encouraged and reinforced when, and only when, they fit into this broader social context, and are discouraged when directed at themselves or otherwise perceived as tangential to the greater well-being of the household. The importance of sharing, particularly food, cannot be overestimated in daily life, and no moral imperative is articulated with greater frequency or conviction. Yet training toddlers to behave morally does not, at first, involve teaching them to recognize the legitimate needs of others, nor does it involve the transmission or "rules" or "norms" to be internalized. Instead, good moral "sense" is first inscribed into daily practices such that it becomes thoroughly embodied and routinized, the most intuitive or natural course of behavior available.

Generally speaking, young children are not prone to sudden displays of needs or wants, and this tendency is reinforced by caring practices. Caregivers tend not to respond to overtly physical or immediate expressions of desire; only serious accidents provoke an immediate response. In the event of crying or calls for help, a quick assessment of the legitimacy or severity of the situation is made, and unless things look very serious there is no immediate intervention. With the exception of very small babies, crying children are often laughed at or simply ignored. Similarly, rather than respond immediately to the desires of her children, a mother tends to intervene with care or food when it suits her. In this way the child stays passive with regard to its food intake, learning not to make incessant requests, as these regularly fail, and instead simply accepting the receipt of food at the convenience of others. In short, sharing is largely dissociated, both temporally and conceptually, from the immediate satisfaction of needs and is not in direct competition with individual autonomy.

As a child grows older, disciplinary practices assume increasing importance in relation to caring practices as the focus of parental interactions. It is also at this stage that the expression of morality becomes a matter of intentional, disciplined action, founded in respect and deliberative recognition of the needs of others, rather than merely learned behavior. As with techniques of care and nurture, Urarina parents use disciplinary measures as a means of asserting the primacy or relative legitimacy of the general household's (or their own) needs over and above those of their children. This is similarly achieved by immediately overriding any expression of will directed at individual rather than group interests. For example, a small child who ignores a request to perform a household chore such as fetching water or firewood, or to provide assistance to another, choosing instead to pursue his or her own game or individual project, will be very sternly reprimanded. If respect for personal autonomy is a core value among adults, this is not a strong feature of patterns of child care, and age-based hierarchies override notions of equality. Obedience is of the utmost importance, and children are subjected accordingly to a particular kind of strict discipline that alternately impressed me with its effectiveness and surprised me with its severity. To my eyes at least, Urarina children were generally extremely obedient, far more than their Western counterparts, leaping into action at the first suggestion of a task to be performed.

When I asked Urarina to state what they considered to be their children's greatest fault or lack, the most common response was nevertheless to lament their proclivity to disobey, to "not want to heed my word" (*canu ere tonorana jerihi*). The solution is usually scolding (*cotaiha*). A child who ignores or disobeys the instructions of his or her caretakers is subjected to an onslaught of verbal recriminations. Strong words spoken with ferocity are used with even very young children, including those still too young to talk themselves. The most common reason for a reprimand is a failure to perform one's duties for the common good of the household. The children, for their part, often seem blithely indifferent to this display, unfazed by the most aggressive scolding, but always eventually capitulate. It should be stressed that this, too, is entirely different from the kind of behavior that would be considered acceptable among adults, for whom the slightest word of criticism would cause immediate offense.

Physical punishment is rare, although not unheard of. It is generally considered acceptable (if uncommon) to hit children lightly in order to teach or discipline them; this is reportedly best done with a slap across the back or head, sometimes on the bottom or back of the legs. Slaps to the face are considered unacceptable, however, as is the excessive use of force. Buchilote's wife once denounced him to the community "authorities" for hitting his son overzealously when it resulted in a slightly swollen lip. The lieutenant governor lost no time sentencing him to seven hours in the communal stockade. Physical disciplining must be undertaken with the utmost care, and how a child is disciplined at this formative age is thought to have lifelong effects. For example, Manuel once brought a large bunch of ungurahui palm fruits back to the village, which subsequently proved "hard" and difficult to peel. This surprised no one, and I was privately warned that Manuel's palm fruits were always like that, because his mother used to hit him with a fan woven from palm fibers when he was young.

Threats of punishment for bad behavior are far more forthcoming than offers of rewards for good behavior. Obedience, subservience, and general good behavior are expected and demanded, and there is no notion of it warranting a reward. When I myself tried to offer future rewards for good behavior, these attempts inevitably failed, for young children seemed unaccustomed to, even incapable of, holding in their minds my promise of a future treat in return for good behavior in the present. Many caretakers instead invoke the specter of Aroba, a forest-dwelling monster, to confront those suspected of waywardness. Hence in lieu of sympathy and consolation, a crying child might be sung a song such as the following:

| ii raarichan arobara canaanai | Aroba[6] will take you, child! |
| nota aroba ii raa ne coina | Look! So that Aroba will take you. |

"We frighten them, so they don't cry," explained Jorge. "If they don't stop crying, Aroba will come and take them." Marcial, one of the oldest men in the community, recounted this story:

> Aroba is someone to frighten the children, so they are quiet and restful. Sometimes the folk would make a mask, and grab some stinging nettles. Someone would come out of the forest to brush them against the children. He'd put on a beard of saki monkey [*Pithecia monachus*] fur, or of piassaba palm fibers. With those stinging nettles they really frightened the children. When that old man called Captain still lived, he did everything, mask and beard and everything. The children would even try to flee by canoe, and he'd follow them, to "nettle" them. The children fled, screaming, and he still followed them by canoe, that Captain. He really transformed into Aroba, and made the children scream, when he lived here.

One likely consequence of the absence of offering rewards for good behavior is a deemphasis on the cultivation of self-discipline with a view to future goals. Indeed, and as already noted, individual needs and desires are construed as most often satisfied either by external circumstances or by third parties that are largely outside of one's control. Hence the notion of work (*amianiaa*) is very often spoken of as an activity directed at the satisfaction of the needs and desires *of others* rather than oneself, and when those others are close family members there is certainly an accompanying sense of duty. When a man is about to go hunting, he is most likely to state that he is doing so because his wife or children are hungry for meat; I never heard any man say that he was hunting to satisfy his own desire for meat. The women's work of making manioc beer is similarly construed as directed primarily at the satisfaction of her husband's desires rather than her own. The enduring preeminence of the economic system of debt peonage, or habilitación—in which goods are received in advance from traders or patrones in anticipation of future repayment—is also due, in part, to people's general unwillingness to produce a surplus with a view to its future exchange for desired goods, preferring instead to incur the obligation to work by receiving goods on credit in advance (see Walker 2012). Instilling an eagerness to meet the needs and desires of others is a primary objective of the disciplining actions of parents—itself a form of subjection—progressively internalized and transformed into the self-discipline needed to attain recognition by one's peers as a mature, moral, fully social adult.

ENSKILLMENT AND GENDER

As they grow older, children also learn to embody, and perform, their gender as a result of direct parental interventions. Girls are dressed in a handmade two-color dress that mimics the traditional women's costume of black (or blue) skirt and red blouse and given the blue bead necklaces and bracelets that she will gradually augment throughout the course of her adult life. As her ability to contribute usefully to the household starts to develop, she will also acquire the series of dispositions and behaviors that pertain to the cultural complex of shame or embarrassment (necoejiha). This is not an exclusively female trait but is nonetheless a central marker of feminine identity, and lies at the core of notions of female propriety. It is central to the initiation of a successful marriage, as discussed in chapter 3. The difference in behavior between a girl of four or five and a girl of around eight is quite striking: the former, while outwardly gendered in her dress, is decidedly "unfeminine" in her actions, laughing and playing with anyone she pleases; the latter, by contrast, has learned to show great embarrassment at the prospect of any encounter with nonkin, especially men, through learned dispositions such as literally "turning her back" (janoriin) to people and above all avoiding any form of eye contact—lest she give the impression, either to her companions or to her interlocutor, that she is seeking an illicit sexual encounter.

Menarche (laatoha) marks the most important transition to adulthood, as only then can a girl be married. Its onset demands her seclusion in a purpose-built hut of palm leaves, the jata, where she dwells or "broods" (looroha) in isolation for a period of ten days. Much like a bird, she is awaiting patiently the fruits of her fertility. It will be recalled that the birth hut, in which infant and mother cohabit for a similar period of time, is also a jata, and in each case there is an implicit analogy to an enclosure in the womb.[7] The jata is constructed in the forest just beyond the community perimeter, often by the girl's mother, who takes her food and water for bathing. It is said that if she were to return to the house during this time she would develop skin sores, and her coresidents, particularly her younger siblings, would fall ill. After the ten days has elapsed her hair is cut short or "thrown out" *(couturi ujui jaoha)*. Left alone, it is said to grow ugly and discolored but cut appropriately it will grow back strong, black, and beautiful. The discarding of the hair emphasizes the element of renewal associated with these rites. From now until such time as she bears a child she is referred to as *ranuna*, "young maiden."

Menstruation itself is construed as a time of seated inactivity and is most commonly referred to colloquially in these terms: as *nelauriau*, "sit," or *amui*, "not go." Menstrual blood *(ichacoarae)* is distinguished from the body's blood *(ichana)* and has a polluting quality. During her menstruation a woman is disqualified from preparing banana drink or manioc beer for her husband, lest he fall ill. She bathes in the forest with heated water, for bathing in the river is said to risk insemination by a dolphin, and should otherwise remain seated at home. During a working party in which I once participated, Maria told everyone the following story:

> A mother sent her daughter with the rest of the folk who were going fishing with *huaca* poison *[Clibadium remotiflorum]*. The girl had her period. They arrived at the stream, and she disappeared. "Where is she, that girl who came with us?" asked the people. They released the *huaca* into the stream, and went searching for her, calling to her. And how the fish jumped! They called and called to her, and they thought they were not going to find her. Every person killed a string bag full of fish each. When the fish were no longer jumping, they saw something moving in the forest, and there was the dog, having sex. And tied to it inside was the girl. "How can you do such a thing!" they called to her. And the folk left her there, taking the dog, and returned to the village. They recounted what happened to the girl's mother, who had sent her. Furious, the mother killed the dog. And the girl, who they had left there, became like a dog. She fell pregnant, and after some time the baby was born, with the face of a dog and the behind of a dog. There they gave it a name, *remae cacunu* [dog's daughter], and they left it there for her mother to raise.

When Jorge later heard my recording of this story, he claimed that a male dog will always seek out a bitch who "has her period" (presumably, when she is in heat), and that was why the dog sought out this girl. Yet although she was "tied" to the dog (as bitches are said to be "tied" to males during intercourse) she willingly accepted the dog as a sexual partner out of sheer lasciviousness *(jailodorojoe)*.[8] In the story the girl's menstruation made her not only excessively wanton, but prone to transformation into animal form. Jorge lamented, "I don't know how it was before, but now the people have learned; now when they are menstruating they don't go off to another part, they stay at home. But not everyone. Some people, even today, still go just like that to the forest, even though they are menstruating."

In effect, menstruation and shame represent related aspects of a girl's nascent fertility. But although a young girl's fecundity may be considered important, even more significant is her newfound right to make manioc beer. This is itself closely associated with fertility, as discussed elsewhere. But it is the ability to satisfy her husband's thirst through her own labor that above all qualifies her for marriage. The other skills she needs, such as sewing, cooking, and weaving, are also related to her suitability for marriage but are perhaps of slightly lesser importance, and their lack is not necessarily an obstacle. Lorenzo told me, "After having her first period, the girl has the right to receive her husband. But sometimes she doesn't know how to cook or wash clothes. After one or two months she can 'resist' her husband. Her mother can help her to prepare her manioc beer. When I married my wife who is with me now, she barely knew how to cook. This didn't matter at all. She quickly learned."

The situation confronting a young man is more difficult, as he has no hope of marriage until he has proven his ability to hunt and make a garden. Parents almost never provide direct instruction to their children; instead, they carefully set an example, which children learn to follow. In fact, most knowledge is deemed to have its origin in sources external to human society, and the parent's role is less to transmit it than provide the conditions for its acquisition. Hence the existence of many different herbal medicines or remedies, or coi, the proper use of which typically brings into conjunction three distinct elements: the plant (or animal) source, which is often eaten; full adherence to the correct regime of fasting and other prohibitions; and an imprinting phase centered on disciplined practice.

The cultivation of blowpipe hunting ability, for example, may be promoted through the consumption of a preparation of bark from two trees known locally as *ueidaje* and *remaae eeura*, boiled and mixed with a well-mashed piri-piri (*joina cobiri*). After consuming the mixture, which is expected to induce vomiting, the lad commences a fast in which the consumption of salt, ripe bananas, gruel, and fish is restricted, in favor of green plantains and manioc. During this period, which may last a month or more, he must go hunting each day and shoot at (and hit) as many animals as possible—even unwanted targets, such as small birds considered inedible. Otherwise the remedy will be ineffectual and not "grab" him and grow in his body.

Similarly, the principal remedy for spearfishing ability involves tying strips of the caustic inner bark of the *bijiurara* tree around the forearm, leaving lasting scars. This is followed by an equally important imprinting phase, in which the novice must throw a spear repeatedly at any nominated target, such as a tree trunk. This is not really "practicing" as we conceive it, for the target is ideally one the aimer is sure never to miss. Rather than improve his aim by continually challenging his existing ability, the remedy "grabs" or "records" the action of actually hitting the target, as a complete event-structure, and literally incorporates it into the body.

A noteworthy feature of such medicines is that the imprinting phase if not completed successfully is liable to leave the novice in a worse state than before he started. Should the lad choose an overly difficult target for practicing spear throwing, for example, the event of missing, rather than hitting, will be recorded in the body. A similar phenomenon adheres to a well-known remedy for strength, which involves drinking a decoction of bark of the chuchuhuasi tree (*Maytenus* sp.), crushed tapir bone, and piri-piri. The fast, said to last up to seven months, prohibits salt, gruel, sugar, manioc beer, and banana drink. All food eaten must be cold: broth without salt, or pure boiled manioc. The drinker should stay "well soaked" all day; continuous bathing day and night is stipulated on the grounds that the remedy must be cold in order to "grow." "Who could possibly put up with that regime?" wondered Lorenzo, acknowledging the diminishing enthusiasm among the young for such arduous feats of self-imposed discipline. The remedy may also incorporate use of an anaconda, which should be killed and the fat extracted. This is stored in a bottle, and may also be used for pains or rheumatism. The strength is said to exit the anaconda and enter the person, leaving the anaconda weak and without strength. Followed correctly, the novice becomes "brave" and "courageous," but if the fast is not properly adhered to, he will emerge weak and slovenly (*medio dejado*). Similarly, I was told that a remedy for becoming a Casanova, a ladies' man, will backfire if not followed correctly, and the novice will become a "poof" (*chivo*).

Strength and hunting ability are coextensive attributes. Persistent failure in the hunt is usually put down to torpor rather than maladroitness. Ritual discourse, such as the *joina baau*, may be employed to overcome such problems and create a skilled hunter (*joinena*). Like others in the genre, the joina baau orchestrates and aligns a series of fragmented perspectives, this time in order to create a continuity between the adolescent boy and certain birds of prey, highly esteemed for their hunting prowess. The chant "blesses" the bile *(lera)* of a hawk *(Leucopternis* sp.), which must be extracted, heated, and finally swallowed, together with a decoction of chiric sanango *(Brunfelsia grandiflora).* This is said to eliminate the novice's indolence or torpor *(nijiaone,* lit., "waste" or "that which is discarded"), creating the conditions for his darts to go "dead straight, like a bullet." All the animals invoked in the chant are birds: the hawk, the "sky hawk," the "kapok hawk," and cojoaaoraain (rendered here as *anojiaain),* the companion and spiritual guardian of game animals. By appropriating their hunting skill, the chant aims to improve the lot of someone whose *nijiaone* (maladroitness, languor) causes their blowpipe darts to "just fail to reach" *(arateen)* their target. The implication is not that darts are "missing" their target per se, sailing past having been poorly aimed, but rather that they are simply not reaching it: a typical example of arateen in quotidian discourse might be *"arateen cauhacanu,"* "We turned back just as we were about to arrive [at such-and-such a place]." As indicated above, a poor hunter's problem is not so much that his aim is off but rather that he lacks the strength or force to propel his projectile all the way to the target. The chant fixes this problem by "straightening out" *(raujia)* his maladroitness, as one might straighten one's course in the river while traveling by canoe.

Blowpipe hunting requires the expulsion of air with considerable force. Nijiaone is located above all in one's breathing *(raca),* and it is in this vital breath *(acarera)* that the vital energy necessary for powerful blowpipe shooting is located. For this reason much of the chant focuses on the inner chest, the ranesijie, and breast or outer chest *(nalaarijia).* The latter refers more to the flesh itself, the former to the vital organs and vital breath contained within. The hawk's quiver *(jare,* found here with the associative marker *co-* and vowel spreading), said to look like cotton wrapped around its foot, encapsulates the desired hunting qualities. The maladroitness finally exits the body, "slipping" out *(ticharaa)* in a way equated with vomiting out.

Learning how to hunt is, for a boy, an important part of the broader process by which he acquires the skills for family responsibility and which qualify him as a fully gendered, and fully social, being. It is the emergent autonomy that comes with enskillment that enables him to participate fully in the realm of the social, through participation in cycles of gifting and sharing. To make a demand on someone is implicitly to assert one's own ability to reciprocate in the future. For this reason, the refusal of a request is highly insulting for an adult—although not for a child—and thus unacceptable, for it effectively negates the asker's hard-won right to assert his ability to reciprocate and hence his achievement of social maturity. Yet requests made of others are often conducted in more oblique ways, and the politics of sharing can be a quite subtle affair.

PATHWAYS OF SHARING

Chajaau lenonee! After months of adjusting to the highly erratic food supply, these words were music to my ears. Come and eat! Sharing in large-scale communal meals was a regular part of life on the upper Chambira, and I had learned to count on at least one such feast every couple of days or so. As Bolon's youngest son scurried off to the next house to continue his round of invitations, I grabbed my favorite small gourd and wandered happily over to their half-built house, where a group of men was already milling around. Before long, Bolon triumphantly set down in our midst an enormous bowl of thick, steaming soup, around which we all sat or squatted. Hidden beneath the immense volume of gravy were a number of choice cuts of brocket deer, the impressive animal with which our host had quietly returned earlier that morning. Good-natured conversation filled the air, addressing a range of topics of communal concern, and Bolon had plenty of opportunity to recount, yet again, the precise manner by which he had prevailed over his quarry. While we scooped out soup with our tiny gourds, his children ferried servings to all the women and young children, who remained in their respective houses. When the large hunks of meat finally appeared from beneath the thick gray liquid, they were carefully selected and dispatched by Bolon to the adult men, who then further subdivided them with their adolescent sons if they had any present. Sometimes the men would cut off a large portion of the hunk before returning it magnanimously to Bolon, who accepted it graciously even though (as the host) he had already eaten, rather as though his share, too, depended on the generosity of others. When he had received many such hunks of meat he began to further redistribute them, supplementing the slightly smaller portions some others had received. The whole process struck me as rather theatrical. Bolon's wife periodically refilled the bowl with soup and replenished people's side dishes of cooked whole green plantains and mashed ripe plantains, thereby ensuring that no one would leave without a full stomach. When all the meat was gone, the meal was formally concluded with a short announcement to each person in turn, following the same precise formula. An extended oration of thanks to Our Creator was spoken by two of the older men, during which no one seemed to pay them the slightest attention, though no one talked or interrupted either. When they had finished, everyone retired, immensely satisfied, to their respective houses to rest.

As elsewhere in Amazonia, the continuous giving away and receiving of food is central to the morality of social proximity and a defining characteristic of Urarina collectivities. Participation in a meal such as the one described above is among the most important events in communal life, and indispensable to the task of building up solidarity within and between residential groups. The verb *lenoniha* means "to eat [a meal]," that is, a complete meal, with meat and plantains, as distinct from *quiha*, meaning simply "to eat." The former is used only with reference to humans and carries with it a sense of occasion, and indeed of gratitude, largely absent in the latter. A meal shared beyond the nuclear household almost always takes the form of a *corerajaa*, a large soup made with grated plantains, usually served with cooked whole plantains as a side dish (figure 6). Occasionally grated manioc is also added, and salt is the only condiment. The corerajaa is considered worth making only with game animals (*cana lenone*, lit., "our food") over a certain size, and has the advantage that a large number of people can be invited to partake in the meal and be guaranteed of satisfaction. Eating together in this way is highly esteemed as central to the practices of living together harmoniously and correctly, a point on which Tivorcio elaborated:

> Requesting our food from Our Creator, eating whatever is killed in the forest, we live well. Our Creator gives us our food, and because he gives it to us, eating it, we may all live as real people [*cacha*]. Should we think otherwise, Our Creator may reprimand us, and our world-epoch [*cana cojoanona*], that which was given to us by Our Father, will be exhausted. That's what the ancients said. And because the ancients said that, I also know this here. When our food is brought from the forest, we can say, "Thanks, oh, Our Creator who is good is giving to us!" Speaking like that, all eat like real people. Even the mestizos, too. If they treat us well, we live well. It is said that all can live like real people, that's why Our Father is telling us, "Ho! Don't do bad things. If you get drunk, get drunk well. Do it like that, dance, live well. If you are drunk, keep dancing, do it like that." Since a long time ago, it has been like that. Because the ancient folk taught us. They carried their thoughts well [*suujua cuaain*], always knowing well their lives. That's what the ancients used to say. I also know this. Knowing this, I too say this.

Many informants similarly pressed on me the importance ascribed to gestures of food sharing as an expression of moral rectitude and a para-

Figure 6.   Sharing a meal. Photograph by author.

mount sign of the "proper" behavior expected of real people, along with getting drunk peacefully and cheerfully—dancing rather than arguing, for example. There is little worse than a person who is stingy *(chunaa)*, and there is certainly nothing worse than to be stingy over than food. One of the very first words I learned in the Urarina language was *raotoha*, "delicious," commonly used to express one's pleasure at eating a particularly satisfying meal. Yet this word is but one of a sizable number of cognates, all prefixed by *rao-* (or its phonetic variant *rau-*), together forming a conceptual complex that lies at the very heart of Urarina notions of the true, the just, and the righteous. One of the most commonly heard of these is *raotojoeein*, "peacefully"—the ideal way to live well with others. Related words include *raotono*, "peace," also "properly" or "truly"; *rautaa*, "to heal" or "to agree"; *rauhi*, "right" or "law"; *rauhicha*, "straight"; *rauhijidi*, "truth"; *rauhijiriin*, "really"; and so on. Some relevant, related expressions are *raotono que te ere taa cacha*, "that man is speaking well"; *raotono que te cuaain rucujue*, "it has been resolved well"; or *raoti erenaa que cuaain*, "speaking with good words." For me at least, one such word above all others seemed to capture something of the essence of the series: *raunacaena*, "to be of good heart," once translated by an informant as "no es miserable"; in other words, the antithesis of someone who is stingy. Sharing a substantial, well-cooked meal with one's fellows and neighbors, in short, recalls the semantic space set up by this lexical series and reasserts the deep sense of harmony and righteousness that pervades it.

Over time, widespread food sharing serves to even out the inherent variability and unpredictability of the food supply. But it also has an important performative aspect. Although people ideally share as widely as possible, a decision must often must be made as to whom to share with based on the quantity of food available, and gradients of food sharing go a long way in defining the boundaries of the solidarity group, or *lauri*. Along with visiting, sharing cooked and uncooked foods is important in asserting relatedness between members of a group and is recognized as a way both of establishing mutual trust and of making one's family and fellows "more like people." Above all, repeated acts of giving, or *belaiha*, are the hallmarks of the strong affective bonds or "love" felt by coresidents living together in close proximity, attaining their greatest intensity within the conjugal unit but steadily extending outward. Importantly, however, Urarina sharing patterns are not entirely egalitarian, as revealed by a closer analysis of the relations between givers and receivers.

Much sharing of food is initiated by the giver and is not prompted by an overt request or "demand" from others. In particular, explicit requests will never be made for cooked food. If someone feels they have been overlooked in the distribution of uncooked food, such as gathered fruits, nonstaple garden produce (such as maize) immediately following a harvest, or small cuts of raw meat, they may openly ask for a share, and people will almost always give something in response to such requests. To refuse or "deny" a request to share is strongly sanctioned; as noted above, stinginess, or *chunaa*, is considered an abominable character trait. Sometimes requests are made spontaneously on the basis of genuine or perceived need, albeit usually for consumables such as batteries or kerosene. In the case of food, people will usually simply wait to be offered it, especially if a shared meal appears likely. Otherwise, they may express their need or lack in a gentler and more oblique manner. A speaker desiring manioc from someone he knows full well possesses it might casually ask, "Is your manioc already finished?" Although the speaker's intention is clear—and the expression would doubtless be considered all too blunt by many—such a strategy has the advantage of permitting the hearer to refuse the request simply by affirming the speaker's pretended "suspicions," namely, that there is no more manioc. I had the strong impression that even a blatant lie was considered far less insulting than refusing a request ("I do still have some manioc, but I cannot give it to you")—although still likely to arouse covert complaints of stinginess.

Generally speaking, the emphasis is placed less on "demanding" than on "causing to be given." Importantly, this "causing" is not coercive but instead rests on gently inducing the appropriate benevolent and caring impulse in others. Knowing that someone has food hidden away somewhere in their house, people will casually say something like, "Oh, we're so hungry, poor us, whatever we will eat today?" The general idea is to let others see you "suffering"—as in the expression *"caichaojoai ii coaraaun,"* "Watching you I feel sorry for you." A person who is ill, for example, is likely to be seen to be suffering and thus will evoke pity.[9] A person who is mourning, or grieving a lost lover or painful separation and crying for pity, is also suffering in this sense *(coaichajoai te chanain).* Someone who evokes pity in another is effectively evoking a desire to give and nurture. Jorge explained as follows: "For example, Bolon over there kills a sajino, and my wife goes to ask him for a little piece. But she is standing right there, not saying anything, she's too embarrassed to ask. So Bolon's wife sees her and says to Bolon, 'Go on, give her a little piece, I pity her.' This is *cairetoaojoane.*"

A similar logic underpins widespread notions that regimes of fasting undergone by those seeking cures and remedies are efficacious because "you have to suffer." One must suffer in order to evoke the "giving" of the remedy, or the pity of Our Creator in order that he give generously, as discussed further below.

This same set of principles or dispositions is also expressed linguistically. For example, in formulating a "request" for something, the diminutive suffix /-jee/ is often used. This normally refers to the small size of a grammatical subject or to its limited physical capacity. Its meaning can extend to counterexpectation, for example, as a surprise about an unexpected action performed by a small or weak person (Olawsky 2006: 543). It is also often used in conjunction with the verb *lanaa,* "to be missing." The resulting form, *lanajeeca,* means literally "a little (of something) is missing"; hence one might say, *lanajeeca carai laano,* to convey the meaning "I need (a little) manioc." The diminutive is employed to downplay the actual need of the speaker, which is conveyed as a hidden appeal. The same sentence without the diminutive suffix (i.e., *lanaa carai laano*) is possible but from a pragmatic point of view might be interpreted as a simple statement of need rather than a request (or alternatively would be perceived as rude). In effect, the suffix /–jee/ functions a deferential marker, used to show respect, modesty, or self-deprecation; it encourages a feeling of pity in others and a desire to give.

This may also be seen in the case of use of the term *atiin*, which makes a request "softer" and thus more polite. Urarina translate the term into Spanish as *por favor* (please), although its primary meaning is "nevertheless," which in turn has the literal translation "insisting." As such, it superficially does resemble a form of demanding. Olawsky (2006: 549) explains this apparent paradox as follows:

> When *atiin* occurs with an imperative, its meaning is clearly employed to convey politeness: by indicating that a request involves 'insisting', the speaker makes his own command so immodest that the opposite is understood. In fact, its use in this context does not imply 'by all means', as one may intuitively want to interpret (based on the meaning of 'insisting'). A more precise characterisation assumes that the speaker himself takes an inferior position by being so pretentious.

Olawsky's claim that the speaker willfully takes on an "inferior" position (albeit through the roundabout route of inappropriate presumptuousness or "pretentiousness") appears somewhat at odds with the egalitarianism claimed for many other Amazonian societies. In a discussion of trade and exchange among the Asheninka, Killick (2011) endorses an argument earlier put forward by Durham (1995) to the effect that, contrary to the classic Maussian model of the gift, no inequality need develop between giver and receiver, nor is the independence or autonomy of the latter necessarily diminished. In the Asheninka case, Killick contends, a gift received symbolizes the bond between giver and receiver, yet the latter "holds no position of inferiority" (2011: 253).

I agree with Killick that both mutual respect and the autonomy of the receiver may be preserved in such transactions, which always implicitly acknowledge the ability of the latter to reciprocate in the future, even if no direct connection or equivalence is drawn between the two prestations. I also agree that debt is often viewed as something positive because it links people together. Nevertheless, the preservation of individual autonomy is not necessarily incompatible with the temporary institution, through the act of soliciting and receiving a gift, of a structure of inequality, figured in terms of an asymmetrical distribution of prestige. In fact, this seems an integral part of Urarina conceptions of ownership, as discussed further below. Moreover, a willingness to assume a position of subordination is not incompatible with the exercise or expression

of agency. These are important points that take us to the core of Urarina
sociality and subjectivity.

UNDER HIS WATCHFUL GAZE

The discussion thus far has concentrated on the giving and receiving of
food once it has already entered the human domain. Yet these dynamics
should not, and indeed cannot, entirely be dissociated from the ways in
which food, especially meat, is acquired or appropriated from the environment. At the end of a large-scale shared *corerajaa* such as the one
described above, one or more of the older men present will usually take it
upon themselves to enunciate a short, ritualized speech of thanksgiving.
This runs more or less as follows:

Inaejia atiin amutoha	It is already finished
caa caohacha ate cosemane	This great race of animal
Cana Coaauneraicha jaotonojoeein	That which was released by Our Creator
atiin Cana Coaaunera notaracae	Still under Our Creator's watchful eye
carijijieein aoharina jerenacaante	I desire mutual nourishment like this
cajaiche cairicha nunera	Support for the poor folk over this side
jaote Cana Coaaunera	Released by Our Creator
usi unolaratianune	Sent to the fire for cooking
carijieein aoharina jerenacaaun	I desire mutual nourishment like this
aiha rijijieein	Indeed, like that
jaote Cana Coaaunera	Our Creator released
ririamaoria cana lenone ne	All the game animals
atiin ocotejecaaun ne	Please let them appear
naria atiin	Please, thank you
Cana Coaaunera notaracae rijijieein	As under Our Creator's watchful eye
bai cuanai comaotianune	Going deep in the forest
rijijieein atiin jaotomi Cana Coaaunera	Like this please released by Our Creator
inaejia atiin aoarinacache	Already we have nourished ourselves
carijieein jaote Cana Inaca	Released like this by Our Father

Evidently, the principal thrust of the speech is to acknowledge the benevolence of Our Creator and humanity's continued dependence on the
divine goodwill. Specifically, it thanks Our Creator for releasing (*jaoha*,
lit., "throw") into the forest a large game animal (*caoacha ate cosemane*,
"good race of fish," an expression used exclusively in ritual language),
where it is "made to appear" (*ocotiha*), awaiting its appropriation by the
hunter and eventual incorporation into a communal meal, where all are

"mutually nourished" *(aoarina)*. Emphasizing that all humans live under Our Creator's watchful gaze *(notaracaae,* "under his eyes"), as "poor people" *(cairicha,* a term translated as *pobrecito* but having roots in the verb meaning "to exert" or "to labor") needing "support" *(nunera),* it implores him to continue this benevolence. In short, it works to redefine the local group as equals, or near-equals, watched over by the higher power on whom all are dependent.

A similar tone and structure pervade the initial requests made to Our Creator for the release of game animals into the forest from the celestial pens in which they are kept and to which their heart-souls return at death. These take the form of lengthy, ritualized monologues pervaded with lexical and grammatical strategies for politeness (such as the extensive use of *atiin*), in conjunction with pity markers *(noane, cairichaa)* and other terms designed to emphasize the speaker's inferiority and elicit feelings of pity and paternal (or maternal) benevolence in the listener (i.e., Our Creator and/or the masters/owners of game animals):

catijia asaje coarajeu atiin	Please look under my feet
Cana Coaaunera neeine	Being Our Creator
eneu bai cuanai comaotia nunaa	I am going deep into the forest
atiin iiche coaaunein	Please, what you created
eneu Ca Coaaunera neeine	You are Our Creator
eneu ii notaracae	You are watching over us
caiche caichanune	I am going suffering
coarajeu eneu ca tijia asaje coarajeu	Look under our feet, look
cabelarae que cacaoateu eneu atiin	Don't let these dangerous creatures harm me
bai cuane comaotianune	I go deep into the forest
atiin chaelae iiche coaaune nejeein eneu	Please [give me] whatever [animal] you have created
atiin iiche ca lenone teein	Please, give me our food
iiche coaaunenojoi	That which you have created
cachanichaune jiniichainte	Together with us, as real people
coaaunaelu calaonunei tein	You created, long ago, our food
atiin lenone cocoaroe	Our scarce food
coujuriu Ca Coaaunera neein neine ajau uain	Be as Our Creator
catijia asaje coarajeu	Watch under my feet
cabelarae que atiin	For dangers please
ca caoatein atiin ca tijia asaje coarajeu	Watch under my feet well
ne caiche caichaain	I suffer, suffering
coatia leeucha que baniateein	It is not for another that I do this
charinaaunte	I'm doing it for me
atiin ca nainatejere atiin	Please help me [to do it]

jaotoine ocoteje caan ne	please, throwing out to me to make appear
ichoi alarijia choae teteriin	in the palm of your hand
isi unelarateriin	sending off to cook
atiin ca cocana neeuri aina	for our children
ii bajaariinera jaorianune coina ne	I am begging to throw to me
aitoonra Ca Coaaunera	listen to me, Our Creator
atiin catijia asaje Cana Coaaunera	please, under our feet, Our Creator

The most potent requests are articulated from a state of hallucinogenic trance, in the genre of ritual chanting known as *coaairi baauno*; as discussed in chapter 6, a cornerstone of shamanic power and agency is the ability to replenish the supply of game animals in the forest by prompting or inducing the compassionate, watchful Creator (also described as *cana inaca*, "Our Father") to give generously to his "children." The presence of game animals in the forest is thus from the very outset explained in terms of divine generosity in the face of human need. This seems a long way from the predatory mode of appropriation often claimed to characterize human-environment relations elsewhere in Amazonia. Buchilote once elaborated this to me as follows:

> A long time ago, at the time of our creation, Our Creator created our food [*cana lenone*, i.e., game animals). He gave us our food, so we could solicit him for it, a very long time ago. Soliciting our food in this way, Our Creator makes it appear, up until the present day. Before that, there was no food. "Whatever will the children eat, the poor little ones? They will surely suffer," said Our Creator, watching over us. That's why Our Creator created our food, together with our forefathers. Thanks to Our Creator, by soliciting him for food, and sending it to be cooked, we can all eat together.

Whether such a solicitation is made by a hunter as he sets out into the forest or by a shaman during a ritual healing session the enunciator will always emphasize that any food granted to him is not for his benefit alone but rather for the benefit and mutual nourishment of the community, who will "all eat together." This strong sense that what is provided by Our Creator is given, not to the hunter alone, but to all, has important implications for how the relationship between the hunter, his quarry, and the wider group should be construed.

Despite the overwhelming emphasis on "individual ownership," discussed further below, a hunter who brings meat back to the community cannot be said to possess the animal outright in any exclusive sense. What this "owner" of meat possesses, to the exclusion of others, is the privilege of custodianship and the rights of distribution (held with his wife, who assumes full responsibility for the animal's preparation). People fully expect him to share the food as widely as it will allow for and will take issue if he does not. Yet who receives a share is largely his prerogative, with the proviso that if he is living uxorilocally his parents-in-law can be assured of a stake. If the animal is big enough to warrant a corerajaa, or large-scale meal to which most households are invited, he will occupy the role of owner or host (baniha). Although this term is usually translated into Spanish as *dueño* (owner), it is distinguished from the "owner," or erora, of a material possession such as a tool or artifact, as discussed below. The baniha assumes responsibility for issuing personal invitations to all the men, without which no one would dream of participating; for setting down the bowl amid the men; for selecting and distributing the meat piece by piece; and for formally concluding the meal with a statement addressed to each adult male in turn.[10] During the meal itself, the baniha eats apart from the rest of the men, implicitly reinforcing his superior status and social distance from the others. Recounting the story of his success provides an additional opportunity for the accrual of prestige.

The kind of ownership enjoyed by a hunter over his meat, or indeed by anyone over resources they have procured from the natural environment, only superficially resembles the kind of ownership that links people to the material artifacts they themselves have manufactured. Recent work on relations with material objects, as discussed earlier, points to the conclusion that "fabrication" is conceptually conflated with "filiation" in Amazonia, such that persons and objects share the same symbolic frame of construction. As Santos Granero (2009) makes clear, the emphasis on craftsmanship endows Amazonian cosmologies with a constructional character that contrasts strongly with the creationist emphasis of other cosmologies such as the Judeo-Christian. Human bodies are themselves artifact-like; a person is not simply born so much as intentially manufactured, as "a complex amalgam of substances and influences" (Santos Granero 2009: 7). This holds true for the Urarina, as use of the baby hammock, among other practices, would amply demonstrate. One consequence of this view is that the "owner" of an entity is also, in a way, its "parent," and vice versa. This can be seen clearly in the fact that the spiritual beings associated with game animals and many other beings and entities in the natural environment, ranging from trees to whirlpools, may variously be referred as either the latter's owner (erora) or as their mother (neba). From an Urarina perspective, these different terms imply inherently asymmetrical relationships of an analogous nature, equally indissoluble and inalienable.

It should now be clear why the game animals "given" to a hunter, either by their owner and mother or by Our Creator, remain the inalienable possessions of the latter, even as and when they change hands. Recognition of this intrinsic filial bond underwrites the emphasis on sharing as the paramount moral virtue. Yet it is precisely because of the expectation that the food will be shared widely that some form of recognition of individual ownership is necessary: it has the essential function of creating and upholding a distinction between the categories of givers (whether "primary" or "secondary") and receivers, without which there can be no basis for the extension of generosity, or for the influence and renown that flows from it.[11]

A further implication of this worldview is that property cannot truly begin with the individual. To the extent that each person comes into existence through a prolonged process of intentional manufacture and nurture on the part of parents, ritual co-parents, and others, they "belong" to these others in the same way that their labor and its products "belong" to them. It might thus be more appropriate to speak of a chain of property that neither begins with individuals nor ends in the resources they procure. Yet the process of manufacture also works the other way: as I argued in the previous chapter, groups coalesce around, and are consolidated by, the persons or selves they jointly produce. For this reason, I suggest, the appropriation of resources by an individual ultimately takes place on behalf of the community of nurture in which his own existence originates. The hunter's meat may be exclusively his (and his wife's) to dispose of but is not his alone to consume.

In short, Urarina sharing patterns seem to occupy a kind of middle ground between unsolicited giving and giving "on demand." This same basic structure can be discerned both in relations between human coresidents and in relations between humans and nonhuman agencies. Autonomy and dependency are brought together here and combined in a way that we might, following Ingold (2000: 69), sum up in terms of an overarching principle of "trust."[12] People do depend on one another, as well as on the natural environment, for food and a variety of everyday services. But they will not act in any way that overtly diminishes the autonomy of those on whom they depend: there is no attempt to coerce others or to impose an obligation. Instead, people seek to elicit positive sentiments of nurturing and helping in others by adopting a subordinate position if necessary, trusting that they will be taken care of and provided for. As Ingold points out, such exchanges may be considered as the surface expression of a deeper concern with "companionship": a relationship that is oriented toward shared activity and that is voluntary, freely terminable, and involves the mutual recognition and preservation of the autonomy of both parties.

The loving or giving (belaiha) that characterizes social relations in the intimate sphere grounds the concept of *beelaicha*, literally, "one who gives or loves," but sometimes translated simply as "friend" (Sp. *amigo*). In the context of a discussion about friendship, Manuel defined the term *beelaicha* for me as "your friend, who holds you in high esteem, who cares for you, who loves you . . . someone who isn't family". When I queried this latter condition, Manuel quickly confirmed that family, too, can be beelaicha: "whoever loves you." But it served to emphasize that the relationship is above all supposed to be voluntary, and based on trust rather than obligation. In fact, Manuel nominated as his beelaicha two men, only distantly related by kinship, who lived close by and often shared food with him. It seemed to me that this did not preclude his close family also being his beelaicha; it was merely not necessary to classify them in this way. The extent to which this ideal of voluntary care actually reflects or translates into reality, however, is not always clear: as I show in chapter 5, the relationship between a son-in-law and a father-in-law is overtly couched in precisely such terms of mutual care and love, but this effectively serves to disguise an underlying sense of tension and anxiety.

In short, and despite their inherent asymmetries, Urarina sharing patterns rest less on any structure or principle of reciprocal obligation than on the existence of trust, in which dependency combines with the mutual recognition of individual autonomy. Yet this mutual recognition is also political: some receivers, at least, are subordinated to some givers. At the same time, sharing constitutes the common purpose that people bring into the productive process itself: a purpose that both originates with and seeks fulfillment through a wider collectivity. The condition of "togetherness" is a paramount value here: people commonly talk about "sharing" using such expressions as "being together we all receive" (*jiniiquin te raaca*) or "being together we all eat" (*jiniiquiin lenonechaca*). I now wish to explore further ways in which this emphasis on the individual emerges from, and is grounded in, senses of togetherness and the collectivity.

IMMEDIACY AND AUTONOMY

Life in an Urarina community allows little privacy. The majority of houses are entirely without walls, and many are situated in close proximity, sometimes at distances of just a few meters. Traditionally two or three families would live under a single roof, each on their own space of stilt palm floor. With the exception of intimate communication between spouses, the interaction between almost any two Urarina is usually witnessed (and often overheard) by others. There are few possibilities for "private" conversations, and normally people would not even try for one. Most communities have about a dozen houses, sometimes less. Notwithstanding the sporadic visits of family living elsewhere, people see the same faces, day in and day out, and know almost everything about their neighbors' lives. Such a social environment, which could be described as "immediate" in the phenomenological sense proposed by Bird-David (1994), is largely conducive to informality. There is little discussion of roles or statuses, and people do not generally relate to each other on such terms. Virtually everyone who lives together is related through kin ties, and all are usually addressed by a kinship term. It is to a large extent actions such as visiting, food sharing, and working together that create and maintain relatedness (figure 7).

The many benefits of mutuality, or of doing things with others, are repeatedly emphasized. People take pride both in "helping" others and in being helped in turn, and there is an inherent duality to this notion: the very verb "to help," *coroatajaa*, derives directly from the numeral "two" (*coroataja*) and could be understood literally as "two-making." For this reason, unskilled children can accurately be described as "helping" their parents, simply by virtue of accompanying them. People continually invite others to join them and also take care not to leave anyone on their own. A person arriving uninvited at the house of another will immediately be cordially invited ("Come on in and visit!"). On my way to bathe in the evenings, the men would invite me to join them, calling out *"chajao necaojoani,"* "Come on, let's bathe," or even more notably call to me to leave with them when they left, saying, "Come on, let's go up," even though I may have just arrived and scarcely entered the water. I also found that getting people's cooperation or participation in a task was always best achieved, not with a direct instruction, but with an expression emphasizing togetherness, such as "Come on, let's go and do X together"—to which the only conceivable reply seemed to be, "Alright, let's go."

Yet Urarina sociality is also imbued with a distinctive emphasis on and prioritization of individual autonomy, which is expressed in various ways. Although food seems destined to be consumed collectively, its production is an inherently solitary affair. Men who go hunting or fishing together will divide the catch well before arriving back in the village, where it is handed to one or more wives, each of whom will even-

Figure 7.   Drinking manioc beer during a communal work effort. Photograph by author.

tually offer a more or less identical meal to the same group of people. Manioc beer similarly has only one "owner," and co-wives will simultaneously serve bowls from their own separate supply to feed their husband's guests.

The individualism of ownership is particularly strong with regard to material possessions, coinciding with a valorization of self-sufficiency. Each person in a community aspires to own at least one of every possible (i.e., potentially ownable) item, regardless of its size, cost, or origin. No one was ever satisfied with the prospect of sharing or borrowing, let alone collective or group ownership, even for expensive (and relatively infrequently used) items like shotguns. All items—one might say all entities, whether living or nonliving—must have one (and usually only one) owner. The rules, institutions, and corporate custodianship required by collective ownership are entirely antithetical to this way of thinking. This was a continual bane to the staff of CEDIA, an NGO trying in vain at the time of my fieldwork to introduce a communal natural resource management program. Similar ideas are found elsewhere in Amazonia: Erikson (2009) provides a nice anecdote for the Matis by way of illustration, relating how he bought the first and only dugout canoe in the community from the neighboring Marubo and offered to let anyone interested use it. The next day he was surprised to find nearly the entire adult male population busy carving paddles, all following basically the same design, blithely indifferent to Erikson's incomprehension of why so many paddles were necessary given that they had only one canoe.

The story of Woodpecker supplies a mythic charter for this moral imperative to make one's own possessions. Woodpecker's ritual co-mother was lazy and neglected to fabricate her own pots, resorting instead to borrowing them from others. Industrious but stingy, the protohuman Woodpecker sat surrounded by piles of fine pots but thwarted her co-mother's requests to borrow one by insisting they were all broken, tapping on the sides of carefully selected cracked pots to demonstrate their worthlessness. It is this same sound that we still hear today, the sound of the woodpecker into which she transformed as a consequence of her actions. The tale is, in a sense, a critique of both actors and highlights that excessive dependency and stinginess are two sides of the same coin, both highly undesirable and to be avoided. Proper sociability requires steering a middle course between these two extremes.

The prioritization of individual autonomy finds ample expression in less immediately tangible areas. Something I often found particularly striking was that people would steadfastly refuse ever to speak for, or on behalf of, another individual. They would not answer a question on another's behalf even when the answer was perfectly well known to them and there was not, at least to my mind, the faintest possibility of ambiguity. The most straightforward question concerning the movements or motivations of another was steadfastly met with an "I don't know" and an implicit or explicit "You'd have to ask him (or her)." At first I found this very frustrating, for I knew that my interlocutor was at the very least in a position to make a pretty good guess. But underlying this refusal to presume to know the thoughts of another was a sense that to do so was, in some important way, an infraction of personal autonomy.

Urarina have no customary greeting and say they did not traditionally greet each other. If they now do so, with increasing frequency, it is presumably a result of mestizo influence. Yet if greetings or farewells are used at all, they are fastidiously addressed to each individual in turn, even if this means repeating the same expression a dozen or more times. It would be virtually inconceivable to employ the second-person plural form to address a group in such a situation. Hence a person leaving the community on a trip to Iquitos, for example, might say something like

"I'm going now, my brother," to each adult in turn, to which the response in each case is a simple "Yes." As a relative outsider, I was the focus of a particularly laborious regime of salutations, and if one person decided to greet me one day, eliciting my dutiful reply, everyone else would tend to follow in turn. There is also a sense here of continually reaffirming the "good" or "tranquil" character of each social relation in turn, especially necessary given that tensions are more commonly expressed through silence than through stern words and argument.

This apparent prioritization of the individual has as its counterpart a far-reaching valorization of individual experience. Most people were generally reluctant to speak about topics beyond the level of their own personal or immediate experience. The construction (and valorization) of knowledge of various kinds on the basis of shamanic practice, particularly through the consumption of psychotropics, is a good example of this basic orientation. The "worldview" or "cosmology" expounded by different shamanic practitioners may vary widely as a result of shamanism's inherent individualism.[13]

Knowledge of the natural environment is similarly acquired almost entirely firsthand rather than received, in some standardized form, along lines of cultural transmission. A question to an informant such as when a particular fruit or flower comes into season, or when a certain animal has its offspring, was always answered with a series of personal anecdotes and observations that relayed, often with great precision, what had been witnessed on some specific occasion or other, even if it had taken place many years ago.[14]

Extensive use of hearsay markers in narratives is a consequence of this general orientation. Although there are few formal evidentials in the Urarina grammar, any information that does not result from the speaker's firsthand experience is heavily qualified by hearsay markers, such as *jetao*. Similarly, people will terminate a discourse or explanation with an expression such as, "That's what the ancients used to say." Such rhetorical devices further highlight that the information contained is not derived from firsthand experience.

Shallow genealogical memory is another striking corollary of this same inclination. I was generally unable to collect genealogical information going back more than one or two ascendant generations. People would regularly claim not to know the names of kinfolk they did not know personally, even though there is no particular prohibition on using the name of a deceased person. For example, Lorenzo claimed he did not know the name of his paternal grandfather "because I didn't exist back then—I didn't know him." The reason for this no doubt lies in part in the avoidance of personal names more generally. Urarina will sometimes go to considerable lengths to avoid using personal names, whether their own or those of others. Relationship terms are unanimously preferred for both address and reference; nicknames are a distant second. Given that most Urarina who come into contact already know the kin relation between them or are able quickly to establish one, there is little need for "real" names in everyday life, and they are easily forgotten. Needless to say, this point made collecting genealogies and general demographic information even more difficult. It was not at all uncommon for a man to be able to remember every detail of his many (living) brothers and sisters and be willing to offer any number of pieces of information, including precisely where they live, but be unable to remember any of their names, whether in Urarina or in Spanish.

Relatively few men are called by their psychotropic names, and while they are not exactly kept secret there is a certain reluctance to use or reveal them. Often when I asked after someone's name, laughter and some embarrassment resulted. People tended to be particularly reluctant to reveal their own names but would often be happy enough for me to ask someone else present at the time. Given the power attributed to names, the sense that they have a kind of compulsive or coercive force and a power to delimit or evoke in some way (see chapter 5), there also seems to be an element of fear and respect associated with them. Their avoidance may thus also relate to a general unwillingness to appear aggressive or coercive toward others.

Yet there is another, equally important reason for what Gow (1991: 151) has termed the "shallow time frame" of Amazonian peoples—of which the inability to remember distant ascendant kin is a prominent aspect. This is the emphasis placed on personal experience in epistemology. This seems to be a widespread feature of Amazonian societies, one deserving more systematic exploration than it has received to date. Commenting on the importance of experience in the way Amazonian peoples represent the world, as something always constituted through action and creation, Gonçalves (2005: 636) has drawn attention to linguistically oriented studies such as those by Urban (1989), who argued that "for the Xavante, the first-person narratives of myths produce a kind of trance-like state, in which the narrator begins to experience the narrative in an individualized way." Basso (1995) has similarly demonstrated that the importance of stories for the Kalapalo consisted less in their representing collectively accepted images that animate social life than in their describing the experiences of individuals exploring alternatives for their lives. Among the Kayabi, Oakdale (2005) has shown how certain ritual performances orchestrate a series of momentary identifications with the personal experiences of others. Gonçalves (2005: 636) observed, "Even in narratives that seem fixed, such as myths and songs, one can discern an important process of individualization that accentuates experience as the basis of this perception, frequently reflected in the first-person telling of the narrative." The case of the Pirahã described by Everett (2005) may represent the outermost limits of this widespread tendency. According to Everett, Pirahã restrict all communication to the immediate experience of the interlocutors: people avoid entirely "talking about knowledge that ranges beyond personal, usually immediate experience or is transmitted via such experience" (623).

This distinctive cultural emphasis on immediate experience has important implications for sociality and personhood. As Bird-David (1994, 1999) has argued for the Nayaka of South India, immediacy inhibits the development of roles, institutions, or statuses: because of the way individuals know each other "vividly" and as "fully real," typificatory schemes are more vulnerable to personal interferences than in "remoter" forms of interaction, where there is greater anonymity. Because relationships are highly flexible, in other words, it is comparatively difficult to impose rigid patterns on them. In the Nayaka case, Bird-David proposed, this leads to a relational view of personhood in which people objectify each other, not as the Maussian "character"—the locus, in everyday life, of different rights, duties, titles, and kinship names—but as kin or relatives, "ones related with." It is the common experience of sharing space, things, and actions that contextualizes people's knowledge of each other: Nayaka "dividuated each other." Yet the question of how or in what sense Urarina personhood is "relational" is a complex one. In the final section of this chapter, a closer examination of linguistic categories, in particular, those pertaining to concepts of the soul, shows how overlapping senses of self pull in several different directions at once, simultaneously expressing countervailing movements toward interiority and exteriority.

INTERIORITY AND ANIMACY

Urarina notions of the person incorporate a concatenation of related, sometimes overlapping qualities, substances, and relations. There is no single term in the Urarina language for "body."[15] People do refer to the *jabereco*, "trunk," a term that excludes the limbs and appendages unless used with a qualifier, such as *saatiin jabereco*, "all the body, everything." *Aura*, meanwhile, means "flesh" (typically in the sense of a hunk of flesh), although both the "trunk" and the "flesh" of the body are nevertheless held separate from the self. I once overheard a conversation in which Buchilote, about to go hunting in the forest, was asked, "What are you taking with you?" to which he replied, *"aura nejesine,"* "Purely [my hunk of] flesh." There is a linguistic strategy to refer to the "self": *raajeniane*, employed in autoreflexive function (e.g., *"caraajenianena chaanu,"* "I did it myself"). There is no denotata, however, and the term can best be characterized as an adverb.

A better starting point for exploring the semantics of local concepts of the self is the following triad of close cognates: *suujui, suujue, suujua*. Although certain preferences guide the use of one over another in specific contexts, all Urarina readily recognize the considerable semantic overlap. *Suujui* (also sometimes *suujue*) is used particularly to refer to the hard inner part or "heart" (*shungo* in the regional Loretan Spanish) of a tree that, in contrast to the outer "flesh," does not rot or disintegrate but simply loses water and dries out. Given that *suujiha* means "to hide," the concealed, hidden "interiority" of the suujui is clearly a defining quality.

The closely related *suujue* is used most often to refer to that interior and nonmaterial part of the person said to ascend to the sky at death—what would usually be translated as "soul" (and which I have throughout translated as "heart-soul"). In chapter 3 I argued that the suujue emerges in an infant as the culmination of a gradual process of "hardening," and in a sense represents the epitome of the quality of hardness. But it is also more than this, and if the suujue is paradigmatically associated with notions of hardness and interiority, it is nevertheless also considered detachable in some contexts, such as dreams and hallucinogenic trance. Hence the capacity of certain birds to sing prior to the arrival of certain types of persons, particularly a benane, or sorcerer, is attributed to the latter's propensity readily to project or detach their suujue. In fact, there seems to be a close, if somewhat mysterious, relationship between the suujue and songbirds, a point to which I shall return below.

Most animals, and particularly the class known as cana lenone, or our food, are also ascribed a suujue. Jorge once warned me against throwing bones of recently eaten animals on the fire, lest the smell scare away other animals and prevent them from approaching the camp. When I asked Lorenzo if bones did indeed have a distinctive smell, he replied that the animal's suujue "flies out of the bones" in such situations "for fear of being burned" and warns its "relatives" to stay away. "Our bones have already been burned, so we must not approach," was his paraphrase of the logic.

Closely related to suujue is the suujua, which is broadly regarded as the seat of thought and affect, associated particularly with notions of compassion *(suujuaa)*. As such, it rather resembles the English "heart" in its metaphoric sense (the literal organ itself, *mojoe*, is ascribed no special importance that I could discern). Importantly, most informants agreed that unlike the suujue, the suujua is a distinctly human quality that is not shared by animals. Although some considered the two roughly synonymous, at least in the human case, it is without doubt *suujua*, not *suujue*, that one hears most often used in everyday conversation, in a variety of idiomatic expressions. It is associated not only with being alive and having a soul, but with being a good, compassionate, and moral person. I would suggest that this implies, first, the capacity to steer an appropriate middle course between the extremes of total self-sufficiency, rather than allowing one's needs and desires to be met by others, and total dependency, thereby failing to meet the needs and desires of others (the story of Woodpecker exemplifies this search for balance). It further implies the self-discipline required to suppress desires or instincts considered antisocial or contrary to the interests of others and instead align one's desires with those of loved ones. This is epitomized by the widespread sharing of food; conversely, stinginess and incest, the two most aggressively condemned forms of immoral behavior, can each be considered failures of self-discipline in this sense.

Moral behavior and the suujua are intimately bound up in notions of "respect" *(suujua acatiha,* lit., "to defend the heart-soul"), which, as discussed in chapter 3, epitomizes good relations between spouses. Real people are supremely capable of this; at the other end of the spectrum are jaguars and bacauha, or enemies (typically the Candoshi), who virtually by definition "don't know how to respect others." Only just falling short of inclusion in the category "real people" are the Cocama, with whom Urarina purportedly intermarried from time to time. As Lorenzo once put it, "The Cocama, they're good folk, nearly real people. They know a lot. They really know how to respect."[16]

The suujua is also associated with the capacity for thought and personal opinion. Hence I often heard the expression *"canu suujua"* used in conversation to mean "my idea" or "my opinion." Yet although the suujua is in many ways an expression of individuality, associated with an interiority largely inaccessible to others, it is also ideally an interiority that closely resembles that of others, one that constitutes the person as an autonomous member of a valued "community of similars" (Overing 2003: 300). This is itself part of a more general positive moral valuation of conformity to established norms and traditions. Hence one of the highest forms of praise people will bestow on something, from a new canoe to a recording of a myth, is simply that it "fits" or "conforms." In relation to persons, the expression *"cana suujua tocoaneein"* literally translates as "like our heart-soul" but means "like-minded." It is often considered the outcome of processes of "taming" or "raising," which is of course a primary process for the production and consolidation of social groups, as agglomerations of analogous selves. Conversely, of someone who behaves poorly or immorally it might be said *"suujua cuaorera,"* loosely "he thinks differently." In context this very fact of difference has negative connotations. Jorge, who as it happened had a fraught relationship with his father, explained the expression to me as follows: *"Suujua cuaorera* means 'that which another person thinks, separately.' For example, on my own, I think to myself, How shall I work? How shall I do good? What things have value? And then, separately, my father thinks differently, he doesn't think of his children like that. *Laaucha suujua cuaorera* . . . he will think apart." With its inherent moral dimension, *suujua* shares something with the concept of *ichao*, "life," which derives from the verb *ichaoha*, "to live" or "to be alive," but also means "manner," "way [of life]," or "nature," as in "that is his nature." The term retains this sense when applied to nonhumans, for example, in speaking of a pig who especially likes rolling in the mud (e.g., *catoaniha ca coosi ichao*, "such is this pig's life"). It is used particularly in the context of discussing the moral shortcomings of others.

None of these terms, it should be pointed out, seem to express a notion of a life essence. This latter concept is more aptly subsumed by the terms *raca*, "breath," and *acarera*, "vitality," "vital breath," or "longevity." Breath is considered almost like a kind of force, associated with physical strength and the will to survive—hence its prominence in the joina baau described above, used to increase strength for hunting. Existing purely in movement, breath is also related to wind (*cujuana*); it may be said of animals such as dogs and tortoises, renowned for their abundance of "breath" (raca), that they "have lots of wind" (*tabai te cujuana sirii*). There is no concept of air in the sense of an invisible medium (a closed bottle is simply considered to be empty), although gasoline vapors—also regarded as a repository of "force"—may be described as wind (*gasona cujuana*).

The suujue is distinguished from the *anocai*, "ghost," which by all accounts comes into existence only at death. This soul or spirit of the deceased induces much fear and anxiety, especially when someone is gravely ill, as its mere touch is said to cause harm or death. Devoid of a body, the anocai is conceived as a malevolent agent, incapable of remembering or recognizing kith or kin. Though deriving from particular deceased individuals, the anocai retains nothing of that person's individual identity or moral sense, which further emphasizes the inherently embodied nature of these qualities.

The suujue (heart-soul) is also distinguished from the corii, or shadow-soul. Some informants claimed that the corii only comes into existence at death and thereafter lingers around on earth, in contrast to the suujue, which ascends to heaven. Others disputed this, however, and common usage of the term, in both ritual and nonritual discourse, certainly implies its presence in some form in the living. The toys supplied by a mother for the corii of her newborn baby is one striking example. A glimpse of a person's shadow or silhouette, moreover, is said to be a glimpse of his or her corii (hence my choice of term for the translation). The shadow itself is known as *beraera* (also *beraecha*), and the term apparently also belongs to that series of cognates relating to notions of care and companionship, which includes *belaiha* (to love or to give as a gift), *beraiha* (to care for or to nurture), and *bedainiha*, "to visit." Importantly, the generic term for companion, *corijera*, is literally "shadow-soul-fellow." Moreover, the corii is closely associated with *cojounaca*, "image," "copy," or "signal." It is the "image" of a person that is often said to be seen in dreams, and is capable of frightening children in particular.

The Urarina concept of corii might usefully be contrasted with the Achuar notion of *wakan*, as discussed by Taylor (1996). Emphasising the intimate link between kinship and memory, Taylor proposed that the *wakan* (usually translated as "soul") refers specifically to an image of the self as reflected in the images of it held by others, which are in turn suffused with memories of nurturing, sharing, and working together. I would suggest that the Urarina *corii* similarly expresses an aspect of selfhood that is closely bound up in intimate, interpersonal ties, particularly those defined by visiting and the giving of food, nurture, and care. Such acts are of course ideally voluntary rather than based in any form of obligation, which is why Manuel chose to define *beelaicha* (a term that clearly subsumes all the above elements) in explicit reference to two men who lived near him and with whom he shared on a regular basis rather than his "kin" genealogically defined.

The corii of a baby in its hammock, as discussed in chapter 2, is especially fond of "playing" with its toys, especially the remnant stub of umbilical cord attached to the rattle; in this way the baby is kept calm and content. I have argued that the rattle itself figures as a kind of replacement placenta, attached to a hammock designed to re-create the enclosed and protected space of the womb. The interaction between the corii and the placenta is effectively consummated at death, when the corii is free to return to the site where the placenta was carefully buried. As such, I proposed, the corii represents something like an echo, or "shadow" perhaps, of the original state of intimate bipolarity, or unity-in-duality, which is ruptured by the act of cutting the umbilical cord. It expresses the notion that the true subject is always accompanied; differently put, that subjectivity always belongs to two or more (Sloterdijk 2011). It is for this reason that the corijera (shadow-soul-fellow) provides the prototypical model of companionship, as a voluntary form of relationship that combines autonomy with dependency while constituting subjectivity. This kind of relationship appears to me as something quite different from the "self/alter" polarity more commonly discussed in the regional literature, and a long way from anything resembling the encounter between "predator" and "prey." As a capacity or potentiality for intimate forms of relatedness, the corii emphasizes that an individual life cannot be represented as a separate point of animation, like an enclosed spark. Subjectivity has a spatial and medial structure, insofar as the true experiencing subject is never alone but always situated in a field of protection and attention.

To recapitulate, the interpretation I am proposing is that the suujue is bound up in notions of individual uniqueness and interiority, especially one's innermost thoughts and emotions, whereas the corii seems inherently associated with reflections, doubles, images, and companions. The latter is present from birth, or more precisely, I think, from the moment an infant is severed from its placenta. Prediscursive and primordial, it represents the shadowy trace of this originary companion, and an existential opening of the individual toward the exterior and to its potential replacements. The suujue by contrast expresses a concept of interiority and containment, as evidenced through its relation to suujui, the hard, hidden, interior of trees; it represents an enclosure, an inward-turning. The suujue is not "given" but is acquired gradually, produced in an infant through the correct behavior of others, especially correct performance of the couvade. Its defining characteristic of interiority and enclosure, which is essential to physical health and well-being, mirrors or refracts that which simultaneously encompasses and unites those who brought it into existence, namely, the child's parents and co-parents.

The suujua is also closely associated with voice, figuring in everyday speech as something capable of "sounding" or "speaking." *Suujuatiha,* "to give heart," means "to advise": someone who "knows how to receive advice" is called *suujuatenacaa;* its antonym, *suujuatenacai,* refers to "someone who doesn't know how to obey advice . . . the advice isn't received in their heart . . . it just flies away." If this is often depicted as a kind of inner voice, it can nevertheless also be external. Such is the case with game animals: the birds that "advise" and "protect" the animal are said to be "like its suujue." We might thus infer that the suujue stands for the discursive aspect of subjectivity, closely related to the capacity to give and receive advice, either to oneself or to others, where this advice is construed as a compassionate form of caregiving, intended to protect and safeguard the well-being of loved ones. It is the voice of a benevolent authority, and one that establishes a firm, interior space and personal sanctuary. Whether its origin is posited as internal or external to the self, it is broadly equivalent to what we might term the voice of conscience: the inward-turning moment of conscience that is a condition of reflexivity.

This returns us to the inherent morality of personhood, and its founding in a submission to the established order. To be a true Urarina, a true person (cacha), is not only to possess the requisite attributes of heartsoul, shadow-soul, vital breath, and so on, but to act in a restrained, disciplined, and conscientious manner toward others. This means especially to show respect to the right people (above all spouses and parents-in-law), where such "respect" is figured in terms of defense of the heartsoul and expressed through proper forms of speech. Linguistic skills, which include the capacity for "true" or "right speech," are of course but one aspect of the many skills learned by children as part of the reproduction of labor power, which is at once the production of gendered subjects. Yet the mastery of the skills required for the practice of one's gender role—and hence full entry into the realm of the social—is simultaneously a submission to gender ideology, the set of ideas that limits the range of people's actions and orients the division of labor. The reproduction of social relations, the reproduction of skills, is not only grounded in individual bodies; it is also the reproduction of subjection.

To master a set of skills is not simply to receive them passively, but to reproduce them in and as one's own activity. Hence the "imprinting" phase central to all remedies for the acquisition of knowledge, in which the novice is obliged continually to practice his newfound skills for a set duration of time. As with training in sharing, which begins at the moment an infant takes its first, faltering steps, it is not enough simply to act according to a set of rules or norms: one must embody rules in the course of action. The care on which Amazonian moral systems are premised is cultivated from the outset as an embodied disposition that is logically and perhaps even temporally prior to the formation of subjects—hence its close association with the shadow-soul.

Learning to behave in a socially appropriate manner clearly does not amount to a mechanistic or voluntaristic appropriation of norms. Learning to share, the cornerstone of morality, is inculcated through repeated practice, almost as a kind of ritual. Like other skills, sharing begins as an embodied disposition that generates certain beliefs, in particular, beliefs in its own "obviousness."[17] But it comes eventually to be founded in recognition of the legitimate needs of others, and evoking such recognition lies at the heart of strategies for soliciting and receiving gifts. This requires the mastery of subtle forms of voluntary self-deprecation or subordination in order to induce a benevolent, paternal, or caring disposition in the giver. Mastery and submission are virtually inseparable here, an apparent paradox explored further below. It is in relations with "outsiders" of various kinds that the incipient power asymmetries already discussed become increasingly apparent. Exploration of these requires a prior understanding of how relatedness is defined and elaborated beyond the household and the principles on which solidarity is founded.

5. Authority and Solidarity

Weary of the interminable feuding, Roberto and his extended family, comprising nearly half the community of Nueva Unión, finally dismantled their houses and cleared a site for a new, breakaway village just a few bends downriver. The dispute between Roberto and his brother Lorenzo was so long-standing that people had trouble remembering how it started. By the time I arrived on the upper Chambira, Roberto's group had just created a modest football pitch and were about to begin their lengthy campaign to recruit a teacher for their handful of pupils. Hostilities were rife and grievances a regular feature of people's conversations. The original community had expanded steadily since its founding some years earlier, and splintering was seemingly inevitable. Nueva Unión in 2007 was one of the Chambira basin's several dozen large, orderly Native Communities, the official landholding units in Peruvian law that follow a one-size-fits-all model for the country's entire indigenous population. Since their introduction in the late 1970s, traditional residence and mobility patterns have been gradually transformed, and the majority of Urarina now live in much larger and more sedentary settlements than anything known previously. This has given rise to a number of new challenges, many of which point to the changing bases of authority and solidarity.

According to early chronicles, Urarina were a relatively mobile group who occupied small, dispersed settlements in interfluvial areas. They reportedly learned to make canoes and to fish only after they were settled on the Marañon River (Veigl 2006 [1785]).[1] They preferred to travel through the jungle on foot rather than along rivers by canoe, staying only as long in an area as the duration of a particular fruit or hunt and constructing makeshift huts of leaves and branches (Costales and

Costales 1983: 124). Traditional mobility patterns were influenced by a combination of sociopolitical and ecological factors, including feuding and access to natural resources, but over the past century access to trade goods—together with a countervailing desire to avoid the worst excesses of exploitative labor conditions—has become increasingly important in determining people's movements. The makeshift shelters observed by Velasco, known as *loanari*, are still in use today, but far more common are a larger, more permanent style of house known as *loreri*, intended to last for at least several years.[2] Virtually all major settlements are now located on the banks of the Chambira and its principal tributaries, where traders and their merchandise are easily accessible.

Though many Urarina still elect to live in small, isolated, and relatively temporary settlements with just their immediate families, all land officially belongs to one or another of the Native Communities, which range in size from several dozen to several hundred residents. These are instantly recognizable by the presence of a school and a football field, both the objects of intermittent bursts of civic pride and collective efforts at maintenance, ranking at the top of an infrastructural hierarchy pertaining to the "civilized" life and slightly ahead, in terms of importance or prestige, of the public medicine cabinet *(botiquín)*, the communal house *(casa comunal)* and the communal holding cell *(calabozo)*. A well-maintained riverbank, with all these conspicuously present, combined with the knowledge that most were founded by groups of adult siblings, can easily give the misleading impression of a united community. The collective identities established under the banner of the Native Community are in fact still relatively weak and do not coincide with the cooperative units that traditionally coalesce around a senior man or group of female consanguines. Traditional methods of conflict resolution are similarly ill-equipped to ensure lasting social integration and prevent the departure of aggrieved parties, and the majority of Native Communities are recognizably divided into smaller factions, often geographically ordered in relation to the river. This often marks the beginning of a process of fission that ends in the departure and resettlement of one of the groups, as happened in Nueva Unión just prior to my arrival.

In this chapter I explore some of the overlapping ties of belonging that characterize life in the Native Community and the organization of solidarity beyond the intimacy of the conjugal body. Of particular interest here is how such ties emerge in relation to constitutive forms of power or authority and their grounding in transformations of personal identity and experience: in other words, how power works through subjectivity in structuring communal life. I build on a number of themes developed earlier, furthering the claim that the construction of selves and social groups are inextricably linked. At the same time, I seek to move beyond claims that corporeal processes of feeding and nurture create commensality in order to explore subjective experience as a locus for creating ties. I begin with naming practices, as opportunities for creating new ties of companionship similar to those of ritual co-parenthood and as principal avenues for shaping personal identities in relation to social groups as well as gender and state ideologies. The gendered dimensions of naming practices have their basis in uxorilocality, which tends to symbolically homogenize females while individuating males. The latent tension between in-marrying men, potentially disruptive of the solidarity largely engendered by women, is explored through an examination of brideservice, figured as a vital but fraught relationship between fathers-in-law and sons-in-law. In the context of increasingly populous and sedentary communities, the role of local leaders in promoting group unity is becoming ever more important, despite important changes in the bases of their authority and claims to legitimacy. In the second half of the chapter I continue to explore the central theme of the nature of solidarity and its relationship to power but focus on the significance of drunkenness as a basis for the articulation of informal friendships and romantic liaisons that complement ties of kinship, and as a heightened, more distributed but less human version of ordinary waking consciousness. This lays a basis for further exploration of extraordinary forms of subjectivity in the next chapter.

THE POWER OF NAMES

Infants receive up to three different names at various points throughout their first year or two of life. Each is referred to by the same term, *curaa*, while deriving legitimacy from its own context of use. The first is bestowed by the mother, who draws for inspiration on salient or idiosyncratic physical characteristics and dispositions already evident in the child's interactions with others. Men I spoke to usually referred to these names as "nicknames" (Sp. *chapa*), and to avoid confusion I shall also refer to them in this way. Nicknames are often humorous and lighthearted and may be regarded as "jokes" or "joking names."[3] To the extent that the couvade restricts physical contact with animals, it is perhaps noteworthy that nicknames often do virtually the opposite in establishing a metaphorical contact between the child and the animal it most closely resembles. Although nicknames are almost always bestowed by the mother,

Lorenzo claimed that a stepfather can also, in some circumstances, bestow a nickname; however, a father can never do so. There are no rules or patterns governing their use or transmission, and no ceremony marks their bestowal: the mother just starts calling her child by this name and it sticks. I had the impression that although women often cease to be called by their nicknames after puberty, many men are called primarily by these names all their lives.

At some point after the first few months of life, and roughly around the time an infant learns to walk, a different kind of name is bestowed, referred to as one's name "within psychedelic trance" *(coaairi jana)*. The name-giving ceremony *(curaatiha*, "to give a name") is performed by a male relative, often a classificatory uncle or grandfather, who is a competent shaman or drinker of psychotropics (coaairi coera). Semantically empty, the name is received from the mother of ayahuasca or brugmansia in a vision and bestowed during the ritual session while the drinker is still heavily inebriated. After smoking a good quantity of tobacco, he coughs, or "vomits up," into the palm of his hand a phlegmlike substance from his ayahuasca- or brugmansia-infused body. This is *coaairi cojoatojoi*, the dartlike media of mystical attack and a manifestation of the power, "goodness," or "value" of psychotropics. From here, the name-dart passes into the fontanel of the infant, still soft at this early stage of development, where it remains lodged irrevocably until death. Knocking one's head is sometimes said to be especially painful because of this "dart" moving around inside. Although most psychotropic names seem to be drawn from a finite stock or repertoire, I could not detect any system governing their allocation, or any sense that names are transmitted across generations. Nor am I aware of any prohibition on more than one person having the same name within a residential community.

The bestowal of a psychedelic name institutes two significant relationships: one within the residential group and the other beyond it. The first of these is between the name giver and the name receiver, who henceforth address each other respectively as *cabaichera* and *cabaichae*.[4] I sometimes heard these terms reversed, in a jocular fashion, such that the older man might call the child "cabaichera" instead of "cabaichae," although there is no confusion as to which is the proper or correct usage. I am not aware of any form of address or relationship instituted between the name giver and either parent. However, in reiterating ties through a form of cross-generational ritual kinship, the relation between a baichae (name receiver) and baichaera (name giver) resembles that between the michua (cord cuttee) and michuera (cord cutter), which is strongly associated with ritual co-parenthood. Yet in neither case did there seem to be any particular formal role or responsibility attaching to this (cross-generational) relationship.

The second relationship instituted through psychedelic baptism is with Our Creator (Cana Coaaunera), for the name is the hallmark of recognition by divine authority. When a person dies, I was told, he or she (more accurately, his or her *suujue*, or heart-soul) will come face to face with Our Creator, who will ask for his or her name, along with details of who bestowed it and how. Lorenzo told me that Our Creator requests the name whenever a person goes to the sky "in order that they can rest"; it is the prerequisite for entry into the sky or heaven *(dede)*. Anyone without a name will be unable to answer. Jorge said, "Our Creator will ask how you were given your name, and you must answer, for example, 'My grandfather gave it to me, drinking ayahuasca.'" He also told me that the name-dart itself, the *cojoatojoi*, returns to the shaman who bestowed it, or otherwise to a powerful tree such as kapok or caupori, where it remains. Lorenzo further claimed that Our Creator actually switches over personal names at death and in this way transforms the deceased person (or rather his or her heart-soul) into another class of being altogether, the arara, or thunder-person.

Relatively few men are called by their psychedelic names, and though they are not exactly kept secret, there is a general reluctance to use or reveal them. Often when I asked after someone's name, laughter and some embarrassment resulted. The names are only known, or at least claimed to be known, by people who are themselves known personally: hence (and as noted earlier) Lorenzo claimed he did not know the name of his paternal grandfather "because I didn't exist back then—I didn't know him." Nevertheless, there is no particular prohibition on using the psychedelic name of a deceased person.

In addition to nicknames and psychedelic names, all Urarina today have Spanish names, which are used in virtually all interactions with non-Urarina and in written documents. A very small minority of young Urarina have only Spanish names. As almost all women are illiterate and very rarely interact with non-Urarina, Spanish names are used primarily by men. Women are liable to forget their own Spanish names and when I was collecting genealogical data often had to be reminded of it by their husbands or brothers; perhaps partly for this reason, most women seemed to be called either Rosa or Maria. It is similarly mostly boys who are formally "baptized" *(baotisaa,* from the Spanish *bautisar).*

The baptism ceremony for Spanish names borrows elements from the mestizo culture, on which it is in some respects consciously modeled. Yet it also contains strong echoes of the more traditional institutions of cord cutting and psychedelic name bestowal. The ceremony is a public one and ideally takes place during a manioc beer drinking party. Thus it is a rite imbued with a distinctly celebratory atmosphere. The school seemed to be a popular location for baptisms, and regional Peruvian festivals, such as the festival of San Juan (not otherwise celebrated in any particular way), are popular occasions for its performance. When the child's father and the name giver have agreed on an appropriate name, a gourd is filled with water and a little salt. Manioc leaves, wrapped in a piece of cloth, are dipped or soaked in the water and used to splash water on the child, in particular, the *corosoelo*, the area at the center of the chest. A few drops of salty water are also dripped from the leaf tips into the mouth of the infant, who is lifted or "held up" by the woman who will become its god-mother (Sp. *madrina*)—typically the name giver's wife—echoing the way infants are "held up" by the midwife at birth.

An oration is performed throughout the proceedings. Some informants were adamant that this should be performed in Spanish, and I was even told that saying the necessary words in Urarina was categorically impossible. This turned out to be more an ideal than a binding condition, for many if not most baptisms took place in Urarina, laudable intentions to perform in Spanish notwithstanding. Despite a similarly widespread sense that a "proper" baptism should be "Christian" in character, to describe them as such from an outsider's point of view would certainly be misleading. Those I heard were addressed directly to the child, and repeatedly emphasized two main points: first, the child is now being given its own name in front of Our Creator; and second, the child's father will henceforth be the enunciator's co-father.

This latter condition marks an important difference from the bestowal of psychedelic names. As in the case of the latter, the child and the name giver begin to address each other as cabaichae and cabaichera. The nature of this relationship seemed rather vague, although Lorenzo did say he felt a special responsibility to the child he baptized and would feel obliged to heal him should he fall ill. However, as in umbilical co-parenthood, the relationship between the two adults tends to be much more significant than the relationship between a child and its sponsor. The two men will begin to address each other as coonfa, and if the name giver's wife assists in the proceedings she too will establish a relationship of co-parenthood with the child's mother.

Unlike psychedelic names, Spanish names are not immutable, at least not until such time as the name has been "officially" recorded in the form of a national identity card, or Documento Nacional de Identidad (DNI). Some people had a tendency continually to change their Spanish names around, a source of endless frustration for the foreign doctors trying to keep track of their immunization records. Moreover, the Spanish system of paternal and maternal surnames was regularly confused or deployed in an unpredictable or idiosyncratic manner. When collecting genealogies I found that full siblings often had completely different surnames. When I queried this I was occasionally told they were given the surnames of one or another grandparent, although for no particular reason I could ascertain. Many surnames appeared to be of foreign origin, and several (e.g., Taricuarima) were identifiably Cocama. Some were converted Urarina words or terms of address, such as Macusi, a word meaning literally "small intestine" and often used as a nickname for the last-born son of any given marriage.

Spanish names are always used in written forms of communication and have a special efficacy that derives from this context. Legitimacy is conferred by state-issued identity documents: the birth certificate *(partido de nacimiento)*, the military card *(libreta militar)*, and, most important of all, the DNI. Although few Urarina on the upper Chambira possessed an identity card at the time of my fieldwork, the esteem in which they were held could hardly be overestimated. Some people at least, especially leaders and Native Community authorities, seemed willing to go to great lengths to acquire one. I myself toiled endlessly (and ultimately unsuccessfully) to help Lorenzo obtain one, and their very elusiveness for those without proper birth documents no doubt accounts for much of their value. Yet I suspect that a great deal of their allure also lies in the power attributed to the written word, which is itself associated with the juridical powers of the state. As Lorenzo put it, he wanted the card "in order to be a citizen, in order to be Peruvian." In fact, the primary reason for wanting the card lay in his strong (and not unfounded) conviction that written correspondence to various state authorities, especially "solicitations" for goods and services, and police incident reports *(denuncias,* deployed frequently against personal enemies), would be accorded greater weight and would be more likely to elicit a favorable response. Confirming one's recognition by the authority of the state, identity cards remit power inasmuch as they make tangible the constitution of a new kind of political subject.

The everyday context in which Spanish names are most commonly used is the school, which similarly derives its prestige from the enhanced access it promises to Peruvian society. This usage is consciously promoted in the classroom by the bilingual teacher, whose general role could be described as precisely that of producing Peruvian "citizens." In fact, despite being nominally "bilingual," with a mandate to teach in Spanish and Urarina in equal measure, the teacher's use of Spanish personal names was about the only Spanish I ever heard spoken in the classroom. The significance of this should nevertheless not be underestimated, given the general sense that names can, or should, play a key role in calling into being that which is named.

An example of this can be seen in the vocatives most commonly used for small children. I rarely heard parents use the address terms for "daughter" *(cacunu)* and "son" *(calaohi),* making these the only vocatives in the relationship terminology not in common use or not preferred in most situations. In fact, and despite having received one or more personal names, small children are most often called *ene* (woman) or *quicha* (man). Although the latter is rarely used as a term of address, the former is used relatively frequently for adult women, possibly reflecting a general tendency to homogenize females in daily life. At first I assumed this was simply a matter of calling children what they "were" by a generic name, to avoid specificity. I later came to suspect it was instead calling them precisely what they were not but should become: "women" or "men." As discussed in chapter 4, babies are essentially genderless in all respects except anatomy; they must grow into their gender, a process with which parents are intimately involved.

Like both psychedelic and Spanish names, then, the vocatives used for children form part of wider strategies for shaping persons through discursive or linguistic means. The act of naming is inherently political, and different kinds of personal names are moreover ways of invoking certain ideas about how persons are constituted. Deriving meaning and legitimacy from distinct ideological contexts, each is associated with its own, largely implicit view of the person. Hence the nicknames bestowed by women prioritize a notion of personhood linked to the practices of domesticity, in which bodiliness and relations of nurture are of paramount importance. They also emphasize bodily uniqueness, which may be why they are used mainly by men, not women, in adult life.

Psychedelic names, by contrast, are bestowed exclusively by (usually older) men. They fix on the "spiritual" dimension of the person and institute an immutable form of personal identity founded in recognition by and submission to divine authority. Our Creator (acting through the mother of ayahuasca or brugmansia as his avatar or proxy) is established as the origin of the subject and remains continuously present in him, in the form of the dart lodged irrevocably in the forehead. The operation of Spanish names is not dissimilar, especially once enshrined in an identity card. As Guzmán-Gallegos (2009) has shown for the Runa of Ecuador, identity cards are seen not only as integral parts of a person's body but moreover as the manifestation and outcome of asymmetrical relations with the church and state. If Spanish names are increasing in importance vis-à-vis psychedelic names, and already considered by some to be more "real" or "legitimate," this may be grounded in a gradual shift in emphasis from Our Creator to the state as primary source of authority in relation to subject formation. As we will see below, this is a theme that also emerges in relation to new forms of political leadership and social organization.

There is a further, no less important characteristic shared by both Spanish and psychedelic names, which relates more closely to the circumstances of their bestowal. In each case, the proper conditions for name giving have as a core prerequisite a state of drunkenness (*ajiha*), deriving from the consumption of manioc beer or psychotropics respectively. Before discussing in more detail local conceptualizations of inebriety and its social significance, however, I wish to examine the dynamics of the local groups known as *lauri*, including their relation to uxorilocality, gender, and the anxieties surrounding brideservice.

GENDERING UXORILOCALITY

That men are addressed by nicknames deriving from their distinctive physical traits or characteristics and most women are addressed by kin terms (or simply as "woman") reflects a broader structural asymmetry between women and men that is intimately linked to the practice of uxorilocal postmarital residence. This is clearly reflected in the relationship terminology, which marks gender strongly: for example, a terminological distinction is made between paternal and maternal grandmothers but not grandfathers; address terms for "grandparent" and "grandchild" are reciprocal for men but not women; and terms for "uncle" (but not "aunt") and "sister-in-law" (but not "brother-in-law") are distinct for male and female ego. More significantly, female consanguines are terminologically homogenized relative to males, or rendered equivalent; hence many women in a residential group address themselves by the same kin term (*aoa*, meaning "sister," "daughter," or "sister's daughter").

This terminological equation reflects the extreme proximity and struc-

tural equivalence of sisters. This is one result of uxorilocality and sororal polygyny, and it gives rise to a sense that the children of sisters are in
some ways more closely related than the children of brothers.[5] Urarina
men tend to claim that uxorilocal residence is common "because the girl's
father wants his son-in-law by his side," but I suspect that one of the key
reasons is that the women themselves want and demand it. Unmarried
females travel infrequently and have relatively little experience of places
beyond their local community; most have never lived away from their
mothers and sisters, and many would reject a marriage if it required them
to do so.[6] Sororal polygyny, which is relatively widespread, is similarly
very often initiated by the second, usually younger sister.

This general principle receives spatial expression, especially during public gatherings. Women tend to sit closely together in tight-knit
groups, often in a single corner of the room or against the back wall,
while men place much greater distance between themselves and therefore
occupy a far greater area. Women of all ages are often addressed simply
as *ene*, or woman, while adult males (unlike boys) would rarely, if ever,
be addressed as *quicha* (man). Female personal names, in both Urarina
and Spanish, also tend to be more homogenous and repetitive, selected
from a smaller stock. This is vastly exaggerated in the case of the latter: while the variety of male names is great, many women seemed to be
called either Rosa or Maria—epitomizing the limits of female individuation, especially in relation to relative outsiders.

Generally speaking, women appeared to me to be more outwardly
conservative or "traditional" than men, more reluctant to learn new techniques, to try out new foods or activities, or to diversify their practices.
They seemed much more likely than men to be skeptical of a new way
of doing something, such as healing the ill using Western medicines or
immunizing their children with vaccinations. Conversely, men appeared
not only more open to such novelties but also much more likely to seek
ways of enhancing their power or ability relative to their peers, in areas
such hunting, spear fishing, healing, flute playing, and the arts of magic
and mystical attack. Men distinguish themselves as leaders by perfect-
ing their oratorical abilities, as well as techniques of diplomacy and dispute resolution. Such knowledge is often inculcated through voluntary
subjection to strict dietary and other disciplinary regimes, which typically require a man to reside in virtual isolation for an extended period,
thereby extricating himself from the countervailing, feminine arts of
feeding and nurture that insistently unify and homogenize the residential group.

This broad, gendered contrast is inscribed into that most salient sociological site, the body. All Urarina women today dress identically, in a highly conventionalized "traditional" fashion: black or navy blue skirt; red blouse; blue bead bracelets; and necklace, also consisting of rows of glass beads threaded on chambira twine. These beads are primarily blue, often with some yellow added, but always with the blue bands grouped together below the yellow bands. All women wear their hair long and loose, in the same style. The overall effect of this body ornamentation is to render all women broadly similar in appearance.

Men, in contrast, wear "Western"-style clothes. Bermuda shorts and short-sleeved shirts are the most common apparel, but many men also occasionally wear trousers, T-shirts, and footwear such as flip-flops or sneakers, all in various colors. Accessories such as caps and especially watches are highly sought after. Men, and only men, increasingly purchase items from traders that enhance their differentiation from their peers. Watches are among the more conspicuous of these; prestige items such as shotguns, radios, or outboard motors—all owned exclusively by men—have much the same effect. Indeed, because only men liaise with the outside world they are more susceptible to the increased avenues for social differentiation it offers.[7]

Such gendered techniques of the body give a dramatic physical expression and salience to subtle but already extant bodily as well as cultural and linguistic differences arising from men's divergent places of origin. The distribution of symbolic or language-based forms of knowledge in particular, such as myths, chants, and oral history accounts, is quite often subject to regional variation, and I found that men from different tributaries were more prone to disagree over matters of history or cosmology. It could of course be countered that such forms of knowledge are by their nature individualistic or subject to free variation, but their relative mastery by or association with men rather than women only strengthens the general argument. Ultimately, as Rival (2005) has argued for the Huaorani, uxorilocality should be understood in part as a political strategy for domesticating and embedding men in the relative safety of matrifocal house groups. From the point of view of the men concerned, however, this is very much a double-edged process.

TWO FACES OF BRIDESERVICE

The term *lauri*, or group, has a range of possible referents depending on context and may be used to refer to virtually any agglomeration of entities, be they human or nonhuman, perceived to share some form of set membership.[8] In daily life the term is most often used to designate a group of coresidents, or deme, generally united around a single man of influence or renown. The composition of such groups may be fluid and variable, strongly affected by mobility patterns, their boundaries always open to interpretation. They are generally most visible for the duration of certain shared tasks or activities, which mobilize the entire group and separate them from a backdrop of wider kin networks. For this reason, to avoid confusion I will henceforth refer to lauri as solidarity groups.[9]

Members of a solidarity group are called *laurijera*, literally, "group-fellow," although the term was often translated into Spanish as "neighbor" (*vecino*), indicating the importance placed on coresidence, or mutual proximity. This is a mode of relationship that is more encompassing, and less intense or intimate, than the corijera, or shadow-soul-fellow. Both forms similarly transcend kinship, though there is greater scope for asymmetry in the former. In contrast to the arai, or bilateral kindred, the lauri does not rely on notions of blood-relatedness or the sharing of physical substance. However, it often overlaps with or centers on the productive alliance formed between a father-in-law and a son-in-law, a relationship as important as it is fraught. Given that postmarital residence is uxorilocal and the only marriage rule presently operative is a prohibition on marrying close kin (a category that generally includes genealogical cousins), the majority of in-marrying men arrive as relative outsiders, if not quite as total strangers, when they take up residence with the new host family. The period of brideservice is variable but typically lasts until the young couple have borne two or three children of their own, by which time they have established themselves as an independent family whose needs increasingly require the husband's full and dedicated labor power.[10]

The relationship between a son-in-law and a father-in-law is characterized first and foremost by mutual respect (figure 8). Lorenzo told me, "I never joke with my father-in-law, even though he can joke with me. This is because I must respect him. I can't ever get angry at him either. I always have to answer him peacefully and properly." Politeness is expressed linguistically using the enclitic /–che/, which is also the plural marker for second person. Indicating a degree of deference and respect, this honorific is used reciprocally, and also between women and men who are not related through marriage or filiation.[11] Women never use the marker /-che/ with other women, even mothers-in-law—a further gender asymmetry that highlights the greater potential tension underwriting male affinal relations and their greater potential for differentiation.[12]

Figure 8. A son-in-law carries building materials for his father-in-law.
Photograph by author.

Lorenzo went on to describe his ongoing (i.e., postbrideservice) obligations to his father-in-law in terms of mutual support, especially material
support in the form of trade goods. This support should ideally be offered
voluntarily, out of respect and goodwill, and certainly not through any
form of coercion. A son-in-law is supposed to care for (beraiha) his father-
in-law, a concept closely related to love and the giving of gifts (both
belaiha) and to high sociability, especially visiting (bedainiha). This in
turn should be reciprocated, and indeed on the surface at least the relationship often seems to work along such lines. One young man told me,
"I work for my father-in-law and we have no problems. He always gives
me meat when he kills something. That's why it was easy moving here
after I married."

The story of Moon's son-in-law offers a neat illustration of this general
idea. The myth, which I will briefly summarize, is clearly a commentary
on the nature of brideservice, and a few key themes are readily discerned.
Moon is a gluttonous father-in-law with a propensity to get into fights,
especially with the celestial jaguar, whose decisive victory would trigger
the apocalyptic collapse of the world or climate (an event discussed fur-

ther in the next chapter). Moon's well-being is secured by his son-in-law, the morning star, who circles around him and whose role is conceived above all in terms of "defense" (*coaaeratiha*, lit., "to give strength"). Yet while it is thanks to his son-in-law that Moon is still persisting and the world has not come to an end, at the same time his fearful and timid nature means he is unfortunately unable to dispatch once and for all his father-in-law's aggressor.

In short, the story directs attention to a pervasive ambivalence surrounding brideservice, whereby a smooth veneer of politeness and respect masks an underlying tension and anxiety, effectively stemming from its excessively asymmetrical structure. The position of sons-in-law is generally considered one of relative vulnerability, for they are largely at the whim and mercy of their fathers-in-law. For example, the relationship between Buchilote and his father-in-law, Fernando, was fraught with a tension that was greatly exacerbated whenever the two had been drinking. Fernando would often violently threaten Buchilote; the latter, unwilling or unable directly to confront his father-in-law in such situations, would periodically retreat downriver for a period of time, sometimes a matter of weeks, until tempers cooled. Buchilote eventually took his wife and two small children to another community, to live with his father, before finally starting his own independent settlement.

Another myth, the story of Lucucoiri, takes this structural vulnerability and latent hostility to an extreme. Lucucoiri was a man famous for killing off his sons-in-law, one by one, until finally he was defeated by a wily son-in-law who turned out to be a powerful shaman (*benane*). As Bolon put it to me, "Long ago, when the ancients had their sons-in-law, it was as though they were raising chickens when there are many foxes around: sometimes you just can't produce many. Just like that, they killed their sons-in-law. They used to say it was the enemies [*bacauha*], but it was them, really."

From one perspective, brideservice is premised on mutual respect, love, and care; from another, it approaches a predatory relationship in which the threat of violence is ever present. These quite different takes on the value of brideservice implicate the different structural positions of women and men, as well as men of different generations. Affinal relationships are considered particularly important in Amazonia because they bridge the divide between the "inside" and the "outside" of the local group: they are the paradigmatic relationship with the Other (Viveiros de Castro 2001: 23). In the case of the Urarina, however, it is the (cross-generational) relationship between father-in-law and son-in-law, rather than the (same-generational) relationship between two brothers-in-law, that is of greatest significance. This may be because it is far less readily masked or neutralized by consanguinity: men rarely if ever make ritual co-fathers with their fathers-in-law, because doing so would require a mother to act as midwife for her own daughter, something widely denounced as unsatisfactory. The father-in-law and son-in-law remain maximally "different" from each other, structurally speaking, which is precisely what makes the relationship so important and fraught.

No doubt due largely to this latent tension between male cross-generation affines, the relationship between father and son is particularly highly valued. In fact, many solidarity groups (lauri) involve a father and son working together. Manuel once told me, "You know, my first three children were all girls. When my wife gave birth to a son, I was truly happy. You see, sometimes fathers want to have sons more than daughters, because the son will accompany him; he will help him with his work." "What about sons-in-law?" I asked. "No, it's not the same with a son-in-law. It just doesn't conform." The importance of father-son companionship in establishing spaces of mutual support and "defense" also receives ample expression in myth. The story of Our Creator's Envoy, for example, tells how Adam offers his food to the people while reassuring them that his own father will "defend" him (cocoaaeratiha). In short, the affinal relationship underpinning brideservice approximates but never fully achieves the ideals of mutual trust and protection typical of other dyadic companionships, where real proximity is more readily achieved. Brideservice nevertheless remains one of the more significant factors conditioning residence and mobility patterns today, and the key principle for the formation of solidarity groups. Yet all these have been substantially altered in the past couple of decades following the introduction into Peruvian legislation, and subsequent adoption by all native peoples, of the new "model" for native settlements, the Comunidad Nativa. Bringing people together in ever greater numbers, these present new challenges as well as opportunities, not least in terms of new forms of subjectivity and new ways of relating to power.

TRUNKS OF THE NATIVE COMMUNITY

On the morning of September 11, 2006, after much informal discussion and amid rising tensions, a communal meeting finally took place in Nueva Unión. Having tried but failed to lure people over to the empty school the previous day, Lorenzo's authority as the incumbent lieutenant governor was beginning to waver, and many were growing weary of his obsessive quest for vengeance and the demands this was placing on local resources. At the top of the agenda was the latest scandal involving his brother Roberto, who had recently struck a deal to let commercial loggers into the area and, worse still, had managed to procure a government-funded mestizo teacher for the tiny school in his new, breakaway community just a few minutes downstream. The well-being of the children caught in the middle of the animosity seemed insignificant compared to the widespread feelings of outrage and betrayal that Roberto's renegade community should receive official recognition and a claim to legitimacy. As the Nueva Unión land title document had vexingly wound up in Roberto's possession, there was, according to Lorenzo, an urgent need for drastic intervention by higher authorities. Hence his proposed appeal to the Urarina justice of the peace, who lived several days downriver, and possibly even to the mestizo authorities in the municipal offices in the town of Maipuco. Though everyone in the community was in agreement in principle, the lengthy journey would require "collaboration," namely, forest products that could be exchanged for gasoline, food, and strategic gifts for the relevant authorities. Although some people were clearly less than thrilled at the prospect of spending yet more time and energy on this uphill battle, mild foot-dragging seemed wiser than open dissent.

Relieved that the meeting was at last taking place and apparently undeterred by the flagging enthusiasm, Lorenzo opened with a lengthy tirade on the "Roberto problem," in which he staked out their collective right to a fair and just decision, and the pressing need to "cooperate" and "coordinate among neighbors." As he spoke, Gilberto the schoolteacher diligently kept notes in the official minute book (*libro de actas*), which would be taken along as proof of their collective resolution. Both were dressed in their finest clothes, the only people present wearing shoes. Eventually it was time for the other community authorities to speak their turn. Samuel, the communal chief (*jefe comunal*), forcefully voiced his agreement with Lorenzo's mission. Gilberto held forth on the need for a peaceful, civilized, and progressive resolution, addressing people mostly in formal Spanish, as though to underscore his message. Finally, Lorenzo's brother Ernesto, president of the Parent Teacher Association (Asociación de Padres de Familia), spoke of the importance of formal education and the need to maintain the school and replenish its resources—notebooks, pencils, fresh paint, and the like, singling me out as a likely "collaborator." Lorenzo concluded the meeting by reiterating at some length, mostly to murmurs of agreement, that the peaceful progress of the children was best ensured if everyone cooperated. The deal now in place, Gilberto dutifully recorded the names of those present in the minute book and stamped it with his personal seal, before taking each man's forefinger and pressing it into the inkpad and then down beside the man's name and finally indicating where he should do the same with his wife's forefinger. Two days later, minute book and modest provisions in hand, Lorenzo, Ernesto, and Samuel set out on their long journey.

Meetings such as these exemplify some of the challenges posed by formal land tenure and new models of social organization and the emerging forms of authority with which these are associated. The strong aversion to any public discord means that communal meetings can formalize an existing consensus but rarely build one from scratch; this is the task of private, informal discussions. Getting people to attend is the greatest challenge and requires a charismatic and persuasive leader. The typical Native Community comprises a loose and imperfect amalgamation of smaller solidarity groups, often centering on a senior father-in-law, alliances between which are extremely unstable and simmering with latent tensions. The traditional chief *(curaanaa)* was a man of renown who exerted loose influence over several smaller groups and is now effectively assimilated to the more formal and ostensibly elected role of communal chief. The latter now typically shares power in a more or less ad hoc manner with the lieutenant governor, also nominally elected, who is the official representative of the Peruvian government.

Most of the characteristics traditionally esteemed in leaders are still valued today, such as oratorical skills and the ability to lead by example rather than by exhortation. New-style leaders are also expected to be knowledgeable, particularly in relation to dealings with outsiders of all kinds, although the focus of this knowledge is gradually shifting away from nonhumans and toward mestizos or Peruvians, reflecting the same secularization of authority hinted at earlier in relation to personal names. As such, the schoolteacher—comparatively well educated and more or less fluent in Spanish—is an increasingly important political player and often holds forth on the values and comportments appropriate to "civilized" life. I often heard him exhort people to be more gracious in defeat at intercommunity football tournaments, for example, and not just returning home in a rage; or to "not be embarrassed like our grandparents were" at the drinking parties that follow, dancing proudly rather than sitting silently among their neighbors and friends. Although illiterate himself, Lorenzo took pride in his collection of official documents of various kinds and sometimes asked me to read aloud from a hefty treatise on human

rights and Peru's native peoples. When I asked him about his role as lieutenant governor, he replied as follows:

> Together with the communal chief, I work properly, I stay watchful
> and vigilant, caring for the inhabitants. I set a good example, so that
> when I die, the others can continue working well. The community is
> struggling to grow because people don't want to stay here—they want
> to move around, for whatever reason. But if the folk here pay atten-
> tion to me, if they understand me, then they'll get everything that
> they're lacking as a community. I'm like the trunk of this community,
> the base. I help it to grow.

Lorenzo's claim to being vigilant and watching over his "people" echoes
widespread notions of Our Creator watching over humanity, as well as
the advice-giving spiritual caretakers of animals, discussed further in
the next chapter. It also conveys an abiding sense of power as generative
rather than coercive; as the "trunk" of the community, Lorenzo helps it to
grow both morally and physically. First, the "power" of political leaders is
sometimes referred to as *nunujui*, meaning loosely support or reinforce-
ment, analogous to a wooden pole propping up a leaning plantain tree
(fanara nunera). This clearly in turn evokes notions of companionship as
a kind of standing-leaned-together. Second, Lorenzo was confident that
if I could help him to obtain his national identity card he could prepare
much more persuasive written requests *(solicitudes)* for assistance from
regional governmental authorities, channeling more resources to the
community and thereby enticing more people. Indeed, Lorenzo prided
himself on his mastery of the art of solicitation and explained to me his
strategy: "You ask for ten gallons of gasoline, they give you five gallons.
You ask for twenty gallons, they give you two. I once asked for forty writing desks for the school and received twenty. Now I'm going to ask for
another twenty, in order to receive ten more."

  To reiterate, the generative capacity of the lieutenant governor and
other new-style leaders implies an ability to persuade and thereby har-
ness the power of higher authorities, in order to appropriate or transmit tangible resources. The duty of care invoked here in turn becomes
a feature of their own relations to residents. This requires knowledge,
experience, and an arsenal of appropriate paraphernalia to ensure one's
recognition by the state, including bond paper, national identity cards,
and personal rubber stamps bearing an official title. Yet this channeling
of higher power also has a more intangible dimension, as embodied in
Lorenzo's concept of the law *(ley)* and its disciplinary force:

The lieutenant governor should have knowledge of the law. He is the continuation of state politics. The government puts people in charge, like the communal chief, he is put in charge by the President of the Republic. Forty years ago, there was law for only the mestizos, there was no law for the Urarina. That's why the mestizos treated us so badly. Now the law doesn't distinguish—it treats Urarina and mestizo equally, woman or man. That's why the mestizos are also afraid of the law. Now, the law itself can punish. The law is for respecting, for working, in order that nothing [bad] happens, with this law that the government gave us.

If this concept of the law approximates an abstract force, it is one that must be wielded by a knowledgeable leader to promote local group unity and obedience. As the local delegate of state power—"the continuation of state politics"—the lieutenant governor has unique recourse to corporeal punishment in order to resolve disputes and maintain order. A capacity previously held only by parents in relation to their children, this marks a radical shift in people's relationship to power, which is traditionally devoid of coercive force. Solitary confinement for a number of hours in the communal cell—a small, makeshift wooden enclosure just large enough for a grown man to sit in—is a common, and greatly feared, punishment for slander, theft, infidelity, or failure to participate in community maintenance works.[13] This newly instituted ability to resolve local disputes, backed by the threat of punishment where necessary, doubtless helps to promote cohesion by preventing the immediate departure of injured parties. At the same time, it is working to forge a new kind of political subject, one directly answerable to the full force of the law. It is difficult to say whether this disciplinary apparatus is promoting the inculcation of new forms of moral conscience in the sense described by Nietzsche (1956 [1887]), for whom the threat of punishment redirected instinctive aggression inward and toward the self, assuming the form of guilt or "bad conscience." It nevertheless represents the same realignment of personal identity given concrete expression in the Spanish name, whose objectification in the form of identity documents assures recognition and a range of new capacities founded in one's subjection to power.

Through a fine balance of encouragement and punishment, local leaders clearly do much to hold the Native Community together, redefining individuals as *comuneros* with equal obligations to an abstract collectivity, no longer bound together by kinship or close affective ties, and as Peruvian citizens answerable to the state and its legal apparatuses. Yet

individual sentiments and affective bonds remain of paramount importance, because people can always vote with their feet and leave the community, and even establish an independent settlement if they so desire—
though today still on land belonging to and therefore under the official
jurisdiction of one or other Native Community. In the remainder of this
chapter, I turn to the role of drinking parties in establishing these affective bonds, rounding out the discussion of how solidarity is engendered
in local groups and in relation to forms of power capable of reconfiguring
personal identities. Drunkenness brings people together in various ways,
to be sure, but also constitutes a distinctive and inherently shared form
of subjectivity.

THE ART OF INEBRIETY

Eejeen! I looked up blearily at the woman standing in front of me with
arm outstretched, head turned away, waiting for me to take the enormous gourd full of manioc beer. She looked tired, and her red blouse was
streaked with white dregs. The last thing I felt like doing was drinking
more beer, but refusing it is impolite, so with both hands I held the gourd
up to my mouth and took a few sips. The potent, bitter taste of alcohol sent
a shudder down my spine. The beer was creamy and strong, still slightly
frothy from the fermentation process. My stomach was now so bloated I
had to sit leaning backward, resting on my palms. "Are you drunk yet?"
asked Luis, his eyes barely able to focus. Looking around at my drinking
companions, I realized many were in even worse shape than I: there was
Rebasi, sitting motionless and staring vacantly into the middle distance;
there was Doinita, snoozing soundly in the middle of the floor wearing
his rubber gumboots. Several women sat in the far corner, talking among
themselves. Our supply of batteries for Balera's radio being long since
exhausted, no one was dancing. Instead, Antonio was playing his bamboo flute, while Carapa dreamily accompanied him on a makeshift drum.
They seemed to be improvising, although I thought I could detect faint
traces of a familiar melody. Damian, our host, was nowhere in sight. Just
as I was wondering whether he hadn't snuck away to eat something, he
suddenly reappeared in our midst, dramatically transformed: he was now
dressed in clean, dark trousers and a brand new checkered shirt, but-
toned right up to the top, which still had crisp crease marks from being
folded around cardboard in its plastic packet. His hair was combed and
slicked back with water; only his bare feet undermined the cogency of
this new look. I suddenly felt like Paul Newman's "Fast" Eddie Felson

in a scene from *The Hustler*, devastated by Minnesota Fats's reappearance in immaculate three-piece suit with rose in the lapel after their all-night session of pool, gambling, and whiskey. Yet it was not psychological defeat that Damian sought; his was a genuinely chiefly determination to lead by example: far from winding down, his attire proclaimed loudly, the party was now entering a new phase of even greater drunkenness.

Drinking manioc beer is inherently both a deeply personal and a highly social activity, the importance of which cannot be overestimated. My willingness to get drunk with people may not have helped my ability to accurately recall the events of more than a few drinking parties but certainly did much to smooth my integration into the community, distinguishing me from other, more "uppity" mestizo visitors. Manioc beer drinking does not take place on a daily basis; on most days banana drink is sufficient to slake a man's thirst and fill his belly after returning home from work. Beer is produced sporadically but in prodigious quantities, and when people drink it their aim is to get drunk; generally speaking, the drunker, the better. Because the beer is very filling people can drink for long periods without feeling hungry. As a psychosomatic state, beer drunkenness has a number of connotations for people, most of which are positive. The most important of these is psychedelic trance, which is often referred to by the same term, *aje*, and not considered a different kind of experience. Any man who goes on a journey, from an overnight hunting trip to a three-week expedition to Iquitos, will expect a generous supply of manioc beer on his return; this is part of his resocialization and a reassertion of his rightful place at home among peers. Beer carries a strong sense of homemaking, a process that ideally extends to include as many others as possible.

Attending a drinking party requires considerable stamina. Yet what is considered most important is not the ability to consume large quantities of beer but to "help" the owner and host by remaining physically present until all the beer is finished. A person incapable of staying awake is expected simply to nap on the floor until he sobers up enough to start drinking again. An invitation to drink beer carries with it a strong sense of obligation, and refusal is severely sanctioned; it takes priority over virtually all other duties. When I first arrived in San Pedro the people had been working hard for many weeks extracting timber. When the logs were finally in the water, waiting to be floated downstream to where they could be sold, several of the women began making manioc beer. Several days of heavy drinking ensued, while the logs sat quietly forgotten in their streams upriver. By the time they finally arrived at the agreed collection point downstream, they had been so long in the water they had

Figure 9.   A woman boils manioc to make beer. Photograph by author.

started to rot. The price they fetched was revised accordingly, leaving people with barely enough to cover the debts incurred over three months' worth of work. When I queried some of the men about this they replied resignedly, "What could I do? My wife kept making manioc beer!" (figure 9). Although the motivations of the women remain unclear, my suspicion is that it had something to do with reasserting a common human sociality after so long working in remote dispersed locations deep in the forest.

Manioc beer carries a heavy moral load, being central to notions of how to live well, "peacefully and contentedly" *(raotojoeein)*, as real people. The apparent excess of moralizing discourse counterbalances the increased tolerance for conflict that drunkenness induces, as well as an ambivalence concerning the illicit affairs that many drinking parties occasion. Almost all the many drinking parties I attended descended at least once into very heated arguments and occasionally into physical violence. All too aware of the ability of alcohol to reduce inhibitions as well as the shame or embarrassment that controls many interactions, allowing long-submerged tensions to burst forth into the open, people explicitly condemn inappropriate drunken behavior and if necessary will stage a communal meeting the following day, when everyone is sober, in order to punish the worst offenders. During one party, while we were both watching, with a mixture of interest and dismay, a particularly heated fight involving two brothers-in-law, Jorge told me, "It's no good doing that while drunk, manioc beer isn't for that. When they sober up, they're going to be very embarrassed. They shouldn't get into their own problems when they're half-drunk. Each side should respect the other. Manioc beer is for having fun together, and for dancing!"

Music and dance are integral to creating the desired celebratory atmosphere in which people can truly enjoy getting drunk and help to promote shared emotional states and a feeling of group unity.During my fieldwork a number of people had portable cassette players, and *cumbia*, a genre of Peruvian popular music, was the preferred music for dancing. As the supply of batteries was erratic, however, and their life spans all too brief in relation to the prolonged drinking sessions, the recorded music would usually be replaced after a while by that of the bamboo flute *(auno)* and drum *(toonto)*.[14] When sufficiently inebriated, women traditionally sang songs, sometimes associated with well-known mythical narratives, while the men accompanied them. The following example implores people to "love life" by getting drunk and dancing together.

canuichane ajeiton	I'm so drunk
dojiara coaae caan	On the power of manioc beer
ichorojoe coaae caan	On the power of manioc beer
canuichene ajeiton ajeiriton	I'm so very drunk
chajao te necoatijiacache	Come on, let's all dance!
canuichane ajeiriton	I'm so drunk
cana ichao	Our life
belaiuriaca cana ichao	Let's all love our life
chajao te necoatijiaoriacache	Come on, let's dance
cana ichao belaiuriacache	Let's all love our life
ichorojoe baca caan	On the juice of manioc beer
canuichane ajeiton	I'm so drunk
ichorojoe baca caan	On the juice of manioc beer

It is this kind of atmosphere that makes drinking parties the ideal occasions for performing baptism ceremonies. In addition to inaugurating the child into the distinctly human form of sociality proper to manioc beer consumption (reflected in the use of a manioc leaf for splashing water on the child), this has the explicit aim of turning outsiders, in particular, male affines, into ritual co-parents. These are joyful occasions, valued by all. When I asked Lorenzo why baptisms always took place during drinking parties, he replied, "It's so the people can dance with enthusiasm!"

The production of ritual co-parents formalizes the process already taking place informally, as it were, through beer consumption: forging and consolidating affective ties between same-sex affines. Involving a third party in this process effectively piggybacks baptism and its social significance onto the act of cutting the umbilical cord as a process for consolidating social groups around the production of individuals. Yet not all drinking songs are concerned with the ritual co-parent relation. Although seducing men is not an explicit goal of most songs,[15] a great many are addressed to paramours, or otherwise concerned with the highs and lows of romantic, extramarital liaisons. For a number of reasons, paramours are also intimately associated with drinking parties, despite the ambivalence of their moral status.

A SECRET LOVE

When people are drunk they become forgetful, and the reserve, respect, and especially shame that usually characterize interactions with others—especially members of the opposite sex—are diminished. This is of course a large part of what allows people to have a good time. Interactions between the sexes are normally subject to heavy restrictions and taboos, and a drinking party offers an unrivaled opportunity for men and women to congregate in common social activity and relax some of the usual norms of propriety. As such, drinking parties also offer an unparalleled opportunity for pursuing illicit and extramarital affairs. Whenever I commented that the women were sometimes too shy or ashamed to talk to me, I was invariably advised to wait until they are drunk, because this is the time their shame is overcome, eclipsed by sexual desire. When drunk a person's ability to refuse the requests or advances of another is said to be greatly diminished. This is one reason alcohol is considered by many to be a crucial ingredient for requesting potential parents-in-law for a girl's hand in marriage.

A great many women and men carry out illicit affairs, with varying degrees of discretion. A paramour, or amujera, is literally a "walking companion" (or walking fellow), in the sense of "going around for fun together." Paramours thus participate in the constellation of "fellowships" that includes sinijera (sleeping fellow), corijera (shadow-soul-fellow) and laurijera (group fellow). *Amuha cuha*, "to go walking" or "to go wandering around," is commonly used to mean "to go hunting," and amujera is similarly euphemistic. The relationships encompassed range from short flings to deep, loving partnerships that last for many years. Paramours are often involved in the most intense affective bonds, and the feelings of nostalgia and longing with which they are associated belong to an entirely different register from conjugality. It is a form of companionship oriented less to production than to the satiation of sexual appetites left unfulfilled by a spouse. The highs and lows of illicit affairs are the subject of many drinking songs, which may be voiced during drinking parties or their melodies simply intoned on a bamboo flute. The following "lover's lament" *(namujera coisichuruana)* tells of lovers pledging their hearts to each other in the face of painful separation.

ca suujua tocoaneein caoatohi	In my heart you are beautiful
canu suujua tocoaneein caoatohi natiin te	In my heart you are really so beautiful
ijiaoera rijijieen naaojoaa	Yet it would seem we are separating
chaelo bana niheh ii baitichanu	I shall at no moment forget you
baitena que aina rijijieen	Like the forgotten ones
nii baitijiauni	I will not forget you
iichoaetichaun ne que aiya rijijieein	It seems as though I leave you behind
nii caatihatacaain	I shall wait in remembrance of you
ta baitirihei ne	You will not forget me either
itacatihatacaain te	We will each wait in remembrance of the other
itajerichaan	And we will love each other

The kind of love treated in the song, itajeriha (to each want the other) is predicated above all on mutual desire. Although this form of deep affection ideally precedes a marriage, it remains conceptually quite distinct from the love enacted between spouses (and close kin), belaiha, which as noted is embodied above all in acts of unconditional giving and which despite being at least as intensely felt has relatively little to do with sexual desire. Separation from a lover similarly provokes an anguish that seems out of keeping with the way people speak about their spouses when separated.

For some women pursuing an illicit affair can have additional, material rewards. Despite their extreme shyness in public, some men confided to me that certain women can be quite forthright, albeit discreet, when it comes to pursuing a lover. Often just a couple of words exchanged in private, or even a knowing look, is enough to communicate the right intention. Men are avowedly helpless to resist such overtures, even when they claim to have little to gain by responding to them. "What could I do?"

asked Jorge rhetorically after telling me of Rosa's discreet request for a length of cloth, payment for which she offered to "discuss in private." "She herself came to seek me out, so I couldn't say no . . . a man is a man." A length of cloth was the going rate for such a transaction, and yet many people did not consider material gain a woman's primary motivation. Jorge immediately connected Rosa's approach to her own husband's suspected recent lechery, which he had recently unearthed, and hence to her understandable desire for revenge.

Despite the prevailing emphasis on erotic love and the satisfaction of sexual desire, the paramour relationship should be understood in the wider cultural context of partible paternity. Any man who has sexual relations with a woman can potentially contribute to the formation of a fetus and hence become a biological co-father. Unlike ritual co-parenthood, there is no formal social or institutional recognition of biological co-parenthood. Yet even though a biological co-father bears no special responsibilities or duties toward his child, this is not a particularly important part of ritual co-parenthood either. Adulterous relationships undeniably play an important role in social cohesion, constituting an additional, if publicly unacknowledged, mode of alliance between residential groups and an incentive to stay in relative close proximity.[16] Yet it must be recognized that the affective dimension stems not merely from sexual intimacy but also from the same kind of joint participation in the reproduction of individual persons that characterize other forms of "extra-kin" ties.

Despite its ubiquity, licentiousness is publicly disparaged and occasionally denounced as immoral. This is evidenced by the assertion that a man who is unfaithful to his wife is unable to cure effectively with psychotropics. An adulterer is denigrated as "without shame," that is, unable to register an appropriate degree of embarrassment or shame in interactions with the opposite sex. In a sense, then, adultery is an extreme consequence of the reduction of "shame" that is the desired outcome of all beer drunkenness. Infidelities can ignite bitter feuds if they become public, sometimes requiring formal, public mediation by the lieutenant governor, who may, after canvassing public opinion, decide on an appropriate punishment or compensation to be paid to the injured party. Between the spouses themselves, while infidelity is not openly condoned, I suspect that a blind eye is often turned; only if some form of public acknowledgment is required by the aggrieved party does it become a serious issue requiring some action to be taken. In any case, it rarely if ever results in the dissolution of the marriage.

A GLANCE BEYOND THE HUMAN

After very protracted periods of drinking and dancing—parties can last for two days or more—a new form of drunkenness begins to descend, notable for its extremity. On such occasions men sometimes feel inclined to intone a genre of ritualized chanting known as *jichorojoe baauno*, "force of manioc beer chant." These are quite different from the drinking songs discussed above, and in fact more closely resemble the *coaairi baauno*, or psychotropic chants, discussed in the next chapter. They emphasize the speaker's extreme drunkenness, as well as the need for all to drink in the correct, jubilant manner as an integral aspect of intergenerational continuity. They look beyond the here and now, as it were, and back toward the ancestors, as well as "outward" to more otherworldly or nonhuman forms of sociality. In fact, by the time a man has become so drunk that he decides to intone the jichorojoe baauno, I would suggest, he is no longer firmly situated in the human domain. Forgetting those around him, he has begun a process of identification with nonhuman others. One version, sung for me by Antonio in an authentically drunken state, ran roughly as follows:

najeein najeeinte	Doing it like this
nedojiaure inara joerateeurera	Your forefathers would get drunk on beer
aihutera	Oh yes indeed
necoatijiacara	Let's dance!
najeeinte chuisi	Really doing it like this
nedojiaurera joerateurera	[Your] forefathers would get drunk on beer
aihutera aihutera	Yes indeed
najeeinra necoatijiacara	Let's dance like this
cana ichao beelaihalajiacara	While we are gifted with life
najeein najeeinte neeurera	Doing it like this they existed
inara rai joerateeurera	Your forefathers who raised you
najeeinra najeeintechuisi	Really doing it like this
nenejeurelura	They existed long ago
coara coarai ichorojoera	Look, look, power of manioc beer
jichorojoei jichorojoe neein	Being the power of manioc beer
caa tabaa enua ne corerania nena	That which is the transform of this giant tree
baqui ne quetera	Made with sweet potato
tijia asajae nia inaate	Underfoot there is fruit
nenacaain caara jichorojoe	There is this power of manioc beer
caara ichorojoe ne	This power of manioc beer
najeein najeeinte chuisi	Really doing it like this

neneurelu inara coitucueracuru	Your forefathers who knew you existed long ago
inara ne nejoerate ne	Your forefathers who raised you
caara coaairi neleru nia chuisi	It has a little of the power of psychotropics
beuruachu eneuneen coitecureracuru	Those who knew how to get drunk would advise
najaneein	Doing it like this
nia cana ichorojoe	There is power of beer for us
nenacaen netaora caa ichorojoe ne	More power of manioc beer thus
caara rai ichorojoe	Power of manioc beer for us
coara coara coara coara	Look! Look! Look! Look!
ajeeinii u u u	I am so drunk . . . oh . . . oh . . .
coara coara coara coara	Look! Look! Look! Look!
caa baquine que tijia asaje	With this sweet potato underfoot
caara ichorojoe	Our power of manioc beer

When Lorenzo later heard this recording, he commented, "That's how the ancients were, those who really knew manioc beer, they would get drunk as though with ayahuasca, with visions and everything. That's how we get drunk too. The ancients really knew [how to do it], and we are replacing them. As the manioc beer is mixed with sweet potato, it ferments. That's why the two sing together."

A distinctive feature of the jichorojoe baauno is that it appears to be articulated from two alternating perspectives, that of the drinker and that of the power of manioc beer itself. I had the impression that this duality or companionship mirrors that between manioc and sweet potato, which is why Lorenzo said that "the two sing together." The fermentation process is called *coaeraa*, which has the literal meaning "to become strong" but where the prototypical meaning of *coaae*, "strength," is the capacity of psychotropics to inebriate. Although everyone recognizes that manioc beer could not exist without women's labor power (not to mention saliva), it is the jubilant interaction between the two plants, manioc and sweet potato, that is celebrated in these songs as the source of the beer's power. Some versions of the jichorojoe baauno that I recorded referred to manioc as *neba baquii que*, "sweet potato together with its mother." Lorenzo explained, "Yes, manioc is like the mother of sweet potato. Don't you see how it stands taller? It defends like a mother too. Sweet potato is very short, that's why they call it *tijia asajae* [underfoot]." Jorge put the matter a little more simply: "Manioc helps the sweet potato to produce. The sweet potato also helps the manioc." Another song, once sung to me by Rosalia, makes a similar point.

canucha ne ajeton	I'm so drunk
baquii que te baquii que	[Mixed] with sweet potato
canucha ne ajeton	I'm so drunk
dojiaracaan	On the force of manioc beer

The term *dojiara*, "force of manioc beer," is used exclusively while in a drunken state, as is *ichorojoe*, which some took to be synonymous. It derives from *roriha*, the large wooden tray in which the beer is prepared by women, but refers more specifically to the potential of manioc beer to induce a state of drunkenness. For this reason, there are also connotations of abundance. As Jorge told me, "The people say *dojiara* when there are heaps of manioc beer already mixed, as for a *minga* or a drinking party. When there's only one or two buckets' worth, they just say *barue*."

The power of manioc beer is personified as a young girl, known as *jichorojoe coranuna*, "maiden daughter of the force of manioc beer." The relationship is again asymmetrical, in that the power of the beer thoroughly "exceeds" *(amuritoha)* the drinker, who consequently needs to be "taken" or "carried" *(amaa)*. Lorenzo explained thus: "The power of the manioc beer looks at us, and doing so it inebriates us. When you're very drunk, you feel very small, you can't even walk. That's because it has overcome us. That's why they say *camaa*, 'carry me.'" The altered state of consciousness, or transformation of subjectivity, brought about by manioc beer is construed as the outcome of an asymmetrical relationship, an intimate encounter with another being. I want to argue that this is not qualitatively different from how "normal" or everyday subjectivity is conceptualized and as such stands to reveal much about the latter. To begin with, there is an essential condition of asymmetry: the beer's power to "look at" the drinker and "exceed" him is responsible for forging his distinct mode of experience, constituting him as "drunk" in and through his subjection to a higher, nonhuman agency. The "power" or "strength" of the latter, its *coaae*, is conceptualized precisely in terms of this capacity to inebriate and to offer recognition and hence to constitute a certain kind of subject. Although it would be tempting to view drunkenness as a form of intersubjectivity, involving a reciprocal gaze or face-to-face encounter, the connotation of two independent subjects entering into relation fails to capture the important element of mutual dissolubility that seems so central to this sense of lived experience as coexistence. The boundary between the drinker and the beer is always highly porous; the two inhabit each other and "sing together," such that we might say that the drunken subjectivity ultimately belongs to both of them. This is, I would suggest, an extreme or even ideal form of companionship, conceived as a state of mutual transparency or solubility, the inhabiting of one within the other.

The superior power of the beer is also a nurturing, protective power, reminiscent of the "mothering" relationship between manioc itself and sweet potato. This relationship is both reciprocal—"each helps the other"—and asymmetrical—manioc "defends like a mother" and "helps the sweet potato to produce." Indeed, the capacity of the beer to inebriate, its strength or coaae, also manifests as a form of defense, and *coaaeratiha* can mean "to give strength" or "to defend." This clearly recalls the defense of humanity by Our Creator and humanity's existential condition of existing "under his watchful eye." Indeed, the protective and unifying intentions of a leader toward his political constituency draws on a similar array of meanings, even if his gradual transformation of their identity—into civilized comuneros—is less immediate or tangible than the effects of manioc beer.

In his endeavor to forge enduring ties between smaller solidarity groups, already riddled with internal tensions and sometimes themselves on the brink of collapse, the new-style leader seeks to tap into and channel the power of the state and the force of the "law," redefining in the process people's responsibilities and allegiances. This is the ideological context in which Spanish-name baptisms take place; they work to produce modern citizens and echo the secularization of power at the level of the person. I have argued that the source of people's "true" or psychotropic name in the "power" or "value" of psychotropics (*coaairi necaoacha*), and subsequent recognition by divine authority, orients people's understandings of the significance of Spanish names and their similar utility in obtaining recognition by the state—as well as others with resources to give, such as NGOs—albeit at the cost of subjection to the law and its disciplinary apparatuses. The basis of power is changing but not its role in forming subjects.

In the present-day Native Community, corporeal processes of feeding and nurture, along with marriage, childbirth, and the temporary bonds of brideservice, are insufficient to construct any real sense of unity beyond the solidarity group. Even the actions of vigilant local leaders can only momentarily forestall the inexorable process of fission. Yet powerful affective ties are forged in moments of shared drunkenness, when feelings of shame or embarrassment are diminished and people drop their guard and have fun together. The flames of passion and romance are also stirred in these moments, allowing secret liaisons and emotional attachments to develop and even inspiring people to baptize children in order to become ritual co-parents to each other. It is tempting to suggest that the experience of drunkenness is particularly well suited to establishing new kinds of companionship, in part because it is itself conceived as "dual," or intrinsically accompanied. This is a theme developed further in the next chapter, which explores experiences of illness and psychotropic trance, the nature of shamanic or sacred power, and other asymmetrical relationships that extend still further beyond the realm of the human.

6.   Mastering Subjection

That most animals, plants, and a host of other nonhumans are said to have some kind of master, owner, or mother is one of the most ubiquitous features of Amazonian cosmologies. In his classic formulation of Amerindian perspectivism, Viveiros de Castro (1998: 471) mentions these only in passing, suggesting that they appear to function as reified personifications, or "hypostatizations," of the species with they are associated, allowing humans to relate to animals on an intersubjective basis. By insisting that the owner, mother, or master is essentially an abstraction drawn from the capacities of the animal itself, the conceptual distinction between the two entities is elided and the relational dynamic between them obscured. A rapidly growing literature has since emerged that takes this figure seriously as an important window into Amazonian lived worlds, and that seeks to understand the underlying notions of mastery and ownership it encapsulates (e.g. Fausto 2007, 2008; Costa 2010; Brightman 2010; Kohn 2007; Bonilla 2005). In what follows I seek to build on this important literature, while emphasizing that subjectivity turns on an intimate companionship with a higher power in a way that is not easily reconciled with schemas of predation.[1] As detailed in the previous chapters, such companionships are typically pervaded by an ethic of care, grounded in an openness to the other that requires a mix of attentiveness, responsibility, competence, and responsiveness. In this chapter I propose that it is precisely this relational dimension that is epitomized by the "master" figure, who is not an abstraction of the subjectivity of the game animal but a conceptual precondition for its emergence.

Much of the literature on Amazonian animism and perspectivism gives the impression that attitudes toward animals are relatively consistent and homogeneous. Yet how Urarina treat and conceptualize animals is highly context-dependent, and the latter figure as persons only under certain circumstances. I begin in this chapter with an examination of the kind of personhood attributed to game animals in postmythical times, drawing on the conclusions of the preceding chapters where appropriate. After discussing ideas surrounding the "default" owners of animals, which are typically assumed to take the form of a bird, I look at how humans can, in some situations, usurp their position as owners and masters, first through widespread practices of pet keeping and second through certain relatively esoteric but nevertheless highly instructive practices directed at the acquisition of shamanic knowledge. This is contextualized in a broader discussion of the shamanic complex and the ontology and eschatology on which it rests.

The discussion of nonhumans is complemented in this chapter by an examination of two extreme or abnormal versions of human subjectivity, those associated with illness and the psychedelic experience. These can be seen as points along a continuum of well-being: whereas illness is marked by vulnerability and an inability to establish proper relations to others, leading to a sense of existential isolation or alienation, psychedelic trance is a state of hyper-well-being founded in a dissolution of individuality that I gloss as "becoming porous," linked to feelings of mutuality and protective, intimate companionship. Like the forms of personhood ascribed to nonhumans, these states thereby help to define "normal" human subjectivity negatively, by mapping out two of its more extreme variants. At the same time, the close correlation of these two states with the relative health or imminent collapse of the wider climate or world-era highlights the connection between personal experience and the broader social and ecological order and the precarious and fragile nature of each.

WHAT KIND OF PERSON IS A GAME ANIMAL?

According to Urarina mythology, most if not all forest-dwelling animals assumed their present form at a decisive moment in the ancestral past, as the result of a dramatic transformational event of speciation. Prior to this, all beings assumed a kind of protohuman form; as Viveiros de Castro (2007) has put it, they were "ontologically indiscernible," or marked by virtual and "intensive" rather than actual and "extensive" difference, albeit often possessing certain distinctive visual or behavioral traits that foreshadowed their subsequent, species-specific mode of existence. Even in those myths ostensibly describing events that took place after this significant moment, animals continue to speak and interact with others in ways that would seem to indicate that their status as "persons" or "subjects," whether human or otherwise, is not in dispute.

The postmythical situation, however, is much more ambiguous. In theory, or at least in the somewhat artificial context of discussions with an anthropologist, the differences between present-day animals and humans are perhaps still not particularly strong. For example, in response to my questions Lorenzo affirmed that animals "have their own families, just like us," and experience a range of emotions, including sadness, happiness, jealousy, and envy. He offered as evidence of animal intelligence the uncanny ability of agoutis to find his garden when it has just begun to produce, to "feed and converse among themselves," and to thwart his best attempts to kill them or scare them away "by blessing [baau] themselves prior to coming, in order that they escape unharmed." Lorenzo insisted that the life or manner (ichao) of animals is essentially "like our own," especially in the sense that "we defend our life, our nature, just like the animals defend theirs—by baau chants," although he conceded that "because they grow up in the forest, it is a little bit different." Many animals are lacking in certain forms of moral sensibility, especially "respect," as evidenced by their treatment of people's gardens and failure to recognize people's rights and privileges as owners.

On the whole, however, most informants seemed hesitant, uncertain, or even downright uncomfortable speaking about animals at this level of abstraction. A far more common form of discourse pertaining to game animals is the hunting story, told again and again by a successful hunter to his peers on returning to the community. The hunter will recount in a matter-of-fact way, with great precision, where he first detected the animal's presence and how he finally succeeded in killing it. People's enthusiasm for hearing such stories seems limitless and unflagging after numerous retellings, as I once experienced firsthand after managing to hit a sloth with one of my own blowpipe darts. Animals are decidedly *not* construed as persons in these stories; or rather, if they are, their personhood—in whatever that might consist—is entirely irrelevant to the unfolding course of events.

Exceptions to this general rule are when animals behave entirely out of character, and these events are more likely to be seen as anomalies heralding impending misfortune. Gustodio once told me an anecdote from his youth, in which he set out hunting in the forest and came across a troop of howler monkeys, one of whom seemed to have her period, like a woman. Another monkey lay down on large branch right in front of him and beckoned to his wife to join him, drawing her attention to their human spectator, and then conspicuously having sex with her. Furious, and sure this was a bad omen, Gustodio shot it with his blowpipe. The monkey fell at his feet, with its legs apart, and continued masturbating. Grabbing a pole, he beat the monkey to death and cut it to pieces. That night his dream confirmed that this was indeed a bad omen, and a short while later his father died. Extraordinary events such as these would not be out of place in the context of a myth or in certain genres of ritual or shamanic discourse. I would suggest that its occurrence in the quotidian context of hunting is what made it a bad omen, for in this context animals are, or should be, "just" animals: food awaiting appropriation by humans, and existing primarily for their potential benefit.

The category of game animals is referred to as cana lenone, literally, "our food." These animals are firmly distinguished from the class known as taebinaae, or savages, whose prototype is the jaguar but which also includes river otters, snakes, bats, and other creatures considered inedible. Urarina affirm that mythical metamorphoses notwithstanding, game animals were placed on the earth by Our Creator, who watches over and cares for Urarina people. Their presence and availability is entirely attributable to the paternal benevolence of Our Creator, who is regularly requested by drinkers of psychotropics to release them from the celestial pen in which they are kept and to which their heart-souls return at death. These shamanic solicitations, and the principles on which they are elaborated, are discussed further below. As discussed in chapter 4, any individual man (not necessarily a drinker of psychotropics) who sets out to hunt may also enunciate a solicitation directly to Our Creator known as Cana Coaaunera bajaa, "request for Our Creator." These resemble a kind of prayer in which the speaker adopts a willfully pitiful and helpless stance as a means of engaging a munificent response, whereby the success and safety of the expedition is assured. In the words of Buchilote:

> Our Creator always throws us something, even though there's not a great number of animals. He always blesses those who go hunting often, so they kill something and nourish themselves with that. Our Creator wants that the animals encountered be killed, even though there's not many. Just like that, when Our Creator so wants it, they kill it, always, and they bring it back and send it to be cooked, in order that we all eat together.

While out in the forest a hunter or his accompanying wife may perform a number of other orations (cojiotaa) in order to aid the success of the hunt. These are addressed, not to Our Creator, but directly to the animal itself, in its potential capacity as a subject. They are perhaps not entirely dissimilar to the Jivaroan *anent*, although I have never heard one employed as a general purpose instrument, used by a hunter to lure, persuade, or seduce his prey (cf. Descola 1994: 260–63). They have specific aims of a more technical nature, and the potent symbolism often has a comical flavor. For example, the following cojiotaa is used for hunting paca *(Cuniculus paca)* by night along the headwaters of streams. Once the location of a burrow becomes known to the hunter, he might return at a later date, with a dog whom he can send in to flush out the hapless creature—provided it has returned there in the meantime.

shoo an jelaiha ii sijiina cainaa uura icha	Hey! Come and return your comb right there, paca!
shoo an jelaiha ii sijiina cainaa uura icha	Hey! Come and return your comb right there, paca!
shoo ii sijina baiteeintera ratiricha icha	Hey! Forgetting your comb you've left it behind, paca!
shoo ii sijina baiteeintera ratiricha icha	Hey! Forgetting your comb you've left it behind, paca!
shoo chaone jaberoco baiteente ratiricha icha	Hey! Forgetting your ball of twine you've left it behind, paca!
shoo chaone jaberoco cainaa uura icha	Hey! Come and give back your ball of twine, paca!
chaone jaberoco baiteeintein te ratiricha icha	Forgetting your ball of twine you've left it behind, paca!
shoo chalasine baiteen te ratiricha icha	Hey! Forgetting your ball of aguaje you've left it behind, paca!
shoo irisine baiteein ratiricha icha	Hey! Forgetting your ball of chambira you've left it behind, paca!

In a similar vein, the following cojiotaa is used in order that the howler monkey *(Alouatta seniculus)*, heard singing early in the morning, will continue all day rather than fall silent, giving the hunter plenty of time to track him down and kill him.

shoo roro ujuae cari que neteei-chaniu quicha charisho ne	Hey! Go and hang yourself from howler monkey's lips, little boy crybaby!
shoo roro ujuae cari que neteei-chaniu quicha charisho ne	Hey! Go and hang yourself from howler monkey's lips, little boy crybaby!
shoo roro ujuae cari que neteei-chaniu ene charisho ne	Hey! Go and hang yourself from howler monkey's lips, little girl crybaby!

The chant aims symbolically to attach an inconsolably crying child to the lips of the howler monkey, preventing it from being silent. A slightly different but equally technical and frustrating problem faced by many a hunter is that of a monkey's tail inadvertently wrapping around a branch after it has been shot, preventing it from falling to the ground. Hence the following cojiotaa:

shoo aara aacari eraurusi nitichara neeura araohata use	Hey! Be slippery phlegm of the cecropia[2] tree, spider monkey tail!
chabana inaatenachara araohata use	Spider monkey tail never gets entangled!
chabana inaatenachara araohata use	Spider monkey tail never gets entangled!
aancari eraurusi nitichara neuriura araohata use	Be slippery phlegm of the cecropia tree, monkey tail!
shoo samaanta nalunecoriu araohata	Hey! Fall like a rock, spider monkey!
shoo anra aaucari eraurusi necoriura araohata use	Hey! Become phlegm of the cecropia tree, spider monkey tail!

A further example targets the edible *querano* lizard, known often to lie on top of dead branches sticking out of the middle of the river. The idea is to prevent or dissuade it from jumping suddenly into the water as one passes by in a canoe, allowing plenty of opportunity to lasso it using a length a rope tied to the end of a pole. The chant brings the lizard into symbolic conjunction with a series of heavy items, in order to immobilize it.

shoo an samaanta te bauhaque	Hey! A rock leans on top!
shoo ajeri te bauaque	Hey! A stone leans on top!
shoo tebe cosaco te bauaque	Hey! A sack of salt leans on top!

The final example is not used for hunting at all but rather to ensure that a certain species of large and exceptionally dangerous jaguar known as *ririeri* does not approach, by imploring a series of monkeys to distract it.

shoo aanra ririeri comasai tichainiura cairi anaira curaana	Hey! Look! Go and have sex with jaguar's wife for me, coati chief!
shoo cairira neeine anai neeine curaana cairi neeine	Hey! Be coati chief for me!
shoo aanra toon ririeri comasai tichainiura cairi cati curaana	Hey! Look! Listen! Go and have sex with jaguar's wife for me, black capuchin monkey chief!
shoo aanra toon ririeri comasai tichainiura cairi carateu curaana	Hey! Look! Listen! Go and have sex with jaguar's wife for me, white capuchin monkey chief!
shoo aanra toon ririeri comasai tichainiura cairi anai curaana	Hey! Look! Listen! Go and have sex with jaguar's wife for me, coati chief!

shoo aanra toon ririeri comasai
    tichainiura cairi unee curaana
	Hey! Look! Listen! Go and have sex
	    with jaguar's wife for me, kinkajou
	    chief!

shoo aanra toon ririeri comasai
    tichainiura cairi carateu curaana
	Hey! Look! Listen! Go and have sex
	    with jaguar's wife for me, white
	    capuchin monkey chief!

Most of the above cojiotaa address animals directly, in their capacity as persons or subjects. It must be stressed that under no account would an animal be expected to understand what was said to it in any other context, especially everyday speech. With the possible exception of the jaguar, even a drinker of psychotropics (coaairi coera) lacks the facility to communicate directly with animals.[3] These cojiotaa instead set up their own space of interaction and have their own form of efficacy, the logic and mechanics of which no one would presume fully to understand, or even inquire into. Their efficacy is evidenced purely by their outcomes: a chant seen to work several times will become trusted and will continue to be used, regardless of how it might "work."

One principle or characteristic nevertheless seems relatively constant throughout all these varied examples, and this concerns the tone adopted. If the pitch of requests to Our Creator is pleading and self-effacing, imploring him to take pity on his "suffering children," that evidenced in these cojiotaa is thoroughly authoritative and commanding. Often beginning with an interjection such as *"shoo"* (roughly, "Hey, you!"), there is no question here who is master of whom, and the efficacy of the chant rests on the expected capitulation of the animal to a higher authority. In fact, virtually all these cojiotaa can be seen as a means of exerting power or influence over nonhumans. That it is also in the general context of these chants that these same nonhumans are represented as most fully subjectivized, or that their essential personhood is least in doubt, is not as anomalous as it may first appear. As I have already elaborated at some length, an intrinsic connection between power and subjectivity is far from alien to Urarina thought. It is given striking expression in a pervasive cosmological concept of singular importance: that of the game master or owner.

OWNERS, CARETAKERS, COMPANIONS

Virtually all entities attributed a power or force of some kind, whether to burn fiercely or to smell sweetly, to produce flowers or to avoid destruction, have some kind of master, mother, or owner, to whom that power is principally credited. The total sum of ideas pertaining to these beings is complex and nebulous and defies easy summarization. The term *neba*, or mother, is used almost (but not entirely) interchangeably with *ijiaene*, "spirit," "owner," or "master," a term also cognate with *ijiaaen* (mestizo) and, arguably, *ijia* (kapok tree), with further connotations of the latter's "whiteness." Although people usually translated *ijiaene* into Spanish as *dueño* (owner), it remains distinct from the everyday owner (*erora*) of a material possession. Cultural conventions seem to guide the use of one term over the other in particular contexts: for example, *nunaa ijiaene*, "owner of the forest," and *usi neba*, "mother of fire," are commonly used, while the reverse, *nunaa neba* and *usi ijiaene*, were generally regarded as acceptable but unusual.

The owners of many entities have both a spiritual and a locational aspect. A particular species of animal is often cited as occupying the latter role, typically one who dwells in the general vicinity. For example, the owner of "rocky rapids" *(caratiri)* is sometimes referred to as *caratiri neba*, "mother of rocky rapids"; at other times it is said to be a kind of crocodile known as *nacanacari*, rarely seen today but instantly recognizable by its short tail and protruding teeth. In a similar vein, the owner of rivers is sometimes referred to generically as *acau ijiaene* (water owner/spirit), while at other times dolphins are singled out as bearing this responsibility.

Perhaps the most important of all such owners is that responsible for game animals (cana lenone), a mysterious figure known as cojoaaorain,[4] generally said to take the form of a small bird (although one informant claimed that it "looks pretty, like a woman, like a young girl"). It was described to me in Spanish as at once their dueño, *madre* (mother), and *cuidador* (caretaker). "All the animals that we eat have their cojoaaorain. . . . It is like a tiny little chicken, who sings 'tiiiii titititi.'" According to Lorenzo, the cojoaaorain "is like a companion who communicates with you constantly, in order to care for your life . . . for your defense." Insofar as animals are "wild," "clever," or "evasive" (*mañoso*), it is understood that this is because their "mother" is constantly "advising" them. When an animal is killed by a hunter, this is essentially because this vital communication had earlier ceased: "The mother didn't advise them that day."

Largely due to the purported ability of cojoaaorain to hear the speech of humans and to see their movements, prospective hunters must take great care not to reveal their deadly intentions. A man about to set out for the forest will under no circumstance utter words such as *nesari*, "hunt"; instead, he will communicate his intentions by saying simply "*amua*

Figure 10.   A hunter repairs his blowpipe. Photograph by author.

curaani" (I'm going wandering) (figure 10). If he plans to target a particular species, a codeword will be used, drawn from the ritual language,
which has an extensive repertoire of formulaic expressions and circum-
locutions pertaining to game animals as well as many other entities, all
said to have been bestowed by brugmansia itself. Alternately, fake or substitute names may be used: people might speak of their intention to look
for grasshoppers, for example, if they are really looking for bush tur-
keys or other small animals. "Fox" might substitute for deer or peccary; or
"toad" for tapir. The danger is always that the cojoaaorain will overhear,
and its animal-subjects will be advised to beat a hasty and fearful retreat
as a result. "When you say it direct, its cojoaaorain goes to warn it. That's
why we speak indirectly."

If the cojoaaorain exists primarily for the defense of game animals, its strategies can nevertheless involve an element of counterattack. Many animals are considered to have the power to inflict harm or
illness through mystical attack or sorcery (*saatiha*, lit., "to shoot with
darts"). This is considered to come from cojoaaorain, who is also said to
be "like its blowpipe darts" *(batohi)*. As Lorenzo put it, "The cojoaaorain
of tapir, or of peccary, has darts, in order to ensorcell the humans. When

we annoy them a lot, it harms us. The animal can communicate with its cojoaaorain in order to ensorcell us."

Some people claimed that cojoaaorain may be solicited directly for game animals, while others asserted that only Our Creator can be requested to "dissuade" or "demotivate" *(suujua aniniaaote)* the owner from its guard work, thus allowing the animal to be killed. Jorge explained the general idea using a personal example. For some time he had been making known his amorous designs on Erlinda, a young girl whom (so he claimed) he wished to take as his second wife. He was not the only man in the community to find her attractive, and her maternal grandmother had taken to sleeping close by in order to fend off unwanted nocturnal visitors. Joajoi, a youth only distantly related to the girl, had recently been kicked out of her house amid great commotion by the grandmother late one night, after being "discovered" in her mosquito net—much to Joajoi's humiliation and the great amusement of the rest of the community. Recognizing this fearsome obstacle in his path, Jorge confessed that he had recently asked Rosalia, Erlinda's maternal aunt, to speak to the old woman (her own mother) on his behalf, in order to persuade her to "release" Erlinda to him—effectively to relax a little her control over the girl, freeing her up for appropriation. Expanding on the analogy, Jorge said, "Cojoaaorain doesn't want to give [animals] to you all by himself, just like that—he is like an employee of Our Creator, and has to be dissuaded from doing his duty." He offered as a second example my entrusting him to look after my outboard motor while I was away in the city: "Should someone come to me and ask to borrow your motor, I would turn them down, because I am supposed to care for it. But if they go directly to you, you could order me to hand it over, and I would obey you. It's just like that with Our Creator and cojoaaorain."

The class of animals known as taebinaae, principally jaguars, enjoys the protection and counsel of a similar type of being, known as *uricho-raaona*. Said to be "like cojoaaorain" (and referred to on occasion as *taebi-naae cojoaaorain*), this birdlike being "communicates with the jaguar for his defense," and his diligence in carrying out this task makes the jaguar notoriously difficult to deceive. Only men of knowledge can see the bird in their visions, and as with the *lenone cojoaaorain*, the bird seems closely associated with the animal's soul. When I once asked Lorenzo if the jaguar had a heart-soul (suujue), for example, he replied, "Yes, it does. This is called its *urichoraaona*. Every jaguar has its own separate urichoraaona." This double existence, a power both internal and external to the subject, is a theme to which I return further below. No doubt due largely to their vocal expressiveness and ability to fly, songbirds seem particularly well-suited to this role as advisers, as well as envoys or messengers of Our Creator. In fact, a number of other birds are also seen as valued sources of information, communicating constantly with a variety of others, both human and nonhuman (see Walker 2010).

If the cojoaaorain is invisible to the naked and sober eye, such is not the case for *janoraain*, another bird who apparently fulfills a similar role, existing "for the defense of the animals." Its reddish brown contours just visible from a distance, the janoraain, most people agreed, is distinct from the cojoaaorain, and some cited the fact that whereas the latter has darts, the former does not. Martín said, "Janoraain always comes from the sky, together with the animal. The animal cannot come alone; it has to have its companion. Janoraain is always maintaining and defending the animals, caring for them, like an owner." Yet the nature of the relationship between cojoaaorain and janoraain remains unclear. It is possible that the two birds represent the spiritual and locational aspects of game owners respectively; or that the latter diffracts the greater power and more abstract companionship of the former into an infinite number of personalized, concrete instantiations.[5] In any event, death is not the only way to prise animals away from their custodians, and humans are not incapable of assuming this role themselves. The most common means of taking over the control of animals is through the capture of live offspring, who are then raised as pets, winning for themselves a great deal of affection in the process.

RAISING PETS

One day Lorenzo returned from the forest with a large dead peccary slung over one shoulder. His son walked alongside, proudly carrying a carefully tied string bag inside which a baby peccary was tirelessly struggling. Just as the large peccary was handed over on arrival to Lorenzo's wife, for cooking, its offspring, now in a state of great agitation, was handed over to his elderly mother, for raising or taming (irilaa). I asked Lorenzo why his wife wasn't given the task. "She can't, because she's pregnant," I was told. "The baby will get sick. If she were to give it food, such as ripe bananas, it would get diarrhea and die." Such ideas, which clearly illustrate the couvade restrictions discussed in chapter 3, highlight the special place pets may come to occupy, almost rivaling that of children. In fact, pets are structurally equivalent to adoptive children, and the term *irilaa* is also used to refer to the task of raising human orphans. The way in which women past childbearing age, such as Lorenzo's mother, would enthusiastically assume initial responsibility for taming and nurturing pets seemed further to highlight similarities to the task of raising children. Structurally equivalent in some ways, as fellow outsiders and dependents, older women always seemed specially attuned to the pets of others. I had already noticed some time before that Lorenzo's mother was liable to remember almost no details whatsoever about a particular person, save the pets they once owned. In any case, she took to her new task with much zeal and for the next week or so was to be seen carrying the animal around wherever she went in a length of cloth, stroking it, feeding it, and talking to it, gently easing it into its new, village-based life.

Though his mother bore primary responsibility for the taming, Lorenzo assisted with the following cojiotaa:

ton ton ton ichecari calaohi mucuun	Oi! Oi! Oi! I'm holding a baby *ichecari* turtle[6]
ton ton jerojoe calaohi ne mucuun	Oi! Oi! I'm holding a baby yellow-footed tortoise[7]
ton ton macaje calaohi mucuun	Oi! Oi! I'm holding a baby macaje turtle[8]
ton ton chabana uraenechara calaohi ne mucuun	Oi! Oi! I'm holding a baby that is never wild
ton ton chabana urajeen natane cuuna coacuin	Oi! Oi! Never thinking of going to its homeland
natane coacuuin nenachara	Never thinking of its homeland
macaje calaohi mucuun	I'm holding a baby macaje turtle
ton ton chabana calanajanachara ajaaonri calaohi ne mucuun	Oi! Oi! I'm holding a baby yellow-footed tortoise that never bites
ton ton ton chabana udaenechara tariacha calaohi ne mucuun	Oi! Oi! Oi! I'm holding a baby yellow-spotted river turtle[9] that is never wild
ton ton ton chabana soronaachara nori calaohi ne mucuun	Oi! Oi! Oi! I'm holding a baby arrau turtle[10] that never flees
ton ton ton chabana erenachara tariacha calaohi ne mucuun	Oi! Oi! Oi! I'm holding a baby yellow-spotted river turtle that never yells

Lorenzo claimed that the cojiotaa was a means of quickly getting the creature to the desirable state, not only of being "tame" *(uratejeen)* but also "like our heart" *(cana suujua rijitojoeein)*, or like-minded, amenable to instruction and friendly cooperation. Humans too, particularly wives, are sometimes spoken of in this way. For example, pleased one day with his wife's willingness to accompany him to Iquitos, Jorge once remarked that she was "very much like my heart" (*jataain canu suujua rijitojoi-hanaja*). When I asked him to elaborate, he explained that she listened to what he said, always obeyed him, behaved "like a good maiden," and followed him willingly. For these reasons, he proclaimed proudly, he loved her very much.

Pets are generally treated well and are a source of pride and amusement. Their behavior arouses great interest, especially when they are recently arrived in the village, and children are encouraged to observe them closely and become familiar with their movements, noises, and other behavioral characteristics. Samuel had a particular fondness for keeping birds and usually had at least four or five living in his house. He once told me proudly that one of his parrots always played with its feathers, or with leaves, when someone had just killed a game animal in the forest. He had arrived at this conclusion purely on the basis of empirical observation.

A large variety of animals are kept as pets, although some are decidedly more popular than others. Birds, especially parakeets, are particularly favored; monkeys are popular with children but less so with adults, who tend to regard them as mischievous and troublesome (figure 11). Certain animals are considered impossible to tame: jaguars, of course, but also the agouti (who may appear tame but always runs away eventually), and the white capuchin monkey (*Cebus albifrons*), who is already the "pet," or iri, of forest demons (*notachanui*) who "care for it a lot" and do not easily relinquish their control. I myself was the proud "owner"—or so I thought—of a pet white monkey, for a total of two days: its miraculous escape from the ropes tying it to the house—or "rescue," as my companions had it—surprised no one but me.

The only pets not taken directly from the forest are dogs, which are kept more for directly practical purposes, namely, hunting, than for the aesthetic pleasures they bring. That said, Lorenzo did once claim that he wanted a dog "to accompany his wife" when he worked elsewhere, adding that "dogs care for the house." Although both men and women care for dogs, it is primarily men who tame them, mostly by walking together in the forest and teaching them to hunt, such that they come to recognize their new owner. A number of other techniques are also used to train dogs, and this animal—like children—seems especially susceptible to the logic of analogic transfer and contagious magic. The tongue of the rufous-collared sparrow (*Zonotrichia capensis*, for example, a bird renowned for being "a great talker," may be rubbed on the tongue of a dog to make it bark better; I have also seen dogs fed wasps' nests in their food, to make them fierce and brave.

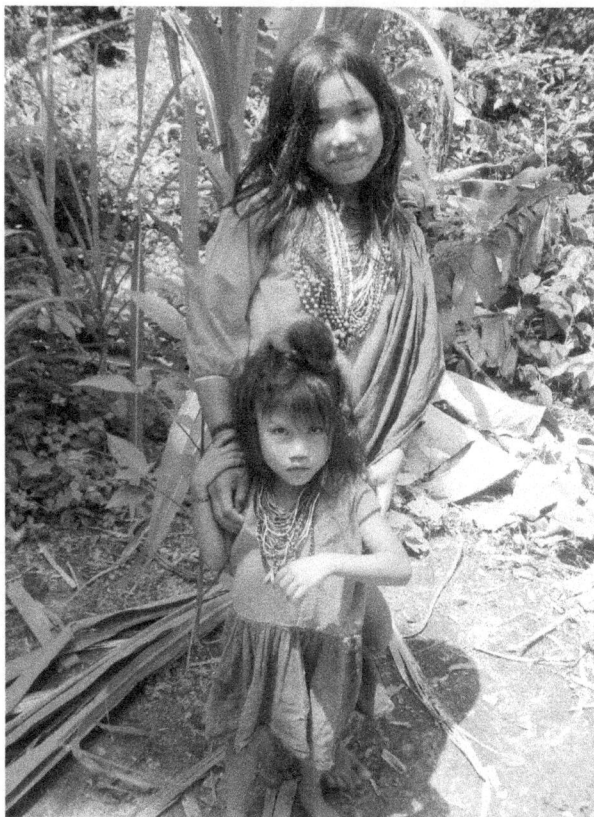

Figure 11. Girls with a pet monkey. Photograph by author.

Once pets have been tamed, people aim to keep them so, by whatever means necessary. I was told never to feed raw meat to my pet parakeet, as this would reverse the taming process and turn it fierce. Pets also call out to their group or family (lauri), who may come to see it occasionally, perhaps circling the community to be near to their "child." "For this reason we need to treat our pets well," said Martín. "So their family will be content, and will appear in the forest rather than run away and hide." Martín pointed out that the greatest psychotropic drinkers always treated their pets "extremely well" and "loved them a lot." Indeed, pets can become the objects of much love and affection. Small children are often inseparable from the baby monkeys who learn to cling to the tops of their heads, burrowing into their messy hair.

The affection shown to pets should not obscure the inherent power asymmetry. At a drinking party one day I heard Rosa sing a joyous song to her favorite pet, a trumpeter bird. While praising it highly for its beautiful voice and ability to foresee the outcome of a successful hunting trip, she entreated it to sing loudly for all to hear. Reminiscent of strategies for raising children, the bird was not encouraged to act with the promise of rewards but rather threatened with starvation should it refuse to comply. Compare now the following "tortoise scolding" (*jerojoe cotaiha*), which I have seen used on captive yellow-footed tortoises, with great dramatic effect, by women whose husbands have recently set out on a hunting trip. Performed while hitting the hapless creature's shell loudly and repeatedly with a long, heavy stick, the chant commands it to use its own lauded powers of communication to make game animals appear in the forest, for potential human benefit.

charai ocoteu ainiane ii
    quiurureencha jerojoe
	Make your kindred appear or we will
	    eat you, tortoise!

ii joaohin ii najari quiururaan
    cotebe teein enujue aina
	Breaking you apart, we will eat your
	    liver with salt and chilli!

iichate coitecuriquin charai
    ocotenein jerojoe
	Only you will know about making
	    your family appear, tortoise!

tabai jiri cana lenone ocoteu jerojoe	Make a bigger animal appear, tortoise!

aineinete icha quiururaan ii najari
    cotebe teu ichate
    coitecujueriquin jerojoe
	Otherwise we will eat you, put salt
	    on your liver, only you will know,
	    tortoise!

Hearing my recording of the above chant brought back memories for Jorge, who told me:

> Yes, that's how it's done. When I was younger, we went to look for tortoises. My father said to me, "If you find a little tortoise, tell me." I found one, and I handed it to my father. He hit it with his machete, saying, "Make your family come out!" Just like that. Another time, my mother sent me, saying, "Go and scold the tortoise, otherwise your father won't find anything!"

Tortoises are widely credited with the ability to perform baau and cojiotaa chants, through which they enjoy a degree of power over the other animals. Presumably for this reason, tortoises are said to be "like janoraain." They are also referred to as *cana lenone comuraje*, the "ritual bowl of game animals," because their shell was made like a bowl or a cap by Our Creator. According to Martín, tortoises can also come in handy on long canoe journeys. If it looks like rain, one simply taps the tortoise on the back, commanding it to "chant" the rain away, lest both get wet. "And sure enough, the rain passes," Martín concluded.

The treatment of tortoises in this way serves once again to highlight an apparent correlation between the amount of power or authority exerted over an animal and the degree to which it is treated as a person or subject—in this case, one with advanced rhetorical and linguistic skills. Our attention is also drawn once again to the power of the spoken word, which here instantiates an enchainment or delegation of authority running from human to tortoise to game animal, bypassing or exceeding that already set up between the game animal and its cojoaaorain. These themes are pursued further below, in the context of a close examination of what are perhaps the most advanced of all pet-keeping practices: those through which an experienced psychotropic drinker engages the small stone bowl known as *egaando*, subjecting it to his authority and subjectivizing it therein. Yet the drinker himself is also constituted in and through relations of power, and the complex hierarchical relationship between humanity and divinity, often mediated by shamans but always permeated by notions of love, care, and dependency, goes to the heart of understandings of what it means to be human and what it means to be moral.

THE DEFENSE OF THE LIVING

> Our Creator created psychotropics for the defense of our world-era and our children. In order that our children are defended and our world-era doesn't collapse, we drink psychotropics. So that our climate is favored. That's what Our Creator said when he passed over to the other side of that which covers us, over there. That's why he left psychotropics for his children, who are all of us. For our support, for our defense against all kinds of illnesses. He left psychotropics in order that all those who drink them will make a bridge for the game animals to pass over to this side. In this manner we are blessed with our mother, and helped with our children. That's what our ancestors said, a long time ago. It's not just anything. In this way, when there are sick people to be cured, Our Creator helps us. Like that, we recover. Otherwise, if Our Creator did not wish it, we would die. Like that, we would die right there, forgotten!

Urarina social life in general, and the consumption of ayahuasca and brugmansia in particular, must be understood against the backdrop of an apocalyptic eschatology in which the world teeters precariously on the brink of annihilation. As Tivorcio's short monologue above indicates, the precipitating factor is the collapse of the "climate" or "world-era" (cana cojoanona),[11] said already to be "scarcely" or "barely" (*alalacaa*) existing, "like an old woman on her deathbed," as one man once put it. "The day is frightened," people sometimes say, "*inae nesonetoa janonaa.*" Sooner or later the sky will finally fall down to the earth, light will give way to perpetual darkness, raging fires and floods will scour the land, and demons will roam freely until no humans are left. This miserable end was the topic of many conversations I had and clearly a matter of genuine concern; a kind of cosmic analogue, perhaps, to the chronic insecurity of the social environment as well as to the existential state of the ill patient—as I will shortly discuss—such that the act of rectification, through the consumption of psychotropics, necessarily acts on all scales at once.

The world-era first threatened to collapse entirely a very long time ago, according to common wisdom, but was saved by one or more brave and knowledgeable men, who drank psychotropics in a concerted effort to forestall the destruction. Such efforts continue up to the present, and all shamans aim to reiterate this foundational act of salvation, though their efforts, while appreciated, are also regarded as increasingly insufficient. As Jorge put it:

> For us, everything is about to become extremely scarce, unfortunately, now that the real shamans have left us. Only we remain, living and standing-leaned-together. The ancients, whose bodies were stronger, who drank more [psychotropics], they have left us, and we are staying behind here. Please, let more psychotropics be drunk! Dear me, our poor world is about to end, our lives, our land, that which is supported by Our Creator. Because it's like this, there is barely anything left in the forest. We can barely encounter our game animals. And because those whose lives are poor,[12] because they eat our game animals, they are already becoming scarce. The animals are silent.

The inevitability of the apocalypse due to the decline of powerful shamans is evidenced by the oft-noted scarcity of game animals in the forest, and older people often assured me that game was relatively abundant when they were children. People also often spoke of a deterioration in the weather, and Jorge testified to a parallel decline in people's behavior:

> When it rains every day, at night and in the afternoon, and the sun never appears, and it stays like that for something like ten days, or more, the women say many things, they say a whole lot of rubbish, like "that person spoke to me thus, he spoke to me thus,"—any old gossip that isn't true. They don't realize that the world is about to end.

Only drinkers of psychotropics are capable of reversing or forestalling the end of the world and its indicators: bad weather and lack of sunlight, the increasing scarcity of game animals, and the erosion of proper sociability. As such, they are known as "our world-era's support" (*cana cojoanona nunera)*: like a pole propping up a leaning plantain tree, I was told, or one who keeps a naturally unstable canoe perfectly still in the water, the shaman "safeguards" and "steadies" the world-era and "shields" or "defends" those dwelling within it. By soliciting Our Creator through the semi-improvised chanting of the coaairi baauno, he effectively creates a "bridge" across which the animals may descend from the sky to the earth, and this image may even describe the shaman himself. At the same time, he solicits or is otherwise instrumental in bringing about fine weather and is the recipient of visions revealing the outcome of future events, ranging from an imminent trip to Iquitos to the recovery of a gravely ill patient.

Serious illness is in fact the most common immediate motivation for drinking psychotropics. Most illnesses are considered the outcome of acts of bewitchment, the result of shocks or intentional attacks by hostile beings in the local environment, sometimes humans but more often nonhumans. All-out sorcery, or attack by blow darts (saatiha), is the cause of the most deadly forms of sickness, and distinguished from other forms of malaise, most notably *buunaatiha*, sometimes described as "like a strong fright." This typically afflicts babies or small children, whose weak or insecurely attached heart-souls are said to make them particularly vulnerable even when one of their parents passes by or somehow comes into contact with something potentially frightening. Typical symptoms are when "a baby can't sleep in its hammock," or alternatively lies completely silent, without crying, without wanting its mother or anything else. Treatments for these ills vary with their severity, although in each case they may be understood as redressing a perceived breakdown in relations to others, resulting in a kind of existential isolation and anxiety.

The first port of call for a mild pain or affliction is usually tobacco smoke, deployed in a procedure known as *totoicha*, or sucking. A large drag is taken from a cigar, and with mouth full of smoke the healer sucks hard on the afflicted body part, then spits and exhales violently and repeats the procedure. Sometimes smoke is blown directly over the patient's body. Like game animals, tobacco's power stems from its "mother," said to be "like a bird" and known alternately as *jiunaca* (connoting the smoke's sweet smell) or *enoata joroora*, "tobacco's lullaby." As Martín explained it, "You hear how they sing to my baby brother over there, to make it sleep? Well, just like that, the bird sings to the tobacco. That's why they call it tobacco's lullaby." Tobacco smoke is actively used to put people to sleep in at least one myth, and as a healing technique is felt to have a soothing, calming effect, somewhat akin to lullaby.

Curing the infant malaise known as buunaatiha requires the performance of the appropriate specialized baau chant, which must be deduced by reflecting on one's movements and activities over the past few days, noting, for example, the particular species of tree or animal or landscape feature one has come into contact with. The words of the chant, as already noted, work to reposition the infant within a wider relational matrix of beings immune to the harm from this particular entity, allowing a contagious transfer of desirable qualities to take place. The baau is usually whispered onto a material substrate to be consumed orally, such as a small bowl of mother's milk or banana soup, and once digested it works to "dye" the blood and make it stronger by "joining with" or "duplicating" it, increasing the child's resistance.

According to some, the purpose of the baau is to "recover" or "return" the heart-soul, which is at risk of permanently exiting the body, resulting in death. Jorge explained this as follows:

> The heart-soul is wanting to leave. It hasn't yet left completely. When someone is really gravely ill, nearly about to die, they don't see that the sky stays very far away. Instead, they see the sky as really close, just there right above them. That's why the deceased go straight to the sky, quickly without delay. When my grandfather was about to die, he told family standing by his side that he would soon roll over and then be in the sky immediately, because the sky was already right there close to him. He already wanted to leave the world.

Martín used a quite different analogy, describing the actions of the baau as "like a policeman," who is uniquely capable of retrieving the heart-soul from the "prison" in which it is "locked." The unique power of the baau to effect a recovery by overcoming one's isolation may be why so many speak of standing-leaned-together or standing-among-two (temereco), a paradigm for healthy living, as discussed in the prologue. Moreover, while buunaatiha usually afflicts only children, adults are also sometimes susceptible to very strong fright *(masina)*—especially if they are already in a weakened state—requiring the performance of the appropriate baau. Jorge described the experience to me as follows:

> For example, you're on your own, with fever, or just without verve, and someone suddenly comes and speaks strongly to you, and you get a fright. And then, after an hour, or half an hour, you feel like you're

all alone, even though you're with your companion. You feel cold, maybe you can hear music, like drums and flutes, because your heart has been really frightened, and your foot is very cold, like ice, and your head is a little bit cold, your nose is very cold, and although you cover yourself with a blanket, you can't feel it. This masina is really wild. If you do nothing, you can die. You feel like you're in the sky, you feel alone, you feel that your family is calling you to dance. And when the people speak close by, making noise, even though they're near you, you feel like they're far, far away from you. Your heart-soul is really, completely frightened.

Martín later told me a very similar story:

> One day after drinking brugmansia, when I was lying down and rest-ing, my brother's son came by and stood on a bee. He screamed, and my mother got a tremendous fright. A little later, she started feeling cold, she began trembling. She had masina. I tried to speak to her, and later she told me that she felt I was only barely speaking at all, that she could only just hear me.

These accounts seem to highlight that aspect of illness experienced as being truly on one's own and alone in the world, a sense of being utterly unable to share our pain or sense of unease despite the good intentions of those around us. For this reason, I would suggest that illness is asso-ciated with a breakdown of proper, healthy subjectivity and in addition to its various physical symptoms, often manifests as an inability to com-municate or achieve proper proximity to others. This would also help to explain why healing chants are concerned above all with invoking and reestablishing a viable relationship with the source of the illness, thereby building up immunity but also plucking the patient out of his or her isolation. Such a conception is slightly different from that described for the neighboring Jivaro by Taylor (1996: 207), who proposes that "sick-ness ... is the suffering experienced by individuals when they become overwhelmed by the ambiguity of the social environment and thereby lose a clear sense of their identity; that is, when their perception of self is clouded by uncertainty."

Among the Urarina, the high level of anxiety stemming from the extreme unpredictability of social and ecological relationships may sim-ilarly help to explain why affliction so quickly turns into a symptom of bewitchment. Yet a further connection is made between the sick patient and the wider cosmos or climate, which is similarly said to be "fright-ened" (*inae nesonetoa janonaa*, lit., "the day is frightened") and in need of shamanic action in order to restabilize. The shaman's cure, far from being an act of symbolic predation (cf. Severi 2002), is essentially defensive: it requires reestablishing a calm, protective space of mutual trust and ontological security, in which the patient can stand or even stand-leaned-together and proximity to others can be elaborated anew. That the shaman is fundamentally a hyper-defender rather than a hyper-predator is further supported in statements that drinkers of psychotropics are "caring for the animals of the forest, just like one cares for children, or for chickens." When a powerful old drinker drinks, I was told, the animals are happy, because they are being protected. They are cared for by the drinker because he does not let them return to the sky; he is also, of course, more likely in this state to construe them as akin to persons. As Martín said, "The really powerful shamans really care for the animals. That's why they always treat pets well." In short, the shaman is again establishing his credentials here as a protector and caretaker rather than aggressor. I now wish to examine in greater detail the nature of the psychedelic experience itself.

BECOMING POROUS

As living plants to be tended, transplanted or harvested, the many salient differences between ayahuasca (inono) and brugmansia (acaa) are reflected in their lexical differentiation. Once prepared as a drink to be consumed, however, both are referred to as *coaairi*, which could be translated as "very powerful one."[13] This power is synonymous with the sensory experience itself, the shaman's inebriety. When queried about the differences between brugmansia and ayahuasca, people's responses were always the same: "They're identical!" Nevertheless, everyone agreed that brugmansia was easily the stronger of the two, and it was sometimes referred to as ayahuasca's "older sibling," partly because much smaller quantities are required for the drug to take effect and partly because the associated visions are more lucid, intense, and powerful. My impression was that brugmansia is drunk more frequently, although both are sometimes drunk in succession: always brugmansia first, then ayahuasca the next evening. As one man told me, "I need to drink ayahuasca in order to sober up from the brugmansia!"

Both ayahuasca and brugmansia are planted, harvested, and prepared for use exclusively by men. Although many women have tried either or both, I never heard of a woman who drank on a regular basis. Most men dismissed outright the possibility that women could become regular drinkers on the grounds that they "don't know" or are "not strong enough." A man usually drinks alone, in his own house, while his wife, who remains sober, "cares for" (beraeha) and "watches over" (notaracae) him. Together with his ritual paraphernalia, comprising feather head-dress, shell breastbands, staff, and fan, she is referred to as coaairi nunera, or psychotropic's support. Occasionally men drink together in groups, in which case there is always a single leader or owner (baniha) who takes primary responsibility for the preparation and organization.

In preparing the psychotropic for use, the shaman performs a special-ized incantation *(coaairi chairetaa)* addressed directly to the plant (or its spirit mother). This is done so the drinker will not "flip out" or "go crazy" *(cajianiha)*, for example, by stripping off his clothes and wandering off into the forest, as many novices have been known to do. The incantation makes explicit the shaman's desire to "play" *(necoatijia)* with the drink, and Lorenzo told me that by playing together the shaman "will stay in the house, peaceful, simply looking up at the sky, not getting up and wander-ing around everywhere. Playing peacefully, not flipping out." The drink is also invited to "pass over me, visit me from above" *(choaje coedaine)*. As already noted, "visiting" is closely related, linguistically and conceptually, to "caring," and together with food sharing is one of the means by which people act conscientiously toward others, resulting in the gradual devel-opment of relatedness. Jorge explained, "For example, my wife comes to care for me when I am lying down: this is *choajae bedaiha*. The ancients used to say, *"ii coedainiha,"* "I'm visiting you for fun."

Ayahuasca and brugmansia are always drunk around dusk, and the experience lasts through the night. Yet the onset of the "force" of the drink is sometimes spoken of in terms of illumination, clarity, or day-light. It is like a very strong light, "very well illuminated," and like many other peoples Urarina use visual clarity to metaphorize knowledge. As drunkenness "descends" on the shaman, he begins to intone the *coaairi baauno*, a genre of ritual chanting exclusive to the psychedelic experi-ence. This may last up to several hours, with rest breaks in between, and is more or less improvised from a stock of formulaic expressions. I was told that although these chants appear to be voiced by the shaman him-self, it is really the psychotropic itself who is speaking, and the shaman has no foreknowledge of what will be said. The words of the chants often state as much and commonly address the shaman—the actual enuncia-tor—in the second person. The use of an archaic ritual language com-bined with unusual and indirect forms of expression make these par-ticularly difficult to translate; people without pretensions to shamanic knowledge invariably claim not to understand these chants, while those

who implied they did were generally unwilling to offer detailed exegesis.
The following exerpt is representative of the general style.

coujuriu curuarauru rai naitono	As in the words of the drinkers [of psychotropics]
rijitocoriin cheteterimi	[He] will make you [inebriated] just like that
coa rai necaohacha socorinacaica	Don't let its greatness frighten you
coujuriu curuarauru rai naitono rijitiin chetemite aonain	Will make you feel [the intoxication] just like the drinkers [of psychotropics] said
ii choajae coedaineine	Shall visit you from above
aonaqui aonain	So that feeling, [you] feel
coa rai caohacha socorinacaica	Don't be frightened of its greatness
ununaincha aonaate	Be still and feel
coujuriu curuarauru rai naitono	Just as in the words of the drinkers
rijitocorimi te aonain cheteine cainono	This ayahuasca will make you will feel
[pause]	
coujuriu cajanona rijitocoriin nein	Being like my day
cana coatijiaete necoatijiaaca	Make us play[/sing] so we play together
tabai nenoijianaa cataante chetenaare	You've been put in the middle of a great darkness
nesoonena cataannaate chete	You've been put in the middle of a great fear
elunai que burichora teinte	Let hear a dangerous thing
coaaunelu cana coaaunera	Created long ago by Our Creator
elunai que te chuisi ijiaene tein	The mother has been put there as something really frightening
coaaunelu Cana Coaaunera chuisi	Really created long ago by Our Creator
[pause]	
coujuriu curuarauru rai	Be as for the drinkers [of psychotropics]
ichoitecueracuru iicha coricha naitono rijitocote	As in the speech of your forefathers' shadow soul
coajian rai nesooiharitiin	Just don't get scared at all
aonatoha nirijitoha nianatiinte chuisi	Even though [you] really feel [it]
eneu ijoerateurera iicha corita	Thus the shadow-souls of those who raised you
nitohaniha jeriha	Want it to be like that
ijanona lucu que chetein neeine ca inono	This ayahuasca will bring you to the dawn of your day

coujuriu ijoerateurera iicha	Will do to you just as the shadow
corichacuru rai naitono	souls of your forefathers were told
rijitocoriin cheteine	
coujuriu canu nunura que nena	Being like that which defends me
rijitocori	
cajianenanajanu rijitoha	It's as though I will go mad
coa rijitojein nesoonetiin	Don't be terrified
aona ununachaun	Feel I am supporting
caohacha nenoijianaa cataante chete	The drinker put you in the middle of
iicha curuaera	a great darkness
nirijitoha jerihate chaelae enoale	You wanted to drink it as though it
baca que aina rijijieein	were just some juice of cultigens
curujuaain neein	
coarai nesoonetoha	Don't be frightened
ununaicha aonaa	Be supported and feel

Much of the language of the chants is formulated as though addressed to the shaman himself, and often those around him as well, including the sick patient. Frequent use is made of second-person grammatical forms, both singular and plural, although third-person and first-person markers (singular and plural) are also employed, creating a sense of ambiguity as to the identity of the agent. The psychotropic continually reassures the shaman and tells him not to be afraid, and that he is going to "go visiting" or "go traveling around." The shaman is also repeatedly told by the chant that "it appears to be your words coming out of your mouth" or that the words appear to be "created from your heart-soul"—while implying that in reality it is not. It is said that the psychotropic can "make you forget everything" or "forget those who are right by your side." The drinker can experience the potentially terrifying sensation of dying or being dead, sometimes described as a process of forgetting: the souls of the deceased are said to forget their kin and may act toward them with malicious intent.

Further reassurance comes with the chants' repeated assertions that all continue to dwell "under Our Creator's watchful eye." They stress that psychotropics were placed on the earth by Our Creator, "for your support." The listeners are instructed to "put yourselves like real people" (*coujuriu cachanichachene*), or to do something "being real people" (*cacha neeine*), always founded in the notion that "while you are alive, you are standing between two, standing leaned together." In a related vein, the ritual provides a forum for the articulation of moral advice or reprimands. One chant I translated described a woman who had sexual relations with a mestizo, thereby contaminating not only her own blood but also that of her husband, who was advised to cure or "purify" himself by personally drinking brugmansia. Another instructed the listeners not to be stingy with food, not to treat their pets badly, not to let daughters have sex with "just any boy," not to hate each other, and finally to live peacefully together like real people.

A cornerstone of the moral claims made by or on behalf of the psychotropics is the continuity evoked with the ancestors. Like the force of manioc beer chant (jichorojoe baauno) discussed earlier, much mention is made of "our ancestors" *(cana inoaesi)* or "our forefathers" *(cana coitucueracuru,* lit., "those who knew us"), who "really knew how to drink without fear." The chant asserts that "just as I spoke to them, so too I am speaking to you now," and that "just as they lived back then, so too you continue the same today." Because he is acting so righteously in drinking the ayahuasca, the shaman is further told that his heart-soul is "shaping up well, becoming beautiful" *(neculucoin),* in order to go to the other side (i.e., to the sky), where it will eventually join the good group of thunder-people *(caohacha laurina arara;* see epilogue).

Coaairi baauno also describe the visions to which the shaman is witness. Ghosts *(anocai),* or souls of the deceased, are a common sight, and may elicit commentary. Many of the themes described above are reasserted: the world-era is routinely described as tired, feeling pity, sorrowful, or already afraid. The process of "extracting our game animals" is also elaborated, and emphasis is placed on the action by which they are "made to appear," which is reaffirmed as central to the human condition, namely, "requesting Our Creator, requesting, you stand together like real people" *(Cana Coaaunera bajae bajaeenchu temerequera cachaniquichene).* Another common expression is *bacurunaa,* or to sing for joy, a term used to describe certain songbirds such as the red-throated caracara *(Ibycter americanus),* who are heard when the weather is "clearing up" and will soon be fine and sunny. This is, of course, an adequate description of the coaairi baauno itself.

It is here that the personal experience of the shaman is of paramount importance: the onset of the visions is itself described in terms of "dawn" or "daylight," and his gradual sobering up, toward the end of the session, does indeed coincide with sunrise. The far-reaching emphasis on personal experience in epistemology, discussed in chapter 4, helps to account for this fundamental homology between the shaman's personal experience and the shift he aims to bring about in the world-era more broadly speaking. The more intense the experience, the greater his efficacy, which is why people are proud of how much psychotropic drink they are able to ingest, and especially how long they stay drunk as a result. Lorenzo would often boast to me, "When I drink ayahuasca, I stay drunk for twelve hours! And when I drink brugmansia . . . twenty-four hours!" The ancients, who were more fearless and whose bodies were stronger, were able to get even drunker, so drunk they "really felt they were about to die." This is reflected in one of the terms used to designate these ancient shamans, of whom few are said to remain today: *ajaenaeinaera*, literally, "those who really know how to get inebriated." The intensity of the experience coincides precisely with the enhanced powers attributed to them. The ritual paraphernalia, of headdress and breast bands, are similarly said to help their owner to "resist" the ayahuasca and thereby increase his tolerance for extreme levels of inebriety.

I now wish to return to the question of who, exactly, should be regarded as the "subject" or author of the words uttered in the chant and the source of the knowledge imparted. As already noted, Urarina say the speech comes from the psychotropic itself, or "from the inebriety." There is a slight conceptual difficulty for us here given that the term *coaairi* refers both to the psychotropic plant and to the visions it induces, either of which may be personified, and not only in terms of a "mother." Lorenzo told me a story about a young woman who always used to "accompany" shamans.

> A long time ago, there was this Inori, a young maiden. The drinker
> of psychotropics, he knew she was there. But they are all finished,
> together with Inori, and we no longer see her. A long time ago, it
> is said she could be heard coming in canoe from our source [cana
> temura], making the sound "cora! cora! corau!" It is said she had
> beautiful green eyes, that Inori woman. The ancients knew her, they
> saw her from directly in front. They drank brugmansia together with
> her, and looking, they saw everything. They saw all our world-era.
> It really seemed they were about to die when they drank, that's what
> they felt. They saw all of our game animals, from where they are
> raised and kept by Our Creator. The shamans said that they dressed
> her, like getting married, and they knew everything. Our ancestors
> knew all kinds of things, but today, nothing whatsoever is known of
> Inori. Really truly up until the very end, those ancient people knew
> everything, but they are completely finished. That's what our ances-
> tors told us.

This story highlights the intimate relationship the shaman can develop with, or through the use of, the psychotropic, who appears here as a possible paramour or even potential wife. Although Inori is no longer visible, many coaairi baauno state that the psychotropic "visits" the shaman as his fellow (jera) or companion (ii jera neein coedaineein).

A closer examination of the coaairi baauno indicates that every once in a while segments are also apparently articulated from the subject position of the shaman himself, and not merely that of the psychotropic. For example, an expression like *ii coitucueracuru*, "your ancestors," seemingly spoken from the subject position of the psychotropic and addressed to the shaman, might soon be followed by *cana coitucueracuru*, "my ancestors," the exact reverse. Similarly, in the exerpt above, all lines are voiced from the perspective of the psychotropic except for two ("being like that which defends me / it's as though I'll go mad"). Here, the subject position suddenly changes to that of the shaman addressing the psychotropic, who is his "defense" or "support." When I asked Jorge about this, he replied, "The man is speaking to ayahuasca, and ayahuasca is speaking to the man. It's crossing [Sp. *esta cruzando*]." Martín confirmed: "Between two of them they are drinking. Just as it makes me drunk, so too it makes you drunk."

The difficulty of identifying the subject position of a sung discourse has been widely noted as a feature of much Amazonian musical performance. Gow (2001: 149) credits Seeger (1987) with showing how "the rapidly oscillating subject positions in Suyá ritual singing culminate in the identification, at the climax of ritual performance, of the supernatural animal composers of the songs and men who sing them." Gow suggests that a similar process is at work in the Piro case and proposes that "the shaman is a switch-point between the experiential domain of powerful beings and humans. Nowhere is there a transcendental assimilation of the powerful being, shaman, and patient. Instead, the shaman's identification shifts back and forth between powerful beings as kin and the patient as kin" (149).

Based on the Urarina data, I would like to propose a slightly different interpretation, according to which there is neither "transcendental assimilation" nor perspectival exchange. The state of drunkenness cannot come purely from the plant but is necessarily the result of the psychotropic existing inside the shaman's body. The two are "playing" together as companions while simultaneously existing in a state of enclosure or containment. The term *aonaa*, ubiquitous throughout these chants, means "to hear" or "to feel," and this is the primary sense modality engaged in the psychotropic experience, not vision as such, despite metaphors of light and clarity and the fact that people do sometimes talk about what they see in their state of inebriety. This further emphasizes the connection, rather than separation, between the two participants. Through these songs the shaman makes transparent the fact that all speech is in some sense beyond the speaker's control: the notion of the utterer as the sole originator of his or her speech is exposed as a fiction. The subjectivity "behind" the words of the song really belongs both to the shaman and to his psychotropic companion simultaneously. They have not entirely coalesced but come together in a complex state of mutual permeability or porosity, in which there is neither full identity nor full difference. "Resonance" might be a better term than "oscillation"; what gives the appearance of the latter is simply the temporal unfolding of the chant rather than the texture of the experience itself. In sum, instead of an oscillation of positions, the shaman attains a "higher" or "more perfect," which is to say more "dual," form of subjectivity. This enhanced or hyper-selfhood is not only a state of super well-being; it expresses a heightened capacity to act in the world. It should nevertheless be stressed that this dissolution of individuality can be very disconcerting at first, hence the repeated admonitions, expressed through the chant, not to be frightened or alarmed as the psychotropic takes hold.

There is also, importantly, a powerful asymmetry here. The psychotropic is inside the shaman's body, inhabiting and "visiting" him in this sense, but also "passing overhead" and "caring from above." The chants describe ayahuasca as "coming down" on the shaman, descending from overhead, almost like a cloak that encompasses him, and overwhelming him. The same principle of a nonhuman agency "exceeding" the drinker was of course already noted as a feature of the jichorojoe baauno, discussed in chapter 5. It is in just such an asymmetrical relationship that "drunkenness" is produced as a form of subjectivity that is in many ways considered "higher" than, while similar in structure to, that characterizing everyday life. It is a similar state of mutual permeability, I would suggest—neither identity nor difference—that characterizes the relation between the heart-soul of a game animal and its nonhuman owner.

It is also in the context of such a relationship that we should consider the act of psychotropic name bestowal. The shaman "births" the child socially, through the bestowal of a name received through his intimate engagement with the power of psychotropics, ideally personified as a paramour or potential spouse. This is also an act of subjection: the formation of the subject through the act of recognition by a powerful, divine authority. Through their joint participation in the formation of the child, the relation between the shaman and the psychotropic is further consolidated. There is a complex transmission of power here, passing through several levels, with multiple participants. The final section of this chapter explores the complex ways in which power is transmitted and refracted in the formation of subjects and in which the mastery of the shaman also emerges as a form of subjection. This is where practices of taming and raising reach their highest level as an art form.

AN OBEDIENT TEACHER

For several years, he told me, Lorenzo had been suffering from a chronic stomach problem. Western medicines, of the kind meted out by the German-run clinic a few days' travel downriver, were all but useless, as the cause was of a different order, one largely beyond their healing scope. During a long canoe journey some years previously, he had foolishly chosen to defecate, for convenience, in the middle of one of the rapids overlying shallow, rocky stretches of riverbed known as *caratiri* instead of mooring the canoe and heading inland into the forest. He was now quite certain that he would one day die as a result of the harm subsequently inflicted on him in revenge. Infants and small children are of course particularly susceptible to these attacks, which may be unprovoked, and I have traveled in the company of men who, despite having left their children at home in the care of their wives, still chose to give these rocky rapids a wide berth by making a detour on dry land where necessary, allowing their travel companions to pick them up in their canoe a little farther along.

Although a particular rocky stretch of riverbed may itself be considered an agent capable of causing harm, such agency seems concentrated in the small, bowl-shaped stones that may occasionally be found lying in their midst. Known as *egaando*, these are both feared and esteemed for their possession in abundance of the tiny darts or dartlike media (batohi) used in mystical attack. The illnesses these stones induce can be cured only by means of the appropriate baau chant, which invokes a series of beings noted for their immunity to attack by egaando, with the aim of integrating this desired quality into the sick child.

At this point in time, the egaando is effectively little more than a hostile concentration of will and "fearfulness." Although occupying a "point of view," and indeed capable of causing harm by "looking," its status as a person is ambiguous, diffuse, and devoid of individual identity. It is not readily distinguished as an entity separate from the rocky rapid in which it rests, or from their shared mother or owner. Perhaps even more significantly, the egaando dwells hitherto outside the moral sphere, lacking those important qualities, such as respect and care for others, that distinguish "real people." An untamed egaando is thus likened to a bacauha, the Urarina's traditional Candoshi enemies—formidable but decidedly subhuman.

If he is not deterred by the difficulty and inherent danger of the task, an egaando may be sought out and utilized by an experienced psychotropic drinker who wishes to increase his power, in particular, his knowledge of and control over the tiny blow darts used in mystical attacks. Along with the kapok and caupori trees, the stone is an important source of this knowledge, as well as a repository of the darts themselves. To utilize an egaando, one must first capture and tame it (irilaa), somewhat in the manner of a wild forest animal. A suitable specimen can be sought out at times of low water level, and is said to resemble the testicles of the white-lipped peccary. Once found, the man immediately blows tobacco smoke on the bowl and places it at the foot of a brugmansia tree, where its cooperation is gradually enlisted through forms of ritual dialogue. The mother of brugmansia and the egaando are directly addressed in turn, in their potential capacity as subjects, with the aim of soliciting assistance, subduing the egaando, and instigating asymmetrical relationships of companionship between the three participants.[14] In contrast to the performative force of the baau, there is no recourse here to external relations of transference. The underlying logic was explained to me as follows: "The man says to brugmansia in his trance, 'Help me, let's play together, such that the egaando, who has power, teaches me.'"

After several days at the foot of the brugmansia tree, the bowl is transferred to a clay jar and brought inside the house. Some claim the jar should be filled with water, to be changed every few days, for if the bowl dries out it is liable to "run away" or ensorcell those in its immediate proximity. In further chants addressed to the egaando the shaman requests it in his new capacity as "owner" to serve him obediently, to respect his family and not cause them harm, and to share its knowledge. Silent at first, the egaando eventually capitulates to the requests in brugmansia visions. It is used as a vessel for drinking concentrated tobacco juice, ingested continuously in conjunction with tobacco smoke. The man must learn to "listen" to the egaando's darts, which sing their songs "through" him as he drinks the tobacco juice. The theme of playing is again emphasized. When I asked who was playing with whom, I was told that "they are getting inebriated, playing together, going around together. The man is getting drunk with the tobacco juice, and also with the darts, he is playing with the darts, going around and around for fun . . . both sides are playing, together with egaando, they are all playing. The darts are making him sing. The darts are always singing. Wherever they are, they always have to demonstrate their manner." Said to resemble tiny worms, the darts are full of life (ichaoha), playful as well as lethal. The egaando "lays eggs" in the song in order "to have grandchildren," "to increase its numbers," and through these songs, through play, the darts are said to "empty out" into the man and multiply.

In exchange for the bowl's continued cooperation, the shaman submits to stringent dietary and other prohibitions. This self-imposed isolation from communal life frees him to "become like the egaando" and communicate with it more effectively. The stone is placed by the shaman's head when he sleeps and will approach him in his dreams, interrogating his motives for seeking it out and fasting with it. He will be asked about his wife, children, and relatives, and the stone may make clear its desire to inflict harm, or to "eat the liver" of one of them. The shaman must have mastered the art of dreaming in order to dissuade it and contain its aggressive instincts. One who lacks mastery of the relevant chants, or the discipline to fast properly, will similarly be unsuccessful in restraining it. Rosa recalled how her father possessed an egaando when she was small but was unable to tame it, and her brother became gravely ill and nearly died as a result.

Rigorous adherence to the fast becomes a form of leverage in such oneiric transactions for ensuring the bowl's continued cooperation. To the extent the shaman's family stay in good health, the egaando is considered to be keeping its end of the bargain, its ability to keep to its word indicating that the taming is proceeding well. After months of fasting the bowl finally enters the moral universe, respectful and obedient, sharing a close affinity with its owner. "A good egaando loves its owner," I was told, and "is like a teacher in the school," instructing him until he becomes a true benane—one with the facility to extract darts from an ensorcelled patient and redeploy them in retributive action. Such figures are the cornerstone of shamanic ideology and continue to command a sense of awe and a prominent place in everyday discourse that seems disproportionate with their now-dwindling numbers. Possession of an egaando, the hallmark of the benane, is enshrouded in a kind of pseudosecrecy, the topic of covert discussions that promote a suitable aura of fear better than any open advertisement. One informant recalled that his grandfather, after many months of fasting with egaando, had successfully tamed it to the point where he could communicate with it in an everyday, waking, nonritual context. He taught his egaando to watch over and protect his house while he traveled upriver on hunting trips, instructing it to "insult," in their dreams, any passing travelers tempted to sleep in the house. Persons so insulted have been known to leap up from their beds, shouting, running out of the house into the night. If they know how to dream, they will have realized that an egaando was responsible.

APPROACHING SUBJECTIVATION

The egaando's progression from an unpredictable predatory force to a petlike subordinate imbued with personality and a moral conscience is glossed by Urarina as the outcome of irilaa, taming or raising. As several authors have noted, taming is commonly associated with a conversion of affinity into consanguinity in Amazonia, a perspective that readily incorporates it within the structural logic of predation (e.g., Fausto 2007, 2000; Taylor 2001; Descola 1997). Yet ideologies of predation and, especially, warfare are far from salient in Urarina thought and practice, which emphasize peacefulness and passive forms of resistance over bellicose action. I would therefore argue that taming can be largely dissociated from warfare and predation and instead incorporated within a broader matrix of subjectivation, or subjection, implying the simultaneous subordination and forming of subjects.

The taming of the egaando can be divided, for analytic purposes, into two stages or axes. These are not conceived temporally but occur in parallel. The first of these is primarily discursive in nature, centering on the deployment of ritual discourse that demands its cooperation. By working in explicit alliance with the mother of brugmansia, revered for its unrivaled power, the shaman seeks to emphasize his position of authority. In his hallucinatory state he continues to address the stone, in its potential capacity as a subject, until it finally responds. This is construed as a kind of capitulation, a recognition of the power of those who call it. We might thus say that the egaando is hailed or interpellated into existence as a subject. Through the performance of ritual dialogues, the stone is positioned in language as a possible addressee, and given the opportunity to achieve and reproduce its own intelligibility: evidenced by its subsequent participation in further songs, such as those of the darts. The chants create a linguistic placeholder for the egaando, establishing the necessary conditions for it to produce itself as a subject, by "turning" toward the authority of the shaman and accepting the identity conferred on it through this founding submission. The egaando aligns itself with authority and responds to its demands, and is thereby endowed with a moral conscience. At the final stages of this trajectory, at least in principle, the egaando is an intelligible and coherent interlocutor even in a non-ritualized, nondreaming context.

In the second stage or axis of the taming process, the egaando agrees to teach the shaman and promises not to harm his family, despite its desire to do so, and the shaman in return undertakes to fast. Trust clearly emerges as a central issue here, as indeed it does in all other forms of companionship. Demonstrating an ability to keep to its word is highly significant in the construal of the egaando as a moral person rather than a mere concentration of dangerous predatory energy. Taming might thus be considered here in terms of what Nietzsche (1956 [1887]) described as the task of breeding an animal entitled to make promises. One who promises must be able to forge a continuity between an original determination and the actual performance of the thing willed, or between a statement and an act, across a time gap in which various other, competing circumstances or temptations might threaten to intervene. This protracted will enables the promising being to stand for itself through time.

The deal struck with the egaando demands the suppression of its instinct to inflict harm and the adoption of social norms, such as respect for others and personal responsibility. It is this good moral sense, evidenced through the performance of self-control and self-discipline, that makes the egaando most like a true person (cacha). It is not quite a consanguine (arai) but more like a neighbor or group fellow (laurijera). From an Urarina point of view, it would seem that the egaando's newfound "consciousness," as represented by its ability to enter into increasingly coherent dialogues, is the form its own will takes, its innate hostility or predatory force, when prevented from simple expression as a deed. It is an aggression turned inward and back on itself: an internalization that creates an autonomous, internal space, producing conscience and the conditions for reflexivity. This generative movement cannot readily be assimilated to a process of familiarizing predation, and the egaando is effectively coaxed or even coerced into a state of full personhood. Its identity emerges in and through its own willful submission to an external authority, on whom that identity depends. This becomes a form of self-submission: consciousness and conscience cannot be separated here; to be moral and to be a fully human person are virtually indistinguishable. In short, the subject is brought forth as and when power is progressively internalized and made "one's own," at the same time founding the distinction between internal and external. This process is arguably never complete, or never fully realized—hence the impossibility of ever fully distinguishing the avian owner of game animals from the animal's own heart-soul.

Urarina claim that a tamed egaando is not only possessed of moral sensibilities, and able to cooperate with others, but is highly dependent on and fiercely loyal to, even "loving," its owner and master. The significance of this newfound emotional bond is more intelligible if we consider that the egaando's identity as a person or subject was, from the very beginning, founded in a kind of "recognition" by and submission to an authority figure on whom it depended in every sense. To embrace that submission, to form a "passionate attachment" to subjection (Butler 1997), is thus equivalent to embracing the very conditions of its continued existence. It is worth noting that the situation of the baby in its hammock, while certainly more complex, does not necessarily differ in general outline from this scenario. As discussed in chapter 2, the baby experiences its physical dependency on the hammock as an intense emotional bond. Only specialized chants (cojiotaa) can placate a crying baby estranged from its hammock. The rattle's gentle messages, which shape and condition its new, human identity, are similarly from a protective authority who offers personalized recognition but to whom submission is mandatory. The skills for achieving personal autonomy later in life can be acquired only through a kind of founding submission to a situation of dependency and attachment.

Subjectivation is never a one-way process, as evidenced by the inevitable ensoulment of the baby hammock. Although a man who fasts with egaando is not himself considered subject to taming or raising per se, his consequent production as a powerful and knowledgeable benane, or sorcerer, is broadly analogous, despite the relationship's inherent asymmetry. As noted, the primary means by which he makes it clear he is upholding his end of the bargain is through rigorous adherence to a regime of dietary and other prohibitions. Fasting is of course widespread in Amazonia, and it is often considered of paramount importance in the acquisition of knowledge. One way of interpreting this is via notions of shared substance. A special diet severs the individual's material relation to the group, cutting the flux of shared food that constitutes the basis of sociability, thus creating the potential for individual transformation and opening up new channels of communication and new forms of sociability. One could argue, in other words, that the shaman severs the material basis of his relation to the group in order to form his own "community of substance" with the egaando, facilitating their communication. Among Urarina, as elsewhere, one indeed finds no shortage of ideas pertaining to food as a precursor to sociability.[15] This would certainly seem at least consistent with Martín's rhetorical remark, "Don't you see that the man is already like an egaando, after so many days of fasting?"

Notions of shared substance are nevertheless not the only dimension of fasting practices worthy of attention, especially given that food constitutes just one part of the total set of prohibitions put in force. In what follows I wish to draw attention to a different aspect of dieting practices, taking as a starting point the subjective position of the faster himself. One of the most commonly voiced sentiments concerning such fasts, whether shamanic or not, is that "you have to suffer" if you want something in return. As emphasized earlier, suffering, pity, and feelings of tenderness or benevolence are very closely connected in Urarina thought, and the demonstration of the former is a key strategy for eliciting the latter. The general sense of give-and-take that characterizes fasting is typically cast in a personalized, rather than depersonalized, way, such that one's "suffering" is moreover simultaneously the satisfaction of another's desires. From the shaman's point of view, he fasts above all because he is under the impression that the egaando wants him to do so. He is eager to maximize the quality of his relationship with it, and hence its usefulness to him. At the same time, this positive incentive is accompanied by a fear of direct punishment, given that if the fast is not rigorously followed the stone might respond violently and capriciously.

A similar rationale is present in many other shamanic practices. One who does not follow the prescribed fast after drinking brugmansia (abstaining from salt and sex, among other things) will be unable to achieve a satisfactory state of inebriation the next time he drinks, because "the brugmansia will be afraid of him." He must not bathe in the river, not for the sake of his own body, but because brugmansia "doesn't like the water" and will cause it to rain. His shamanic paraphernalia are worn "because brugmansia likes us to wear them," and he paints his face with achiote "to appear more friendly to brugmansia." A shaman who wears these items and paints his face thus puts himself in a positive state of mind in which he may confidently expect to be well received by brugmansia in his inebriation and their "playing" interaction to be a positive one. In the eyes of those around him—and hence further reinforcing his own subjective experience—the egaando and other shamanic paraphernalia are all important parts of a broader performance that objectifies his status as a powerful man of knowledge and a unique individual, distanced from the group in terms of both physical substance and specialized knowledge. His chants, enunciated in a specialized, ritual language that is partially obscure to laypeople, can be seen to serve similar ends.

In short, although it may seem to us that the shaman's dietary regime is entirely self-imposed, it cannot be construed this way if it is to be

deemed efficacious. From the point of view both of a shaman's own subjective experience and the performative force of his actions on others,
undertaking to fast, like wearing the requisite paraphernalia or painting one's face with achiote, is a means of establishing a positive affective relationship and couches his encounters with nonhuman agencies in
terms of a transactional reciprocity. He has ostentatiously fulfilled all the
requirements for achieving an intimate and mutually rewarding relationship with a powerful nonhuman agency capable of imparting valued esoteric knowledge, an act for which such a relationship is a necessary precondition. His "mastery" over the egaando, his power, as it were, is not
a form of coercion, dependent as it is on the latter's willingness to share
its knowledge. Although entered into voluntarily, the shaman accepts
that any infractions of this relationship's terms and conditions will be
met with severe punishment. The expansion of the man's knowledge,
assumed to coincide with his moral progress—in short, the production
of his specialized form of subjectivity as a benane—is thus contingent
on his prolonged and voluntary submission to a particular disciplinary
regime. The reciprocal tenor of this relationship, through which powerful benane are produced, echoes that important process, discussed in
chapter 4, by which infants learn to achieve recognition and validation as
individual subjects in and through those actions that meet the needs and
desires of others. As a general rule, people come to be themselves—the
particular kinds of person they are—only in such shared spaces of intimacy and mutuality.

In concluding this account of the egaando's moral journey, it is worth
drawing attention to where we must part company from perspectivist
assumptions. Egaando are indeed considered to be alive, to possess animal or vegetal souls (or both) and a mother/owner, yet such attributions
would seem almost incidental to their gradual positioning as subjects.
The ability to occupy a "point of view" does not guarantee or index personhood, and their changing subjectivity relies not on a soul or body but
on shifting relations to its owners and masters. This opens up important questions of variation foreclosed by the perspectivist recourse to
overarching inversions: how and why, for example, animism and perspectivism are not unilaterally applied to nonhumans and may often be
restricted to particular species, "those which perform a key symbolic and
practical role" (Viveiros de Castro 1998: 471).

As I have already suggested, the notion that the mother/owner figure is a personification, or hypostatization, of the species with which it
is associated, or even of an animal's predatory energy or "jaguar part," is

in danger of conflating the relation between the individual and its species and their mother or owner. It will already be clear that the figures
of cojoaaorain, urichoraaona, and janoraain are of an entirely different
nature or order than the animals they advise and protect, and can hardly
be viewed as reified versions or transformations of them, even though
they are perhaps not entirely separate entities either. Similarly, the
egaando and its mother or owner are referred to interchangeably when
the former is still in the river, yet this is not the case once it is extracted,
where the egaando alone is addressed directly, and the shaman attempts
to usurp the power of its erstwhile master. There is a kind of duality or
even multiplicity here, in which power is refracted across several levels
at once.

Based primarily on Yanomami ethnography, Viveiros de Castro (2007)
has made an intriguing characterization of Amazonian spirits as nonvis-
ible and noniconic "images," awaiting actualization from a virtual "background." At one point in the analysis, he picks up on the Yanomami leader
Dawi Kopenawa's use of the Portuguese term *representante* (representative or delegate) to describe these images, noting its importance in the
political vocabulary of indigenous leaders in Brazil. He then correlates it
with Alfred Gell's (1998) use of the "diplomat" to illustrate the concept of
aniconic symbol: "'The Chinese ambassador in London . . . does not look
like China, but in London, China looks like him.' We can paraphrase this
by saying the *xapiripë* [shamanic spirits] do not look like animals, but in
the mytho-shamanic context, animals do look like them" (Viveiros de
Castro 2007: 160).

The political connotation is a welcome addition, but in the Urarina
case, at least, such an interpretation would be to reverse the proper flow
of delegation and invert the necessary hierarchical ordering. The animals
stand in an indexical, not symbolic, relationship to their owner, while
the latter is often spoken of as "employee" or "envoy," not of the animal,
but of Our Creator. I have argued that the mother/owner figure might
better be understood as an accomplice in the creation of shared, protective spaces inside which persons may come into being while at the same
time representing the "voice" of authority that alone is capable of confer-
ring and safeguarding personal identity. Power and speech are closely
connected in Amazonia, just as authority is often expressed verbally,
which is why songbirds—which are almost "pure voice," rarely seen but
highly esteemed as divine messengers and mouthpieces—are such logical
choices for the form assumed by the owners of animals.

To be a living being means always to be accompanied. In Martín's words, "Every animal has to have its companion"; or as Lorenzo put it, "No one can live alone." Yet one's companions are rarely one's equals in every sense, and asymmetries pervade the lived spaces within which all beings dwell. As these shift and transform, so too do the possibilities for achieving a stable individual identity. Realignments of attachments and dependencies—often, though not always, expressed in bodily modifications or transformations—would go some way toward accounting for the variable and sometimes transient nature of subjectivity in Urarina lived worlds. Hence prior to their incorporation within the human realm, game animals, or the egaando, are only "people" in a very limited and partial sense, more potential than actual. It is through a more radical form of subjection to human owners and masters, in which lines of authority and dependency are gradually redrawn, that the former state is converted into the latter, and they achieve fuller recognition as subjects with whom communication is possible.

The mastery exhibited by the shaman—his capacity to defend and care for the living—requires in turn his own submission to a higher power. His incorporation of the psychotropic and yielding to its power—which echoes the control of the game animal by its spirit mother—is a cogent strategy for achieving his ends. His enhanced selfhood reflects a state of resonance, an inspiration or cohabitation through which the speaking subject becomes dual or distributed. As a condition of extreme well-being and vitality, one that beautifies his heart-soul, this bold inebriety contrasts radically with the weakened state of the sick patient, whose dangerous openness to hostile pathogens in the wider environment reflects a breakdown of the protective spaces established with others, and an excessive isolation. Aside from any debilitating physical symptoms, this may be experienced as a terrifying inability to attach to or be cared for by one's peers, an enduring anxiety or state of fright that echoes the condition of the climate itself and epitomizes the vulnerability of the lone individual.

Epilogue

An Accompanied Life

Old Gustodio lay motionless as the visitors started to arrive, the only sign of life the barely detectable rise and fall of his blankets. One of his sons, a quiet lad named Amiuri, gently fanned air over his tired body. I stared at the floor in front of me as one person after another slowly wandered over and climbed the steps to the house, easing themselves down onto the stilt palm floor. Nobody spoke a word. From far away across the river I could hear the whistling of a tinamou. The heavy atmosphere that clung to the house like a thick fog was unlike anything else I had experienced in the field. After a while there were at least two dozen people of all ages seated under the dilapidated roof or standing around nearby, looking over in silence at the near-lifeless body. Among them were two of Gustodio's daughters, now old widows themselves. I noticed how exhausted Gustodio's young wife looked, as she tried, unsuccessfully, to ease a little banana drink through his lips. He was beyond eating and drinking now. She gave up, and we all sat together, sharing the silence, for what seemed like hours.

My mind wandered back to when we all buried one of Gustodio's former wives some months ago. She had been wrapped tightly in her own woven sleeping mat, sealed up inside an old canoe, and floated downstream to the cemetery. I remembered how when she was still able to eat old Gustodio had traveled all the way upriver to San Pedro by canoe, together with his new family, to try to heal her by drinking psychotropics. I thought about what Martín later claimed to have overheard her say to him on her deathbed: "It's your fault I'm sick, your fault for having sexual relations with your own family! You will surely suffer in the celestial fire for a lot longer than I will. You too will die before long." I don't know how many years had elapsed since he abandoned her, but her bitterness didn't really surprise me. Most of the people I knew on the upper Chambira could readily trace their ancestry to Gustodio and one of at least four successive wives that I knew of. I also never heard anyone spoken of with such profound respect. I lost count of how many times I exhausted informants' knowledge and patience with my endless questions, to have them tell me I should really be asking old Gustodio, not them, as he knew so much more and had in any case taught them most of what they knew. They would often comment that he still lived wandering from place to place, never staying still, despite being so old, just like the ancient people did. One of the last remaining benane, Gustodio was the only man I met who refused to speak a single word of Spanish.

It was Gustodio himself who once told me a story about mortality. It described how the very first people, when they grew old, would lie down by the hearth and let themselves be heated by it until their skin shriveled up like a plastic bag in the flames before falling away to reveal a young, healthy, beautiful body underneath. Only the snakes and lizards possessed this knowledge now, and the trees who change their leaves, season after season. Gustodio's body, on the other hand, would have to enter the cold earth and "be lost."All this to the great dismay of Our Creator, who, I was assured, did not want it to be that way. The wailing laments that follow every death center almost exclusively on this terrible fate of the body: "Never again will I see your body standing / Your body is going over there into the ground / Never again will you stand your body with our food / Your poor body is going to suffer . . . " According to local folklore, as a veteran drinker of psychotropics, Gustodio's passing would soon be followed by a sharp deterioration in the weather. Portended by the forlorn singing of the dove, the sky would darken dramatically, the wind would howl in pity, and the pouring rain would herald this ominous step closer to the world-era's imminent collapse.

Unlike the body, nobody lamented the fate of the soul. As a veteran drinker of psychotropics, Gustodio's soul would be "beautiful," despite his former wife's admonitions; after passing through the celestial fire, it would immediately be received by the araracuru, or thunder-people. As I understood it, the thunder-people both defended earthbound humans from their celestial vantage point and welcomed their souls when they finally ascended to the sky to rest. Jorge had once explained this to me:

> A long time ago, the noble thunder-people groups were created, together with the creation of the sky. The noble groups, our grandparents, and our sky, were created for us by Our Father, lasting up to the present day. Our Creator lifted and set up our sky so that when

the mestizos want to make us suffer, they will be reprimanded by the noble thunder-people groups, our grandparents. When the mestizos want to harm us, or when the mestizos speak [badly] to us, they come out in our favor and defend us strongly over here. Our Creator put the noble thunder-people groups in place in order to defend us up until the present day, and for the heart-souls of our psychotropic drinkers [coaairi coera], those forgotten ones, so that they arrive over there, in front of where the noble group-companions are, in beautifully painted hammocks.

As beacons of virtue, the souls of psychotropic drinkers are justly rewarded after death, received and harbored by the noble thunder-people groups (*caoacha laurinacauru araracuru*). But others, too, can still enjoy this privilege; Manuel once told me that when any sick person dies, the thunder-people will receive him or her as hosts welcoming guests to their celestial abode, treating them according to the kind of life they led. Only those who pursue an immoral life—stingy, belligerent, incest-commit-ting—will be deprived of the privileges awaiting the righteous.

There is nothing for those whose life is poor. When a person who lives with their family [i.e., commits incest] dies, they are received by demons who burn and punish, like Moconajaera, who burns their souls. Those who live with the mestizos go to rest with the mestizos, not with the Urarina. They don't go to the sky, they go to another place. Hence they don't see their families ever. They will never see the faces of their families.

The sky is said by many people to be "like a city, like Iquitos"; less often, "like the beaches of the Marañon River: well swept, with no [leaf] litter anywhere." Those who reside there "seem like they are going around in a passenger ferry—pure hammocks everywhere." The image of a celestial resting place free of vegetation and filled with beautifully painted ham-mocks is certainly striking. As we have seen, the principal owners and users of hammocks are infants, who exist in a state of extreme depen-dency and vulnerability. Always an infant's closest companion, the ham-mock with its rattle provides a nurturing, protective space that eases the transition from intrauterine life, largely by replicating it. At death the shadow-soul is thought to be reunited with the true placenta, which was carefully buried in the birth hole, while the heart-soul ascends to the sky where it, too, is completed and enclosed within the beautifully painted hammock, thus in a sense reduplicating, in the celestial abode, the fate of the shadow-soul on earth.

Death mirrors birth in some ways, to be sure, but inasmuch as birth is a kind of dawn, linguistically and conceptually, individual death, like the end of the world-era, is always marked by darkness and night. Sociologically, the two processes are very different indeed: if birth unifies and consolidates residential groups, death is an occasion for their partial dissolution. The deceased's house is burned, along with all other material possessions, and its remaining inhabitants seek refuge elsewhere.

But what of the mysterious thunder-people and their "noble groups"? Common wisdom has it that the heart-souls of the virtuous reside next to them, joining with them as laurijera, neighbors or group companions. Lorenzo thought that Our Creator eventually transforms each heart-soul into a thunder-person, by bestowing on it a new name, to replace the old. In contrast to the arai, or bilateral kindred, present-day earthly lauri are founded not in shared blood or bodily substance but in coresidence and physical proximity, as difficult as it might be in practice to distinguish these criteria of group membership. In their celestial "noble" or "beautiful" version, such lauri are not only humanity's destiny but in a sense their origin too: they are composed of "our grandparents" or "our ancestors." Is this another variation on the classic Amazonian theme of "Other-becoming"? Could it be that these noble thunder-people groups represent a transposition into the celestial realm, a divinization or apotheosis, of the clans that once structured life here on earth? As Viveiros de Castro (1992: 254) has emphasized, the Other does not really function as a mirror in Amazonia, as it does in the West, so much as a destiny or a pole of attraction. Yet unlike the Araweté case that he describes, where gods incorporate the dead by devouring them, the Urarina subject is never the victim of divine cannibalism. It is not an omnipresent ontological predation that makes this society possible.

"We always must accompany someone who is dying," Manuel once told me. "We should stay watching until the very end." Even as he spoke we both knew well that this latter ideal was rarely if ever actually met. "Sometimes . . . sometimes people leave the dying person because they're afraid, returning the following day to check on him. Sometimes they take a dying person to the forest, to die there." Once the visitors had left the abandoned house where old Gustodio was laid out, they did not return, not even the next morning, when the sorry family departed by canoe, headed downriver to where the young wife's kinfolk were living. Wanting nothing more to do with the whole affair, the rest of the community of Nueva Unión had slept together in the three houses located farthest away, on the other side of the football field, fearing that his malignant ghost might torment them when it exited his body shortly before his death.

These dreadful moments just before death are the closest thing to solitude in a life that is always, and in so many ways, lived in the company of others. As I have argued throughout this book, to be alive and to be a full moral person means always to be accompanied in the Urarina lived world.

This emphasis on companionship, as the defining condition of possibility of the subject, does not square well with the theory of perspectivism, which positions the subject within a matrix of predation, affirms the structural significance of affinity and alterity rather than intimacy, and posits the figures of the enemy and the animal—rather than the companion—as transcendental determinations of Amazonian thought. Yet it can be argued that the perspectivist reading of Amazonian ethnography is biased toward the highly predatory cosmology of a relatively restricted sample of language families, notably the Panoan, Jivaroan, and Tupi-Guaraní (Henley 1996).[1] This downplaying of regional variation could be considered in terms of a relative lack of interest in concrete political and historical processes, arguably a legacy of structuralism. The articulation of perspectivism in terms of a generic struggle to turn others into kin usefully introduces a theory of power, yet there are good reasons for viewing "familiarizing" processes in terms of more concrete regional and historical dynamics, according to which, for example, weaker groups were systematically victimized by stronger groups. Recent research on ancient patterns of exoslavery and servitude points to the prevalence of strongly asymmetrical relations between groups linked together in heterogeneous regional power systems (Santos Granero 2005a).[2] Dominant slaving societies saw their weaker enemies as slave-breeding or servant-breeding populations, "marked with the stigma of servitude even before they were actually defeated and subjugated" (Santos Granero 2005a: 166). Not all forms of institutionalized subjection relied on physical coercion: common arrangements included attached servant groups and subordinated tributary populations (168 n.). Gender difference and imagery again emerge as significant here, as masters were seen as occupying a masculine position and subordinates a feminine one.

If the Urarina do not espouse the predatory view, it may be in no small measure for historical reasons, including the shape taken by regional power dynamics. Subjectivities, and the local theories that surround them, do not emerge in political and historical vacuums. The same might be said of ontology, which is often treated as static and timeless. As scholarly interest increasingly turns to networks of trade as well as of exploitation, slavery, and violence on a regional scale, there is a need to more adequately situate ontological claims in regional and historical contexts, in a way that does justice to significant, long-term, intergroup differentiations. Though I have only fleetingly addressed Urarina ethnohistory, precursory analysis of a large corpus of stories, combined with what little written historical information is available, points to some important recurring themes. One is that the Urarina have traditionally been forced to occupy a relatively subordinate position vis-à-vis their more powerful and warlike neighbors, such as the Candoshi and Cocama. Although violence pervades many accounts of interactions with these groups, Urarina rarely see themselves as aggressors and instead identify themselves as righteous or noble victims with the moral high ground. Jivaroan enemies are feared, much like jaguars, but also roundly denounced as belligerent "savages," deficient in terms of respect, self-discipline, and other quintessentially human qualities.[3] Mestizos, too, figure prominently as conquerors and overlords, maintaining their dominance through brutality as well as cunning. These power asymmetries, to be sure, are not legitimized by love or protection.It would not quite be accurate to claim that Urarina identify themselves as prey rather than predators on the axis of predation, despite their admission of vulnerability. If anything, it is the figure of the pet to which they feel a certain affinity. Pets are, of course, in Amazonia at least, typically the captured and domesticated offspring of prey animals slain in the hunt. Partly for this reason, pets are likened to orphans, bereft of parents and deserving of pity—hence the tendency for singers to describe themselves as orphans in drinking songs as a way of humorously eliciting engagement from their listeners. Yet the pet is not simply another figure emerging from the matrix of predation, for what is perhaps most significant is its capacity to become enmeshed in asymmetrical relations of loving care. Pets are the recipients of much affection and bring joy to their owners, often children, who care for them and grow attached to them and who above all accompany them, for pets are nothing if not good company. In emphasizing the figure of the pet—and avoiding in the process the simple valorization of predation—the Urarina are perhaps pointing to a fundamental feature of all human existence. To be a true subject is first and foremost to be accompanied, to be situated within an animating field of care and protection.

The figure of the companion elaborated here may well be a transformation of sorts of another relation that has received far more attention in Amazonia: the political ally, quintessentially an affine, which Viveiros de Castro (2010: 43) acknowledges is more important, sociocosmologically, than the outright enemy. Yet there is a certain tendency toward proximity in the actual Urarina brother-in-law relation, as I have shown: an instability that resolves itself into companionship in the form of ritual co-parents, who collaborate in producing new members of the community. Once again it is the process of creating life rather than destroying it, of producing persons and enabling their autonomy, that seems here to be most sociologically productive. In any case, one senses that the key unit of ethnosociology is not the individual but the accompanied self or dyad.

In emphasizing that the self is made through accompaniment and cannot be reduced to a stable or unitary point of view, I am not simply proposing that perspectivism may be valid for some parts of Amazonia but not for the Urarina for historical or cultural reasons of the kind just discussed. Perspectivism powerfully pinpoints the problematic foundations of culturalist arguments of this kind, in which nature is effectively bracketed out for the purposes of making cultural comparisons. On the one hand, it may well be that the predatory configuration of the dyad is a particular case of a more overarching, pan-Amazonian concern for the relational grounding of the subject and its medial or distributed qualities. On the other hand, the Urarina direct our attention to certain fundamental aspects of human experience that apply to us all, regardless of our ontological commitments. In other words, the Urarina lived world that I have sought to elucidate may offer profound insights on fundamental human existential predicaments relating to our constitutively accompanied way of being.

In seeking to understand the basis of Urarina companionship, the series of jera relationships is a good place to start: in order of increasing inclusivity and indeterminacy, sinijera (sleeping companion, spouse), amujera (walking companion, paramour), corijera (shadow-soul companion), and laurijera (group companion). All have an important voluntary dimension and are not "given" in any sense; all mediate, or transcend, the antinomy of affinity and consanguinity. In the end, their salience for Urarina might even be in part a consequence of a relatively essentialized view of the latter, characterized in terms of moral duties and obligations. The unmarked form (jera) implies an integral, dyadic relation, meaning roughly "the other one" or "its pair," as well as "next to" (cf. *jerajejein*, "side by side"): the left leg is the jera of the right leg. But the missing sock of a pair is simply its *laucha*, "other," as is the second of two sons or brothers, or two polygynously married wives. There is an all-important sense of dependency here—although not, strictly speaking, of equality. Much shamanic practice is concerned with developing and nourishing such fellowships with nonhuman agencies; chants implore the shaman to "be a companion" *(jera neeine)* of the mother of the psychotropic he has consumed.

Such ideas may not be peculiar to the Urarina: the Piro shaman's song, we are told, is simultaneously a "learning" and a "joining in with"; as one man explained it, "The shaman is singing to his companion, to what he sees" (Gow 2001: 147). The central concept here, we are told, is *gipxaleta,* "to accompany, to help another."

Might there be an ultimate source, a basis, for the concept of an integral, dyadic relationship founded in proximity and dependency? When a newborn child first comes into the world, it does not come alone but accompanied. As Sloterdijk (2011) has put it, all births are births of twins. Recognition of a vital and formative attachment to the placenta, one that endures emotionally or spiritually even in the face of physical separation, is a strikingly widespread phenomenon, though it tends to receive little more than passing acknowledgment from anthropologists. Yet the idea that the placenta is forever joined to the fate of the infant with whom it shared the maternal womb is ubiquitous. Among the Amazonian Matsigenka, the umbilical cords and placentas of newborns are carefully buried in the floor or patio of the house where they are born, and this site "remains a central point of reference and territorial identity throughout the lifetime and, apparently, beyond it" (Shepard 2002: 209; see also Descola 1994: 121). Transformation of this relationship is often recognized; hence among the Airo-Pai hammocks are associated with the envelope of the placenta (Belaunde 1994: 109 n. 5). There are countless examples beyond Amazonia (see Davidson 1985 for an overview). Concluding one comparative study, Leach (1950: 24–25) writes that "what becomes of the afterbirth either influences or determines the whole life-story of the child. It is variously believed to embody his own soul-substance or his guardian spirit, to be either his brother, twin, or actual double, or to be so mystically and inseparably connected with him that its treatment or fate will shape his skills, luck and fate."

A brief survey of the literature is enough to convince one that modern Western culture is virtually unique in its indifference to the fate of this organ. Might this have more than a little to do with the dominant Western ideology of individualism—a similarly striking denial of our constitutively accompanied nature? According to Sloterdijk (2011), who considers the issue at some length, it would be difficult to overstate the importance of our original and defining condition of accompaniment in the womb, as a result of which our being is always a being-together; we necessarily always inhabit a shared intimacy with others. Western psychoanalytic theories have long built on the insight that the subject achieves independence through a constitutive loss that cannot be mourned, though

Sloterdijk proposes that the primary attachment is not to the mother. It is instead to that diffuse, shadowy presence, later objectified as the placenta, which is not experienced by the fetus as an object so much as a coinhabitant within an intimate, enclosed space: the first "there" from which the first "here" is conceived. It is this loss—dramatized in the act of severing the umbilical cord—that drives a lifelong quest for reunification and an incessant tendency toward the pair. Much as the placenta operates as an exchange point between maternal and fetal blood circulation, the quintessential companion is thus a kind of membrane, a semipermeable zone of mediation between the subject and the outside world.

The reverence with which the placenta is treated by Urarina and the care with which it is buried in the birth hole are not without foundation. If they do not manage an elaborate series of myths or cosmological principles concerning twins per se—as do so many other Amazonian groups—it may be precisely because this conceptual complex has undergone something of a transformation, reemerging in a different mode or register. Urarina do not identify the placenta with the guts of the child, as do the Piro (Gow 2001: 112). The severance of the umbilical cord, as the single most defining moment in the constitution of the individual, does not result in the closure of the guts and the production of an interiority, in the form of a stomach that can be filled with food. It results instead in the appearance of the shadow-soul: equally a prerequisite for entry into human sociality and the establishment of certain indispensable interpersonal relationships. The separation of child and placenta is not a simple division of "one" into "two"; the fetus and the placenta coexisted inside the womb as a kind of bipolarity, what Sloterdijk dubs a dual unity: a perfect duality characterized by intimate cohabitation in an interior space. The placenta is not a "first design" (Gow 2001: 140) for Urarina but a "first companion."

Severing an infant from its placenta is a defining moment in the transition into human sociality. It opens up a space, a potential, a gap to be filled by others—but not others who are only, or necessarily, "related insofar as they are different from each other" (Viveiros de Castro 2001: 25). There is an important middle ground, somewhere between "identity" and "difference," which is what I suspect the shadow-soul is all about: a register of relatedness that is not necessarily antipredatory so much as nonpredatory, nonaffinal just as much as it is nonconsanguineal. The umbilical cord is testimony to the possibility of separating from "communities of blood," strictly speaking, in order to enter a world marked by exchanges of other kinds of fluids: breath, for example, or manioc beer, or words, shaping personal identity with reference to a wider defining community with whom analogous forms of intimacy are possible. From this perspective, the basis of sociality and cooperation is less a matter of mutual comprehension than of being with others who are subtly but irreducibly different from ourselves.[4] Separation from the placenta launches a desire for reunification that persists throughout a life, testimony to the fact of being alive and enmeshed in relations of proximity but also, crucially, distance from others. For to be fully rejoined with the original companion means no longer to be a true person, a real, living human being—hence the widespread notion that such reunion is for the dead, for the souls of the deceased. To be alive is to exist in a state of longing. Hence the dyadic tendency in human sociality: it is only within the pair that we really come to be who we are, and it is within such spaces that we are re-formed and renewed.

Urarina people recognize that in the ambiguous transitional phase that immediately follows this first constitutive "cut" for the subject, the relatively minimal subjectivity of body ornaments and other artifacts make them well suited to playing an accompanying role. The hammock, in particular, sets up a protective space or field within which the child can safely dwell and come into existence as a fully human being. Unable to defend itself, a baby is always in need of care—so often articulated, especially in these early stages, as "shielding" (bujuaa). Much later in life, this same structure of protection or defense will be echoed in many other relationships, including ritual co-parenthood and especially matrimony, combined with a strong sense of mutual respect—which is itself ultimately construed as a defense of the heart-soul. These relationships, which lie at the heart of Urarina sociality, are pervaded by an attitude of attentiveness and attunement that does not inhibit individual freedom but enables it. Yet an equally important connotation is that of containment or enclosure: constructing spaces of refuge, as it were, which range in scale from the hammock or the birth hut to the world-era itself, as a kind of precariously supported bubble, always on the brink of catastrophic implosion. The "climate control" enacted by drinkers of psychotropics is ultimately all about the preservation of such interior spaces, postponing the apocalypse by soliciting from a caring, watchful Creator the ultimate gift of all: time.

Care and the giving and receiving of nurturance are central to Urarina sociality and concepts of self , as of course they are in most Amazonian societies. They are expressions of love (belaiha), albeit grounded less in the eros of mutual desire than in acts of unconditional giving (belaiha), whether of food or other forms of nurturance, along with visiting (bedainiha) and other forms of caring (beraiha). This kind of love is not only performed by kin: one's *beelaicha* is anyone who gives to you freely. Finally, a genuine caretaker (beraera), such as a wife caring for a husband while he drinks psychotropics, is like that person's silhouette or shadow (beraera or beraecha), which of course is also just another manifestation, or instantiation, of the shadow-soul. Neither "identity" nor "difference" but intense proximity and a reciprocal, if asymmetrical, entanglement.

Asymmetry is an important, perhaps indispensable component of such relationships. Care is so often expressed in terms of vigilance and attentiveness, watching over or keeping an eye on a loved one in need, in order to shield or protect him or her from harm. In an important sense, this is humanity's existential condition, nurtured and protected by pitying, beneficent divinity: the thunder-people in the first instance and ultimately Our Creator. The giving that characterizes such relationships flows primarily in one direction and legitimizes power asymmetries. Not only humans become subjects by such means: many other beings, too, can count on an attentive mother or owner who is continually protecting and advising. Thus a game animal's well-being, indeed survival, is entirely dependent on the vigilance of its avian caretaker and guardian; the reverse is not the case. Yet the owners are in turn the subordinates, or "employees," of Our Creator, who delegates tasks to them much as a mother delegates to the hammock, or Moconajaera to the traders, who control the distribution of "his" goods (or, breaking it down still further, as one trader delegates to his employees or envoys). What may at first appear to be a dyadic relationship is thus very often the coalescence or condensation, or idealized representation, of what is ultimately an enchainment, a hierarchical network.

From the point of view of the subject, this asymmetry has a further, important consequence. Care, nurturance, and protection are not always gifts freely given; often they must be evoked or solicited. Notions of care and the self are embedded in a relational ethics predicated on responsiveness and receptivity to others as well as broader conceptions of what is good and valuable. To know who one is means in part to be oriented in moral space. Along such lines, gestures of solicitation of care or protection become a principal vehicle for the expression of agency. A variety of more or less subtle strategies may be deployed, in appropriate contexts, to emphasize one's status as "helpless" or "suffering," in order to elicit the appropriate nurturing impulses in others. Such contexts range from the whimsical and lighthearted (as in a ritual co-mother placing herself in the position of an orphan in a drinking song) to the earnest (drawing attention to one's suffering state in order to elicit compassionate gifts of food) to the deadly serious (as in a shaman soliciting time, health, or game animals from Our Creator after drinking psychotropics). As one man put it, "We always request Our Creator, who is truly there for us, to give us all kinds of things." Underlying this possibility is the widespread view that "Our Creator watches over us with pity and compassion," and a central role of shamanism is carefully to mediate and reinforce this fundamental relationship in order to make visible and tangible otherwise hidden resources.

There are important implications here for how we might think more about power in Amazonia, and possibly elsewhere. Though we might be accustomed to thinking that submission consists in simply yielding to an externally imposed dominant order, or that it is characterized by a loss of control or autonomy, we find that it instead turns out to be a form of mastery, and a venue for the expression of agency.[5] This is why the question of subjectivity cannot be divorced from discussions of power, which can pervade the most intimate spheres of human existence. Legitimate forms of power have little or nothing to with a leader enforcing his will on others; Urarina leadership is based on the capacity to inspire and mobilize people for voluntary collective action of various sorts, and to generate valued forms of togetherness. Because of the emphasis on autonomy and the recognition that it emerges from relatedness, real power—at least that which is socially valued and promoted—is ultimately the power to create selves and social groups.

One of the central problems of social and cultural theory for at least the past century has been how to accommodate the role of the person or subject. Are human subjects actors who create relationships, or do they act instead as the precipitation of relationships? This conceptual dilemma has been discerned at the root of endless dichotomies of individual and society, equality and hierarchy, or autonomy and relatedness. I have tried to show how these are all, in effect, false oppositions. In contrast to both the perspectivist and traditional Western treatment of the subject as at base a unique location or vantage point—arguably embedded in the modernist assumption that the subject can be treated as if its existence did not depend, at every stage, on its intimate relations with others—the category of the subject might more usefully be approached as less a point of view than as an animated field of attachments and dependencies.

Because of the many senses in which persons are "crafted" rather than simply "created" in Amazonia, the conceptual framework advanced by Gell (1998) may help us to pursue these issues under a different light.

However, there is an important proviso here, for although notions of agency are central to my analysis, they clearly cannot be reduced to any simple dichotomy of "agent" and "patient" or of "primary agent" and "secondary agent." In the final analysis, virtually any entity or phenomenon attributed some kind of efficacy, or capacity to act on the world, provokes an abduction to a superordinate being or power. The cosmological concept of the owner or mother is premised on all-pervasive indexicality. Only Our Creator, resembling in this sense a kind of Prime Mover, exists "above" this logic, standing for nothing but himself. Humans, for their part, inevitably first index the agency of their parents, as the visible products of their hard "work," and second that of myriad nonhumans, whose capacities are introjected or enfolded into the developing self through the hammock and other forms of ritual discourse. There is no room for a concept of the fully autonomous individual, in this view, because agency and subjectivity always belong to two or more.

Casting a glance back in time, by considering the archaeological records of complex, hierarchical societies in prehistoric Amazonia, might shed more light on Urarina strategies for representing and managing asymmetrical relationships. The organization of many such societies seems to have been ranked or stratified in sociopolitical hierarchies, composed of regional and local chiefs, nobles, commoners, and subordinate individuals such as servants, client foragers and farmers, and captive slaves (Roosevelt 1993: 260). In addition to large-scale organized warfare for defense and conquest, systems of exchange and gift-giving were much more elaborated than today. Roosevelt also discusses some intriguing pottery: both male and female images are represented with shamanic paraphernalia, such as stools, rattles, and special hats, and "as alter ego figures with an animal on their shoulders. A concept of hierarchy and subordination may be discerned in the imagery representing small human figures as appendages or supports to large ones" (263–64). An emphasis on entanglements at various degrees of asymmetry is not, in short, a recent phenomenon.

Nevertheless, the steady transformations in the bases of power and authority that have taken place over recent decades direct attention to new and emergent forms of subjectivity. While the everyday prominence of Our Creator shows little sign of diminishing in the near future, the Peruvian state is an increasingly important player when it comes to elaborating personal and group identities and allegiances. Such a scenario, so common to indigenous peoples worldwide, highlights the need for the kind of wide-ranging approach that explicitly aims to bridge psychic, social, and political dimensions of subject formation, ranging from the most intimate spheres of human existence to the interpellating effects of official ideologies and state bureaucracies. Though it remains to be seen just how peoples like the Urarina will develop their own modalities of citizenship at a time when indigenous rights and identities are under considerable pressure from above, careful ethnographic attention to the processes through which persons and groups are created and reproduced will remain essential for understanding how these difficult transitions play out at the level of individual, embodied experience at the same time that they help to illuminate a more fundamental paradox of human existence, as being at once uniquely alone in the world and always lived in the close company of others.

On the day of old Gustodio's departure, Lorenzo and the other residents of Nueva Unión were more concerned with the painful business of forgetting the dead. To make matters more difficult, the gloomy weather just around the corner would serve as a reminder of their loss. Perhaps a dove would sing in mourning, as is often said to happen when the sky grows dark and the apocalypse looms. A celebration of life may be the only adequate response in such times. At least the abandonment of the deathly ill by the healthy is also a preparation for the new mode of sociality soon to be entered into, alongside the thunder-people. The living will go on living, loving their lives, if they are fortunate.

cana choajae coricha	Dove of our sky
nesocoritiin niane cana choajae banara	When our sky grows dark
coricha corite corite corine	Little dove, little dove
nesocoritiin niane cana choajae banara	When our sky grows dark
saatono nedojiariin nedojiaaca	For the last time let's get drunk
saatono	Until the very end
Cana Coaaunera notaraae	Under Our Creator's watchful eye
dojiara coaaecaan ajeton	I'm drunk with this force of manioc beer
nesocoritiin nia cana choajae bana	When our sky grows dark
corite oeque	Hear the dove's song
corite corine	Little dove, little dove

Notes

1. Generally speaking, the term *person* is used to designate a social agent; it is a moral and legal concept that refers to the individual as part of a social order. The person typically comprises both spiritual (or psychical) and material (or biological) components. The term *self* is most often used to emphasize the human being as a locus of experience, designating an individual's awareness of a unique identity (Harris 1989), whereas *subject* implies the capacity to have experiences or hold intentional states such as beliefs or desires. These terms should not be entirely conflated; nor is it practicable or desirable, in my opinion, to seek to maintain any absolute or rigid distinction between them (see also Bloch 2011). In any case, we almost inevitably draw on available cultural concepts of the person organize our experience and to conceive of ourselves as conscious beings (Harré 1983; see also Morris 1994).

2. See, e.g., Marriott and Inden 1977; Strathern 1988; Shweder and Bourne 1984; Kondo 1990; Geertz 1973; Conklin and Morgan 1996. See also Spiro 1993 and Bloch 2011 for critiques of the tendency to overdraw the contrast by confusing the lived experience of self with cultural (or "meta-") representations.

3. It is this crucial element of multinaturalism that perhaps above all else distinguishes the Amerindian version from the "perspectivism" of Western philosophy, as developed especially by Liebniz and Nietzsche.

4. As Viveiros de Castro (1998: 470) neatly expressed it, "animals (predators) and spirits see humans as animals (as prey) to the same extent that animals (as prey) see humans as spirits or as animals (predators)."

5. Viveiros de Castro (2010: 47) has stated this clearly: "All of the inhabitants of the cosmos are people in their own department, potential occupants of the deictical 'first person' position in cosmological discourse: inter-species relations are marked by a perpetual dispute surrounding this position, which is schematized in terms of the predator/prey polarity, agency or subjecthood being above all a capacity for predation."

6. The Urarina were generally distinguished by early chroniclers from the now-defunct Itucale, a possible subgroup who spoke an identical language and to whom they were evidently closely related. The Itucale have been described as inhabiting the lower section of the Chambira, while the Urarina resided farther upriver (Figueroa 1904: 382). This accords well with Urarina oral historical accounts.

7. Candoshi is usually ascribed to the Jivaroan bloc. Omurana is now extinct but thought to be either an isolate or a member of the Zaparoan language family, while Iquito, Jebero, Cocama and Yameo belong respectively to the Zaparoan, Cahuapanan, Tupían, and Peba-Yaguan families (Olawsky 2006).

8. Unless otherwise stated, transcriptions of discourse, including all myths and most extended quotations, were made in Urarina first and then translated into Spanish with the help of an assistant. Though time consuming, such a strategy allows for a more sophisticated reading, and with experience one is able to pick up on many of the connotations and nuances present to a native speaker but almost certainly lost in translation. The orthography I have adopted for written Urarina is based on that developed by the SIL linguists Ron and Phyllis Manus and so has the advantage of consistency with the standard currently in use in bilingual schools for literacy instruction. A summary is given in the prefatory pages.

9. At the time of my fieldwork there was no published dictionary or grammar of Urarina. Knut Olawsky, a professional linguist then working on the language, was kind enough to give me a draft copy of his grammar, which he was then still preparing for publication, as well as a basic lexicon compiled for his own personal use.

10. The territory occupied by the Urarina today, encompassing the Chambira and Uritoyacu watersheds, is large and admits of some degree of cultural and linguistic heterogeneity. Generally speaking, the density of contact with non-Urarina and the presence of imported goods decrease as one travels upstream from the mouth of the Chambira. However, even the communities farthest upstream have at least semiregular contact with itinerant traders; conversely, I found that even the communities closest to the mouth of the Chambira maintained a strong cultural identity and had their own rich mythologies and traditions of shamanism and ritual discourse. Much further work would be required to uncover the real extent of this regional variation. Nevertheless, while most of the ethnographic and linguistic material presented here is from the upper Chambira, properly speaking, I suspect it will be broadly applicable for all Urarina communities in the Chambira basin. I was not able to visit the Uritoyacu River, where there are also Urarina settlements.

CHAPTER 2. VITAL SHIELDS

1. See, e.g., Henare, Holbraad, and Wastell 2007; Hutchins 2005; Ingold 2007; Knappett 2002.

2. Emergence is in some ways analogous to the baptismal and other "second birth" practices identified by Bloch and Guggenheim (1981), with the proviso that in this case there is little evidence that the "natural birth" is devalued or supplanted as part of a broader gender politics.

3. This construction is common to virtually all baau chants. While *calabi* is simply a ritualized or archaic form of *calaohi*, "son" or "offspring," the derivation of *aino* is less clear. A couple of informants claimed it referred to the marbled swamp eel *(Synbranchus marmoratus),* but others disputed this interpretation. All agreed that it refers to the child itself; it is "our child," to which the children of various "others" are compared.

4. *Podocnemis unifilis.*

5. Probably *Dirouia hirsuta.*

6. Known as *supaichacras,* or "devil's gardens," in the regional Spanish, these clearings have been found to be caused by ants living in symbiotic relationship with *D. hirsuta,* which would explain the predominance of this particular species.

7. "Index" is understood here in the Peircean sense of a physical or causal relationship between signifier and signified.

8. Similar associations may be widespread in Amazonia. The neighboring Achuar, for example, propose that the placenta is a metaphorical "house" for the fetus, and one that the "true soul" of the deceased may reoccupy in a second intra utero existence underground (Descola 1994: 121).

9. Lorenzo proceeded to tell me that Mamiti's wife once went to urinate in the bushes, leaving her baby and hammock in the indifferent care of an older sibling playing idly nearby. The baby fell gravely ill, and Mamiti, who promptly drank brugmansia to diagnose the problem, duly reported that a spirit had been swinging the hammock with the baby inside it.

10. Following Bourdieu (1990: 250–62), we could say they are united by a transfer of schemes across domains of practice.

CHAPTER 3. CONCEIVING THE CONJUGAL BODY

1. See, among others, Seeger, Da Matta, and Viveiros de Castro 1979; Gow 1991; McCallum 2001; Vilaça 2002; Rival 1998.

2. For discussions of comparable ideas pertaining to the taming of women among the neighboring Jivaro and Candoshi, see Taylor 2001; Descola 1997: 124; Surrallés 2003.

3. *Ujue* can mean either "semen" or "feces." Semen is also sometimes referred to as "that which is thrown out by men" *(quicheicha jaonojoi).*

4. While there is much to be said for Vilaça's claim that humanity is produced through a kind of ongoing dialogue with nonhuman entities, the extensive use made by Urarina of the baby hammock suggests that transformations arising from corporeal associations with other species are far from undesirable in principle. More important, her claim that the couvade works to particularize the child from an "undifferentiated universe of subjectivities"

is not consistent with the material presented here; nor is Rivière's distinction between physical and spiritual creation, reformulated by Vilaça (2002: 363 n.) in terms of a "dividual" model of the person in which "body" and "soul" are related in terms of figure/ground reversal (see also Viveiros de Castro 2001). I propose that what Rivière refers to as the "spiritual" development of the infant is at once its physical development and that these processes cannot logically be separated.

5. As I see it, this potentially limits the applicability of the interpretations of the couvade by Rival (1998), Vilaça (2002), and Menget (1979), which essentially focus on the pragmatic and symbolic dimensions respectively of food taboos.

6. *Crypturellus undulatus.*

7. *Nothoprocta* sp.

8. Unidentified. Said by informants to have a large head with a red beak.

9. The hog plum tree is a continual nuisance in the task of clearing gardens: felled, with branches chopped up by a machete, it will still grow back. Only by burning can it be killed or "lost." The tree grows anywhere and is often found by riverbanks; when in season, its fruit, though generally considered unpalatable, is produced in prodigious quantities, covering the ground like a blanket.

10. *Heliornis fulica.*

11. *Anhinga anhinga.*

12. *Tigrisoma* sp.

13. *Chloroceryle* sp.

14. This is consistent with Rivière's (1995) proposal that an association between hardness, durability, and invisibility may be widespread in the region.

15. That the term "to give birth" is often pronounced with a long final vowel, *janohaa*, does not alter the fact of polysemy, which is of course also common to many other languages.

16. *Co-* is an associative prefix linking *janonaa* to the 1pl pronoun *cana*, with resultant vowel spreading across the *j*. Though use of *cana* as a qualifier might be taken to suggest that the end of "our" epoch might be followed by another, even implying a repeated cycle of cosmic deaths and rebirths, this was not a proposition on which my interlocutors could be drawn to speculate.

17. For a discussion of the connection between women (especially female procreative power and the ability to menstruate) and shamans among the Barasana, see Hugh-Jones 1979: 125.

18. Prior to Gudeman's (1971) analysis, most authors agreed that the institution was principally concerned with furthering social solidarity, either by intensifying and/or sanctifying existing ties or by creating new ones (e.g., Redfield 1941; Hammel 1968). Mintz and Wolf (1950) showed how, depending on contextual factors such as the potential for social and economic mobility, it may operate either "horizontally," that is, between members of the same group or social class, or "vertically," linking members of different social groups. Pitt-Rivers (1958) later suggested that a similarity exists in

Andalucia between the roles of ritual kinsman and brother-in-law and drew a further analogy between compadrazgo and complementary filiation (see also Gudeman 1971: 46).

19. *Peje* is a derivation from the Spanish *pez*.

20. Among the Warí, for example, the killer becomes father to the enemy's spirit (Vilaça 1992: 105). See also Fausto 2000, 2007.

21. Or what Fausto (2007: 509), for example, dubs their "jaguar part."

22. More like the Araweté spouse-swapping ritual friends (Viveiros de Castro 1992: 167–78), they are perhaps "anti-affines" without thereby being "consanguines."

CHAPTER 4. MUTUALITY AND AUTONOMY

1. See, e.g., Kilbride and Kilbride 1990.

2. Independent crawling does not appear to be encouraged or acknowledged as a developmental stage.

3. See Rival 1997: 149 for a similar observation for the Huaorani.

4. Cross-cultural research does in fact point to considerable variation in average onset age of walking and other motor development milestones (see Adolph and Robinson in press).

5. Known locally as *canaanai tijia barala, canaanai leleura,* or *luluna cobiri.*

6. Aroba is also the term for the giant otter *(Pteronura brasiliensis),* though informants state the two meanings are unrelated.

7. The menstrual hut of the Piro, associated with the transformation of a girl into a woman, is similarly considered analogous to the womb (Gow 2001: 162).

8. Alberto compared the girl to those Urarina women who willingly have sex with mestizos "without shame," simply because they desire it, an act all Urarina men disapprove of.

9. Taylor (1983) also notes that the Jivaroan verbs for "to take pity on" and "to suffer" are closely related and share the same root.

10. This proceeds according to the formula *"inae amutoha X,"* "it is finished already," where X is that person's kin name. X then responds, *"inae inaaera,"* where *inae* means "already" and *inaaera* means "he who knows/is able," which I was told refers in this context to Our Creator.

11. As Ingold (1986: 228) has expressed it, "a pretence of appropriation has to be constructed ideologically, in order that it may be cancelled out socially." This situation has more in common with groups such as those in Northwest Amazonia, for whom exchange is structured by a principle of reciprocity, than for more egalitarian groups such as the Huaorani, where sharing occurs "on demand" and is generalized to the extent that "givers never become creditors, nor receivers debtors" (Rival 2002: 104).

12. This mix of autonomy and dependency nevertheless remains quite distinct from the "giving environment" or "cosmic economy of sharing" mod-

els developed by Bird-David (e.g., 1993) for describing human-nature relatedness among egalitarian, "tribal" societies elsewhere, despite the similarly prevalent recourse to a parent-child metaphor.

13. See also Chaumeil 1998 for a discussion of this point.

14. Personal gossip constituted a striking exception to this general rule. To my enduring surprise, people would often instantly appear to believe virtually any piece of gossip or news of scandal to reach their ears, no matter how seemingly preposterous or outrageous. This general credulity was all the more striking given people's insistent empiricism in all other areas of knowledge.

15. This is also true of some other Amazonian societies (see, e.g., Turner 1995: 165; Overing 2003: 306).

16. I suspect that relations with Cocama were not always amicable in times past, but they never seem to have occupied the same "enemy" status as the Candoshi.

17. See also Bourdieu 1990: 66–79 for a discussion of this point.

CHAPTER 5. AUTHORITY AND SOLIDARITY

1. People I spoke to similarly asserted that their ancestors did not know how to make canoes and were highly mobile in comparison to the present day.

2. These loreri were formerly built to grander dimensions and housed an entire extended family under the same roof. Formally headed by a single mature man, they were in practice centered on a nucleus of female consanguines, which in-marrying men would join during their period of brideservice. Each coresident couple had their own separate stilt-palm platform for sleeping, with bare earth between. In 2005–7 most loreri were somewhat smaller, measuring around 4–6 meters by 2–3 meters, and more or less intended to house the nuclear family; new dependent couples typically constructed a small, separate dwelling alongside.

3. Some typical examples include Cati (black monkey), after a distinctive early haircut that allegedly gave resemblance to this animal; Alao (spider monkey), referencing long arms; Bucu (bone), referencing thinness; or Seeonjoa (big), from perceived chubbiness. Sometimes such nicknames are corruptions of Spanish words: Doinita (a diminutive corruption of the Spanish *doña*); or Buchilote (from the regional Spanish nickname Buchisapa, meaning pot-bellied).

4. The prefix *ca-* is the cliticized form of the first-person possessive pronoun, and *-era* is the agentive suffix.

5. Rival (2005: 292) makes a similar observation for the Huaorani.

6. Residential arrangements are nevertheless always open to negotiation, and there are in practice many couples who chose to live virilocally. This appears to be a much more common option if the bride's parents have divorced or if the girl is herself already a divorcee. In any case a groom who

does not intend to complete brideservice would certainly be expected to make these intentions clear to his potential parents-in-laws when seeking their permission for the marriage.

7. The generic association of men with the "outside" (including the world of the mestizos and modernity more generally) and of women with the "inside" is similar to the case of the Jivaro (Seymour-Smith 1991), among others.

8. In ritual language and in myth, for example, *ca lauri*, literally "our group," encompasses all Urarina and means broadly "our world," as opposed to the celestial world or the afterlife.

9. My use of the concept of solidarity group is indebted to conversations with Jürg Gasché. It should be noted that the term *lauri* may also be used to refer to a number of now-defunct clanlike "groups," probably larger in size but of uncertain composition, whose names persist in collective memory. For a more extended discussion of this possible clanic system of social organization, and of Urarina kinship and the relationship terminology more generally, see Walker 2009b.

10. At this point many men desire to return to their natal community, although this is subject to negotiation, and some couples compromise by establishing a new, independent settlement or satellite residence. Most men on the upper Chambira seemed to be living in the general area in which their fathers were born, even if the latter were no longer living there, and there appears to be a tendency for men who have completed brideservice to eventually join with their siblings, especially male siblings, to form new settlements. These men and their families become a new core group that others, especially in-marrying men, gradually join, thus temporarily mitigating or reversing the long-term effects of predominant uxorilocality.

11. Olawsky (2006) claims that a man is also expected to use the politeness marker with the husband of his sibling's daughter, i.e., his sibling's son-in-law.

12. This gender asymmetry, which seems directly related to the practice of uxorilocality, is also reflected in the suffix /-ana/. This too is used primarily (though not exclusively) by men as a politeness marker in the context of referring to (but not addressing) cross-generational affines.

13. According to some, communal jails have existed in some communities for several decades as tools of corrupt self-appointed mestizo bosses who would all too eagerly punish any sign of disobedience.

14. I was told that people also formerly made panpipes *(chojoana)* from bamboo, although I never saw one. For many people the eclipse of traditional music is a powerful symbol of social change and the source of much ambivalence. Although himself the proud owner of several cumbia cassettes, Lorenzo told me, "Earlier, the people didn't listen to music from the radio. Instead, they played their own music with flutes, and for that reason Our Creator helped them plenty, giving them lots of time and good weather." Gustodio similarly nominated shifting musical tastes as the most salient cultural change he had witnessed in his lifetime.

15. Unlike, for example, those sung by the Piro (Gow 2001: 166).

16. For example, I was once told surreptitiously that the reason a certain cluster of houses in Nueva Unión were sited so close together had to do with their inhabitants' penchant for semisecretive spouse swapping.

CHAPTER 6. MASTERING SUBJECTION

1. For many of these authors, and perhaps for many of the Amazonian peoples with whom they are concerned, to be a subject or an agent is first and foremost to be a predator, or to be caught in a polarized world of predators and prey. Hence, for example, the suggestion that the "master" is an abstraction of the animal's agency or "jaguar-part" (Fausto 2007). The approach I take here is nevertheless closely aligned with the work of Bonilla (2005), who pays careful attention to the perspective of the subordinate party in the relational dynamics of masters and subjects.

2. *Cecropia* sp.

3. Lorenzo once described how a man of knowledge whose manioc plantation was being "badly treated" by a deer drank ayahuasca in order to request Our Creator for assistance, by sending a jaguar or a snake to attack the deer.

4. Also known as cojoaaora in some areas.

5. Alternatively, to return to the terminology adopted by Viveiros de Castro (2007), the identity of janoraain is actual and extensive while that of cojoaaorain is virtual and intensive.

6. Possibly *Platemys platycephala*.

7. *Geochelone denticulata*.

8. Probably *Phrynops gibbus*.

9. *Podocnemis unifilis*.

10. *P. expansa*.

11. *Cana cojoanona* can be read literally as "our days" and is translated by Urarina into Spanish as *tiempo*, with the same intended dual meaning of "time" and "weather." It is also construed spatially, as akin to an enclosed space formed by the land joining seamlessly with the sky and effectively floating on an endless sea of water. The stem verb, *janoha*, "to dawn," can also mean "to give birth," as discussed in more detail in chapter 3. The end of time correlates with a deterioration in the weather, from fine and sunny to cold and dark.

12. *niauene ichaonaa*, "without life/manner." Alberto elaborated: "those outside God, who have sex with their family, who don't recognize their God."

13. It was difficult to decide how best to translate *coaairi* into English, and in the end I settled on "psychotropic." When speaking in Spanish, informants translated *coaairi* variously as "ayahuasca," "*toé*," or the mother of either (e.g., *su madre de toé*).

14. For a fuller description of the taming of an egaando, see Walker 2009a.

15. For example, as described in chapter 3, often no words at all are spoken between newlyweds for days, sometimes weeks, after getting married. A wife who wishes to initiate some form of contact may offer her husband a bowl of

cooked banana drink—a gesture considered a necessary precursor to their verbal communication.

EPILOGUE: AN ACCOMPANIED LIFE

1. Though Henley (1996) was referring specifically to Viveiros de Castro, a similar charge could be made concerning Fausto's (2000, 2007) use of comparative material, despite his drawing on a wide range of sources. Fausto (2000: 937) concedes that in the Upper Xingu, "the peaceful circulation of goods, bodies, and identities dynamizes the system," while groups such as those in Northwest Amazonia have a more developed generational or vertical transmission of identities, which attenuates their reliance on horizontal capture for social reproduction. Yet little is made of these distinctions, and such regional differentiation is suppressed in the quest to articulate a generic model of a predatory cosmology. The Huaorani, for example, are said to articulate their identity around the subject position of "prey" in their dealings with a hostile outer world (Rival 2002; see also Bonilla 2005), while Santos Granero (2005b: 611) has pointed to a growing number of studies emphasizing that the Arawak-speaking peoples in particular "represent a style of being 'native Amazonian' that differs in important ways from that of the Tupí-Guaraní, Jivaro- and Carib-speaking neighbours who have been taken as paradigms for the formulation of purportedly pan-Amazonian modes of sociality and kinship ideologies."

2. For example, the Conibo, the largest and most powerful of the Panoan-speaking societies of eastern Peru, constantly raided and enslaved their weaker semiriverine and interfluvial neighbors, including fellow Panoan peoples such as the Cashibo, Amahuaca, and Remo, as well as the Arawak-speaking Asháninka, Ashéninka, Machiguenga, and Nomatsiguenga (Santos Granero 2005a: 156).

3. See also Londoño Sulkin (2005) for an argument concerning perspectivism's need for a more robust appreciation of the role of the morality in determinations of identity.

4. The natural tendency of humans to cooperate, according to Sennett (2012), remains a potentiality unless cultivated through interaction and being with others. His work may be read as implying that Western thought concerning the basis of cooperation has tended to overemphasize the cognitive dimensions of the process of understanding others while downplaying the importance of being together and the physicality of togetherness.

5. As Butler (1997: 116) puts it, the "lived simultaneity of submission as mastery, and mastery as submission[,] . . . is the condition of possibility for the emergence of the subject."

Bibliography

Adolph, K. E., and S. R. Robinson. In press. "The Road to Walking: What Learning to Walk Tells Us about Development." In *Oxford Handbook of Developmental Psychology*, ed. P. Zelazo. New York: Oxford University Press.

Alès, C. 2002. "A Story of Unspontaneous Generation: Yanomami Male Co-Procreation and the Theory of Substances." In *Cultures of Multiple Fathers: The Theory and Practice of Partible Paternity in Lowland South America*, ed. S. Beckerman and P. Valentine, 62–85. Gainesville: University Press of Florida.

Basso, E. 1995. *The Last Cannibals: A South American Oral History*. Austin: University of Texas Press.

Belaunde, L. E. 1994. "Parrots and Oropendolas: The Aesthetics of Gender Relations among the Airo-Pai of the Peruvian Amazon." *Journal de la Société des Americanistes* 80: 95–111.

Bird-David, N. 1993. Tribal Metaphorization of Human-Nature Relatedness: A Comparative Analysis." In *Environmentalism: The View from Anthropology*, ed. K. Milton, 112–125. London: Routledge.

———. 1994. "Sociality and Immediacy: Or, Past and Present Conversations on Bands." *Man*, n.s., 29 (3): 583–603.

———. 1999. "Animism Revisited: Personhood, Environment, and Relational Epistemology." *Current Anthropology* 40: S69–S91.

Bloch, M. 2011. "The Blob." *Anthropology of This Century* 1. [On-line.]

Bloch, M., and S. Guggenheim. 1981. "Compadrazgo, Baptism and the Symbolism of a Second Birth." *Man* 16: 376–86.

Bonilla, O. 2005. "O bom patrão e o inimigo voraz: Predação e comércio na cosmologia Paumari." *Mana* 11 (1): 41–66.

Bourdieu, P. 1990. *The Logic of Practice*. Cambridge: Polity Press.

Brightman, M. 2010. "Creativity and Control: Property in Guianese Amazonia." *Journal de la Société des Américanistes* 96 (1): 135–67.

Butler, J. 1997. *The Psychic Life of Power: Theories in Subjection*. Stanford: Stanford University Press.

Carsten, J. 2004. *After Kinship*. Cambridge: Cambridge University Press.

Castillo, G. 1958. "Los Shimacos." *Perú Indígena* 16–17: 23–28.

———. 1961. "La medicina primitiva entre los Shimacos." *Peru Indígena* 20–21: 3–94.

Chaumeil, J.-P. 1998. *Ver, poder, saber: El chamanismo de los Yagua de la Amazonía peruana*. Lima: CAAAP/IFEA.

Conklin, B., and L. Morgan. 1996. "Babies, Bodies, and the Production of Personhood in North America and a Native Amazonian Society." *Ethos* 24 (4): 657–94.

Costa, L. 2010. "The Kanamari Body-Owner: Predation and Feeding in Western Amazonia." *Journal de la Societé des Américanistes* 96 (1): 169–92.

Costales, P., and A. Costales. 1983. *Amazonia: Ecuador-Perú-Bolivia*. Quito: Abya-Yala.

Davidson, 1985. "The Shadow of Life: Psychosocial Explanations for Placenta Rituals." *Culture, Medicine, and Psychiatry* 9 (1): 75–92.

Dean, B. 2009. *Urarina Society, Cosmology, and History in Peruvian Amazonia*. Gainesville: University Press of Florida.

Descola, P. 1992. "Societies of Nature and the Nature of Society." In *Conceptualising Society*, ed. A. Kuper, 107–26. London: Routledge.

———. 1994. *In the Society of Nature: A Native Ecology in Amazonia*. Cambridge: Cambridge University Press.

———. 1996. "Constructing Natures: Symbolic Ecology and Social Practice." In *Nature and Society: Anthropological Perpectives*, ed. G. Palsson and P. Descola, 82–102. London: Routledge.

———. 1997. *The Spears of Twilight: Life and Death in the Amazon Jungle*. London: Flamingo.

———. 2005. *Par-delà nature et culture*. Paris: Gallimard.

Dumont, L. 1972. *Homo Hierarchicus*. London: Paladin.

———. 1986. *Essays on Individualism: Modern Ideology in Anthropological Perspective*. Chicago: University of Chicago Press.

Dundes, A. 1988. "Introduction." In *The Flood Myth*, ed. A. Dundes, 1–7. Berkeley: University of California Press.

Durham, D. 1995. "Soliciting Gifts and Negotiating Agency: The Spirit of Asking in Botswana." *Journal of the Royal Anthropological Institute* 1 (1): 111–28.

Durkheim, E. 1973 [1898]. "Individualism and the Intellectuals." In *Emile Durkheim on Morality and Society*, ed. R. Bellah, 43–57. Chicago: University of Chicago Press.

Erikson, P. 2009. "Obedient Things: Reflections on the Matis Theory of Materiality." In *The Occult Life of Things: Native Amazonian Theories of Materiality and Personhood*, ed. F. Santos Granero, 173–91. Tucson: University of Arizona Press.

Everett, D.L. 2005. "Cultural Constraints on Grammar and Cognition in

Pirahã: Another Look at the Design Features of Human Language." *Current Anthropology* 46 (4): 621–46.

Fausto, C. 2000. "Of Enemies and Pets: Warfare and Shamanism in Amazonia." *American Ethnologist* 26 (4): 933–56.

———. 2007. "Feasting on People: Eating Animals and Humans in Amazonia." *Current Anthropology* 48 (4): 497–530.

———. 2008. "Donos demais: Maestria e domínio na Amazônia." *Mana* 14 (2): 329–66.

Ferrúa Carrasco, F., J. Linares Cruz, and O. Rojas Pérez. 1980. *La sociedad Urarina.* Iquitos: Organismo Regional de Desarrollo de Loreto.

Figueroa, F. 1904. *Relación de las misiones de la Compañia de Jesús en el país de los Maynas.* Madrid.

Geertz, C. 1973. *The Interpretation of Cultures.* New York: Basic Books.

Gell, A. 1998. *Art and Agency.* Oxford: Clarendon Press.

Gibson, E. J. 1988. "Exploratory Behaviour in the Development of Perceiving, Acting, and the Acquiring of Knowledge." *Annual Review of Psychology* 39 (1): 1–41.

Gonçalves, M.A. 2005. Comment on Everett, Daniel, "Cultural Constraints on Grammar and Cognition in Pirahã: Another Look at the Design Features of Human Language." *Current Anthropology* 46 (4): 636.

Gow, P. 1991. *Of Mixed Blood: Kinship and History in Peruvian Amazonia.* Oxford: Clarendon Press.

———. 2001. *An Amazonian Myth and Its History.* Oxford: Oxford University Press.

Gudeman, S. 1971. "The Compadrazgo as a Reflection of the Natural and Spiritual Person." *Proceedings of the Royal Anthropological Institute of Great Britain and Ireland,* 45–71.

Guzmán-Gallegos, M. 2009. "Identity Cards, Abducted Footprints, and the Book of San Gonzalo: The Power of Textual Objects in Runa Worldview." In *The Occult Life of Things: Native Amazonian Theories of Materiality and Personhood,* ed. F. Santos Granero, 214–34. Tucson: University of Arizona Press.

Hammel, E.A. 1968. *Alternative Social Structures and Ritual Relations in the Balkans.* Englewood Cliffs, NJ: Prentice-Hall.

Harré, R. 1983. *Personal Being: A Theory for Individual Psychology.* Oxford: Blackwell.

Harris, O. 1989. "The Earth and the State: The Sources and Meanings of Money in Northern Potosí, Bolivia." In *Money and the Morality of Exchange,* ed. J. Parry and M. Bloch, 232–68. Cambridge: Cambridge University Press.

Henare, A.J.M., M. Holbraad, and S. Wastell. 2007. *Thinking through Things: Theorising Artefacts Ethnographically.* London: Routledge.

Henley, P. 1996. *South Indian Models in the Amazonian Lowlands.* Manchester: Department of Social Anthropology, University of Manchester.

Hornborg, A. 2005. "Ethnogenesis, Regional Integration, and Ecology in Prehistoric Amazonia: Toward a System Perspective." *Current Anthropology* 46 (4): 589–620.

Hugh-Jones, S. 1979. *The Palm and the Pleiades: Initiation and Cosmology in Northwest Amazonia*. Cambridge: Cambridge University Press.

Hutchins, E. 2005. "Material Anchors for Conceptual Blends." *Journal of Pragmatics* 37: 1555–77.

Ingold, T. 1986. *The Appropriation of Nature: Essays on Human Ecology and Social Relations*. Iowa City: University of Iowa Press.

——. 2000. *The Perception of the Environment*. London: Routledge.

——. 2007. "Materials against Materiality." *Archaeological Dialogues* 14 (1): 1–16.

Izaguirre, B. 2004. *Historia de las misiones franciscanas y narración de los progresos de la geografía en el oriente del Perú*. Vols. 11–12. Lima: Asociación Librería Editorial Salesiana.

Kilbride, P. L., and J. E. Kilbride. 1990. "Sitting and Smiling Behaviour of Baganda Infants: The Influence of Culturally Constituted Experience." *Journal of Cross-Cultural Psychology* 6: 88–107.

Killick, E. 2011. "The Debt That Binds Us: A Comparison of Amazonian Debt-Peonage and U.S. Mortgage Practices." *Comparative Studies in Society and History* 53: 344–70.

Knappett, C. 2002. "Photographs, Skeuomorphs and Marionettes: Some Thoughts on Mind, Agency and Object." *Journal of Material Culture* 7: 97–117.

Kohn, E. 2007. "Animal Masters and the Ecological Embedding of History among the Ávila Runa of Ecuador." In *Time and Memory in Indigenous Amazonia: Anthropological Perspectives*, ed. C. Fausto and M. Heckenberger, 106–29. Gainesville: University Press of Florida.

Kondo, D. K. 1990. *Crafting Selves*. Chicago: University of Chicago Press.

Kramer, B. J. 1977. Las implicaciones ecológicas de la agricultura de los Urarina. *Amazonía Peruana* 1: 75–86.

——. 1979. "Urarina Economy and Society: Tradition and Change." PhD diss., Columbia University.

Latour, B. 1996. "On Technical Mediation—Sociology, Philosophy, Genealogy." *Common Knowledge* 3 (2): 29–64.

Leach, M. 1950. *Dictionary of Folklore, Mythology, and Legend*. Vol. 2. New York: Funk and Wagnalls.

Lévi-Strauss, C. 1972. *The Savage Mind*. London: Weidenfeld & Nicolson.

Londoño Sulkin, C. 2005. "Inhuman Beings: Morality and Perspectivism among Muinane People (Colombian Amazon)." *Ethnos* 70 (1): 7–30.

Marriott, M., and R. Inden. 1977. "Towards an Ethnosociology of South Indian Caste Systems." In *The New Wind: Changing Identities in South Asia*, ed. D. Kenneth, 227–38. The Hague: Mouton.

Mauss, M. 1983 [1938]. "A Category of the Human Mind: The Notion of Person; the Notion of Self." In *The Category of the Person: Anthropology,*

Philosophy, History, ed. M. Carrithers, S. Collins, and S. Lukes, 1–25. Cambridge: Cambridge University Press.

McCallum, C. 1996. "The Body That Knows: From Cashinahua Epistemology to a Medical Anthropology of Lowland South America." *Medical Anthropology Quarterly* 10 (3): 347–72.

———. 2001. *Gender and Sociality in Amazonia: How Real People Are Made.* Oxford: Berg.

Menget, P. 1979. "Temps de naître, temps d'être: La couvade." In *La fonction symbolique: Essais d'anthropologie,* ed. M. Izard and P. Smith, 245–64. Paris: Gallimard.

Mintz, S. W., and E. R. Wolf. 1950. "An Analysis of Ritual Co-Parenthood (Compadrazgo)." *Southwestern Journal of Anthropology* 6 (4): 341–68.

Morris, B. 1994. *Anthropology of the Self: The Individual in Cultural Perspective.* London: Pluto Press.

Nietzsche, F. 1956 [1887]. *The Genealogy of Morals.* New York: Anchor Books.

Oakdale, S. 2005. *I Foresee My Life: The Ritual Performance of Autobiography in an Amazonian Community.* Lincoln: University of Nebraska Press.

Olawsky, K. 2006. *A Grammar of Urarina.* Berlin: Mouton de Gruyter.

Overing, J. 1989. "The Aesthetics of Production: The Sense of Community among the Cubeo and Piaroa." *Dialectical Anthropology* 14 (3): 159–75.

———. 2003. "In Praise of the Everyday: Trust and the Art of Social Living in an Amazonian Community." *Ethnos* 68 (3): 293–316.

Pitt-Rivers, J. 1958. "Ritual Kinship in Spain." *Transactions of the New York Academic Society* 20: 424–31.

Redfield, R. 1941. *The Folk Culture of Yucatan.* Chicago: University of Chicago Press.

Reeve, M.-E. 1993. "Regional Interaction in the Western Amazon: The Early Colonial Encounter and the Jesuit Years: 1538–1767." *Ethnohistory* 41 (1): 106–38.

Rival, L. 1997. "Modernity and the Politics of Identity in an Amazonian Society." *Bulletin of Latin American Research* 16 (2): 137–51.

———. 1998. "Androgynous Parents and Guest Children: The Huaorani Couvade." *Journal of the Royal Anthropological Institute* 4 (4): 619–42.

———. 2002. *Trekking through History: The Huaorani of Amazonian Ecuador.* New York: Columbia University Press.

———. 2005. "The Attachment of the Soul to the Body among the Huaorani of Amazonian Ecuador." *Ethnos* 70 (3): 285–310.

Rivière, P. 1974. "The Couvade: A Problem Reborn." *Man* 9: 423–35.

———. 1984. *Individual and Society in Guiana: A Comparative Study of Amerindian Social Organisation.* Cambridge: Cambridge University Press.

———. 1995. "Houses, Places and People: Community and Continuity in Guiana." In *About the House: Lévi-Strauss and Beyond,* ed. J. Carsten and S. Hugh-Jones, 189–205. Cambridge: Cambridge University Press.

Roosevelt, A. 1993. "The Rise and Fall of the Amazon Chiefdoms." *L'Homme* 126–28: 255–83.

Rosengren, D. 2006. "Transdimensional Relations: On Human-Spirit Inter-action in the Amazon." *Journal of the Royal Anthropological Institute* 12 (4): 803–16.

San Roman, J. V. 1975. *Perfiles históricos de la Amazonía peruana*. Lima: Publicaciones CETA.

Santos Granero, F. 1991. *The Power of Love: The Moral Use of Knowledge amongst the Amuesha of Central Peru*. London: Athlone Press.

———. 2005a. "Amerindian Torture Revisited: Rituals of Enslavement and Markers of Servitude in Tropical America." *Tipití: Journal of the Society for the Anthropology of Lowland South America* 3 (2): 147–74.

———. 2005b. Comment on Hornborg, A., "Ethnogenesis, Regional Integration, and Ecology in Prehistoric Amazonia." *Current Anthropology* 46 (4): 611–12.

———. 2007. "Of Fear and Friendship: Amazonian Sociality beyond Kinship and Affinity." *Journal of the Royal Anthropological Institute* 13(1): 1–18.

———. 2009. "Introduction: Amerindian Constructional Views of the World." In *The Occult Life of Things: Native Amazonian Theories of Materiality and the Person*, ed. F. Santos Granero, 1–29. Tucson: University of Arizona Press.

Sartre, J. P. 1969. *Being and Nothingness: An Essay in Phenomenological Ontology*. New York: Washington Square Press.

Seeger, A. 1987. *Why Suyá Sing: A Musical Anthropology of an Amazonian People*. Urbana: University of Illinois Press.

Seeger, A., R. Da Matta, and E. Viveiros de Castro. 1979. "A construcão da pessoa nas sociedades indigenas brasileiras." *Anthropologia*, n.s., 32: 2–19.

Sennett, R. 2012. *Together: The Rituals, Pleasures, and Politics of Cooperation*. New Haven: Yale University Press.

Severi, C. 2002. "Memory, Reflexivity and Belief: Reflections on the Ritual Use of Language." *Social Anthropology* 10 (1): 23–40.

Seymour-Smith, C. 1991. "Women Have No Affines and Men No Kin: The Politics of the Jivaroan Gender Relation." *Man* 26 (4): 629–49.

Shepard, G. 2002. "Three Days for Weeping: Dreams, Emotions, and Death in the Peruvian Amazon." *Medical Anthropology Quarterly* 16 (2): 200–229.

Shweder, R. A., and E. J. Bourne. 1984. "Does the Concept of the Person Vary Cross-Culturally?" In *Culture Theory: Essays on Mind, Self, and Emotion*, ed. R. A. Shweder and R. A. LeVine, 158–99. Cambridge: Cambridge University Press.

Sloterdijk, P. 2011. *Bubbles: Spheres*. Vol. 1: *Microspherology*. Cambridge, MA: MIT Press.

Spiro, M. 1993. "Is the Western Conception of the Self 'Peculiar' within the Context of the World Cultures." *Ethos* 21 (2): 107–53.

Stolze Lima, T. 2000. "Towards an Ethnographic Theory of the Nature/Culture Distinction in Juruna Cosmology." *Brazilian Review of Social Sciences*, special issue, 1: 43–52.

Strathern, M. 1988. *The Gender of the Gift: Problems with Women and Problems with Society in Melanesia.* Berkeley: University of California Press.

Surrallés, A. 2003. "Face to Face: Meaning, Feeling and Perception in Amazonian Welcoming Ceremonies." *Journal of the Royal Anthropological Institute* 9 (4): 775–91.

Taylor, A. C. 1983. "Jivaroan Magical Songs: Achuar Anent of Connubial Love." *Amerindia* 8: 87–127.

———. 1996. "The Soul's Body and Its States: An Amazonian Perspective on the Nature of Being Human. *Journal of the Royal Anthropological Institute* 2 (2): 201–15.

———. 2001. "Wives, Pets, and Affines: Marriage among the Jivaro." In *Beyond the Visible and the Material: The Amerindianization of Society in the Work of Peter Rivière,* ed. L. Rival and N. Whitehead, 45–56. Oxford: Oxford University Press.

Taylor, C. 1989. *Sources of the Self: The Making of Modern Identity.* Cambridge: Cambridge University Press.

Tessman, G. 1930. *Die Indianer Nordost-Perus.* Hamburg: Friedrichsen, de Gruyter & Co.

Turner, T. 1995. "Social Body and Embodied Subject: Bodiliness, Subjectivity, and Sociality among the Kayapo." *Cultural Anthropology* 10 (2): 143–70.

Tylor, E. B. 1861. *Anahuac: Or Mexico and the Mexicans, Ancient and Modern.* London: Longmans, Green, Reader, & Dyer.

Urban, G. 1989. "The 'I' of Discourse in Shokleng." In *Semiotics, Self, and Society,* ed. B. Lee and G. Urban, 27–51. Berlin: Mouton de Gruyter.

Van Velthem, L. 2003. *O belo é a fera: A estética da produção e da predação entre os Wayana.* Lisboa: Assírio and Alvim.

Veigl, F. X. 2006 [1785]. *Noticias detalladas sobre el estado de la provincia de Maynas en América meridional hasta el año de 1768.* Iquitos: CETA.

Velasco, J. de. 1979 [1789]. *Historia del reino de Quito en la América meridional.* Quitos: Imprenta del Gobierno.

Vilaça, A. 1992. *Comendo como gente: Formas do canibalismo Wari'.* Rio de Janeiro: Editora da Universidade Federal do Rio de Janeiro.

———. 2002. "Making Kin out of Others in Amazonia." *Journal of the Royal Anthropological Institute* 8 (2): 347–65.

Viveiros de Castro, E. 1992. *From the Enemy's Point of View: Humanity and Divinity in an Amazonian Society.* Chicago: University of Chicago Press.

———. 1998. "Cosmological Deixis and Amerindian Perspectivism." *Journal of the Royal Anthropological Institute* 4 (3): 489–510.

———. 2001. "GUT Feelings about Amazonia: Potential Affinity and the Construction of Sociality." In *Beyond the Visible and the Material: The Amerindianization of Society in the Work of Peter Rivière,* ed. L. Rival and N. Whitehead, 19–44. Oxford: Oxford University Press.

———. 2007. "The Crystal Forest: Notes on the Ontology of Amazonian Spirits." *Inner Asia* 9(2): 153–72.

———. 2010. "The Untimely, Again." Introduction to P. Clastres, *Archaeology of Violence*, 9–52. Los Angeles: Semiotext(e).

Walker, H. 2009a. "Baby Hammocks and Stone Bowls: Urarina Technologies of Companionship and Subjection." In *The Occult Life of Things: Native Amazonian Theories of Materiality and Personhood*, ed. F. Santos Granero, 81–102. Tucson: University of Arizona Press.

———. 2009b. "Transformations of Urarina Kinship." *Journal of the Anthropological Society of Oxford online* 1: 52–69.

———. 2010. "Soulful Voices: Birds, Language and Prophecy in Amazonia." *Tipití: Journal of the Society for the Anthropology of Lowland South America* 8 (1). [On-line.]

———. 2012. "Demonic Trade: Debt, Materiality and Agency in Amazonia." *Journal of the Royal Anthropological Institute* 18 (1): 140–59.

Winnicott, D. 1971. *Playing and Reality.* London: Routledge.

Index